REALWINE

PATRICK MATTHEWS
REALWINE

THE REDISCOVERY OF NATURAL WINEMAKING

MITCHELL BEAZLEY

for Pamela Matthews

REAL WINE

by Patrick Matthews

First published in Great Britain in 2000 by Mitchell Beazley, an imprint of
Octopus Publishing Group Limited, 2–4 Heron Quays, London E14 4JP.

ISBN 1 84000 257 3

A CIP catalogue record for this book is available from the British Library.

Commissioning Editor: Rebecca Spry
Design: Colin Goody
Illustrations: Clifford Harper
Managing Editors: Adrian Tempany, Hilary Lumsden
Editor: Helen Spence
Production: Nancy Roberts
Index: Ann Barrett

Typeset in Goudy and Meta Plus
Produced by Bath Press, Bath, England

CONTENTS

INTRODUCTION 7

1 CHOOSING A SITE 17

2 PLANTING THE VINEYARD 47

3 SOURCING THE VINES 73

4 CHOOSING GRAPE VARIETIES 97

5 GROWING THE GRAPES 121

6 MAKING THE WINE 151

7 MATURING THE WINE 179

8 DEALING WITH WINE FAULTS 205

9 MAKING MONEY 231

APPENDIX ONE 257

APPENDIX TWO 261

FRANK SCHOONMAKER – TWO PERSONAL TRIBUTES 274

BIBLIOGRAPHY 278

INDEX 281

ACKNOWLEDGEMENTS 288

INTRODUCTION

This book belongs in the proud tradition of gardening books sold to flat-dwellers, or recipe collections read for entertainment value by people busy microwaving a frozen pizza. In fact, I would guess that most "how to" manuals (especially when bought by hopeful partners) end up in the hands of people who are unlikely to do anything more energetic than turn the pages.

Wine drinkers tend to be more interested than the average consumer in how their product is made. The wine trade has mixed feelings about this. A certain inquisitiveness is good for business, but you'll also hear complaints about the tedium of spending all day on a stand at a consumer fair answering boring questions. But perhaps one of the best things about wine culture is the habit of asking questions.

Recently a British supermarket wine guru raised the concern that the labelling of ingredients might "confuse people". Her worry is compounded by the fact that some of the methods and ingredients of modern winemaking sound distinctly unappetizing. People might not support or understand the use of fungicides, herbicides and synthetic chemical additives, or modern machinery which adjusts the levels of water, vinegariness or alcohol.

There are now two broad categories of wine: one that results from mass-production by fermentation scientists, and wine made by simple, conservative methods. The makers of what some people call "McWine" borrow the imagery of vintages, regional styles and oak barrels because that's what the public wants to see. Traditionalists like to counter by throwing open their cellar doors; their best marketing tool is to show the customers exactly what they are up to.

This story is largely told through the eyes of Californians. British readers may object that they don't drink much California wine and that much of what reaches this country is unimpressive. The point is that wine culture has been mapped by newcomers, just as American black music was brought into the mainstream between the wars by white enthusiasts.

The British may have written the most about European wine, but it's the Americans who have rolled up their sleeves and got to work in the cellar, alongside their French hosts and teachers. The result is a network of Californians (as well as Australians and New Zealanders) with a unique overview of traditional grape growing and winemaking. This can be seen as an influx of European ideas and culture into America to compare with the arrival of Viennese psychoanalysis, modernist architecture or the great European film directors. The *Académie Internationale du Vin* is a kind of superleague of the world's top wine estates, in which Europeans predominate. But at a seminar in December 1994 on "natural winemaking" the keynote speech was delivered by an American, Paul Draper of Ridge Vineyards.

I could have given an account of the rediscovery of tradition in an Australian context with many fine Australian examples.

But the belief among most Australians is that they have got it right and the French have got it wrong, and that the techniques designed to simplify the bulk handling of grapes are not simply more convenient and cost-effective, they also make better wine.

This was also the attitude of most Californians until fairly recently. But from the 1970s onwards there was a new willingness to learn from Europe. Now, traditional winemaking has all but become the new orthodoxy. A big winery like Robert Mondavi, which pioneered stainless steel fermentation tanks in the 1960s, is switching to wooden fermenters for its top wines. Natural yeasts rather than cultivated strains are in vogue, and filtration is frowned upon. Recently, the big Australian firms have also begun to consider these approaches.

Of course, France is not peopled only by traditionalists. The University of Bordeaux and other institutions have improved their theoretical understanding of what takes place when wine ferments. A less happy development has been the arrival of chemical treatments in the vineyards. And, as well as learning from the French, the Americans have encouraged them to stand their ground, whether as importers, as writers or as friendly rivals. Aubert de Villaine, proprietor of Burgundy's most celebrated estate, the Domaine de la Romanée-Conti, describes his American friends as a "beacon". Henri Jayer, the other great man of the village of Vosne-Romanée, warns fellow growers against using agrochemicals and high-tech winemaking, pointing out that even the Americans are turning away from them.

Is this the tale of a conflict between the traditionalist craft workers – "William Morris types" – and "scumbag corporate winemakers"? Sometimes yes, as in the case of the outright fake wines discussed in Chapter Four. But as Mel Knox, the California winemaker and barrel importer who identified this dichotomy observes, most people are driven by a love of wine. It's a bohemian kind of industry. If you're a winemaker who handcrafts unfiltered wine from organic grapes using natural yeasts, big firms might seem menacing and faceless. Nevertheless, working for one of the big boys – the likes of Gallo or Southcorp – is still very different from a lifetime in the corporate hierarchies of, say, IBM or Exxon.

Some Californian pioneers, such as Martin Ray (1904-1976), made a rigid distinction between non-authentic wine and the real thing, of which Ray saw himself as a unique exponent, (This conviction did not make him happy or popular.) Generally, however, the artisanal and industrial philosophies are intertwined. The Australian titan Southcorp first gained international recognition and accolades by taking grapes from old, low-yielding vines and turning them into wine, with methods learned first-hand in Bordeaux. The Trinchero family at Sutter Home in Napa tapped into wealth and fortune in the early 1970s, when they accidentally left some residual sugar in a rosé Zinfandel, which became the hugely successful if critically derided "White Zinfandel". "We had the common sense to give the consumers what they wanted, instead of what we thought they should buy," Bob Trinchero bluntly told the author David Darlington[1] "I'd rather be a live heretic than a dead traditionalist." But the Trincheros remain steeped in their family's Italian wine culture.

Anne-Claude Leflaive runs her family's domaine in Puligny-Montrachet, and is Burgundy's top exponent of biodynamic, chemical-free grape growing and winemaking. But this represents a complete turnaround, one that she has effected since succeeding her father. The late and much-loved Vincent Leflaive believed in spraying and had abandoned ploughing in favour of weedkillers.

In fairness, "techno-wine" is only moderately manipulated compared to much of what we eat and drink. A Moët & Chandon scientist told me how he was developing yeasts to release proteins into the wine. Champagne needs proteins to stay fizzy, but these were being lost through an overuse of fining and clarification agents. He had previously worked for a giant brewery, who, he said, would simply have used additives to tighten up the foam.

It's a question not of doing wrong, but more of selling yourself short. The traditionalists set themselves an extraordinary task: to make a piece of ground speak through the medium of wine. As Paul Draper told the *Académie Internationale du Vin*: "Wine is different from other alcoholic drinks, in that you have everything necessary to make it present in the raw material. It's due to this simple fact that wine, since the dawn of Western civilization, has been the essential symbol of transformation, both physical and spiritual. I sometimes think that my colleagues in the New World forget that the power and meaning of wine come from nature and from a natural process, not from man or an industrial process."

Draper attacks the idea of setting out to manufacture a great wine. High prices don't automatically improve wine: someone spending a week's salary on a single bottle is seeking an intense sensory experience, but wines tailor-made to provide this – and to win in competitive blind tastings – can sometimes be barely drinkable. The English wine writer and tutor Michael Schuster, who is an exceptional taster, says that one of the least enjoyable events he recently took part in was a comparison of vintages of the world's most expensive wines, Pétrus and Le Pin. They were impressive, but they weren't enjoyable.

And what exactly is the point in being impressed by a wine? Some wine merchants occasionally ask themselves this question. "I've been wondering about so-called 'great wine'", one of them told me recently. "I mean it's good, no-one's denying that, but how good is it? Good enough for all the fuss that's made about it?" There is no disputing that hype is at an all-time high. Prices keep going up; wine writers have become media stars; winemakers are spending more time keeping up their public profile on the tasting circuit than in the vineyard; books pour off the presses.

My excuse for adding to their number is to put forward a momentous but unlikely-sounding proposition: that the best wines are also those that contribute to a beautiful and diverse landscape and employ small-scale farmers, as well as reflecting their maker's skill and integrity. By this I don't mean the most "politically correct" wines, but the best tasting. Wines are the sum of a series of choices. *Real Wine* argues that the more these choices respect both nature and people, the better the wine will be.

My book emerges in the shadow of two mighty predecessors, *The Art and Science of Wine* (Mitchell Beazley, 1992) by James Halliday and Hugh Johnson (published in the United States as *The Vintner's Art*) and *New Classic Wines* by Oz Clarke (Websters/ Mitchell Beazley, 1991). Halliday and Johnson triggered a public row over technique, with the authors' defence of filtration savaged by Robert Parker. Their book is essential for anyone interested in what wine growers get up to, although it draws the sting from controversies. You don't hear the distinctive cries of the two factions, inveighing against "unscientific dogma" in one camp and crying *"ils massacrent nos terroirs"* in the other. It's a bit like implying that only a difference of emphasis separates the Vatican from the fundamentalists of Bob Jones University.

Oz Clarke's book gave me a shock recently. My impression had been that this was a manifesto for those who believe that "technology matters more than terroir", built round the careers of selected modernist winemakers. But the case studies weren't how I remembered. There are some modernists, such as the Australian Rosemount, but it's mostly an old-fashioned group, with little in common except that they operate outside the classic French wine regions. It is hard to think of a more passionate *terroirist* than Paul Draper of Ridge (although he hates the tag: "It's been turned into an advertising gimmick"), or a less technical winemaker than Serge Hochar of Chateau Musar in the Lebanon. It's rather like the celebrated California versus France blind tasting held in Paris in 1976 by Steven Spurrier. This made headlines round the world because the French tasters gave the top places to a California Chardonnay and Cabernet Sauvignon. But this was no victory for "modern" wine styles; the winning wines were so European as to fool France's leading wine writer and the proprietor of its most celebrated wine estate.[2]

In the chapters that follow, Draper and others explain what they do and why they do it; there is also an historical background. The difficulty is where to start. Wine is a relic of the Neolithic period, the heroic age of multi-substance abuse. "Traditionalist" winemaking began only as a reaction to a rupture with the continuity of centuries: in France this was the direct result of the late 19th century phylloxera epidemic that destroyed French vineyards; in America it was the man-made disaster of Prohibition.

Although I have never made anything more ambitious than elderberry wine, I hope that these stories will interest and enthuse people who produce or sell wine. I also hope to shed some light on why different wines taste as they do, by describing how they were created. Production processes do not always make a gripping story – seasoned winery visitors tend to rush past the bottling line

– but there is a distinguished precedent for dwelling on them. Virgil, court poet to Augustus, the first Roman emperor, devoted his second book of poems, the *Georgics*, to details of stock rearing, bee keeping and viticulture on an Italian farm. The subtext was a call to cosmopolitan Romans to return to the republican virtues of their ancestors. Today, when we are infinitely more divorced from the natural world than the Romans, there is all the more reason to linger a little over the origins of what we eat and drink.

(1) Darlington, David, *Angels' Visits: An Inquiry into the Mystery of Zinfandel.* Henry Holt and Company, New York, 1991.

(2) The winning white was a 1973 Chardonnay from Chateau Montelena, founded in 1882 in northern Napa County. Its red counterpart was a 1973 Cabernet Sauvignon from a recently-planted vineyard at Stag's Leap, also in Napa. Steven Spurrier remembers the Montelena as being "very lemony, Puligny-style". The group tasted the whites and the winner of this group was announced before they moved on to the reds. Spurrier thinks this was the main reason that a rather light red wine was chosen ahead of 1970 Mouton-Rothschild and 1970 Haut-Brion. "The tasters were all determined not to let a Californian win the reds. The Stag's Leap wasn't at all typical and when they came across a beautiful, cheerful Cabernet they all thought it was French." A Ridge Montebello 1971, which Spurrier found to be a dead ringer for a Bordeaux, was placed after the French first growths; the heavier, more "porty" California wines came last.

1
CHOOSING
A SITE

Bob Haas spent three years scouring California, looking for the right place to plant a vineyard. It was six years before John Alban found what he was looking for. Josh Jensen did it in two frantic years, sleeping by the roadside in his Volkswagen van – an experience that did little to prolong his marriage – and testing soils with eyedroppers full of sulphuric acid to detect limestone. Many Californians have displayed the obsessiveness in their search for the right soil and climate shown by their forebears, the 49ers, in their quest for gold.

Few Europeans would behave like this, but they don't need to. In Europe your choice of site and grape variety are dictated by tradition and, as Californian winemaker David Ramey emphasizes, tradition is the result of experimentation that has succeeded.

Cistercian monks built walls round the different vineyards in Burgundy to show where the flavour of the grapes changed in response to geological variations. One American commentator argues that the role of the vines is not to supply the taste of a grape variety but to act as a conduit, transmitting the essence of land and soil. Even "modernist" Burgundian growers hold this view. In a recent brochure Patrice Rion of Prémeaux describes one of his evolving wines as tasting of "cherries", another of "may blossom" and another of "a hayfield after rain". Yet they all come from the same grape variety and have been made the same way: the differences are created solely by variations in the limestone soil within the space of a few kilometres.

Old-fashioned viticulture comes from the world of the mixed farm, when vines were planted on free-draining slopes with poor soil. Now those who invest in vineyards look for flatlands suitable for modern farm machinery. A hot, dry growing season maximizes yields and reduces the incidence of disease. No-one loses sleep over soil types: "it's just dirt", in the words of one Californian, the late Bill Jekyll, since echoed by many Australians.

This attitude isn't confined to grape growers: hydroponics is the branch of agriculture that grows greenhouse crops in an inert porous medium and feeds them with a chemical solution. Modern vine growing could be likened to a sort of outdoor hydroponics, with the vines drip-fed water via a network of underground pipes. This approach finds little favour with environmentalists, who point to the damage caused to the world's soil covering by modern farming techniques.

But the big wine companies who are powering the expansion in the world's vineyards regard this emphasis on specific soils and places as an irritant. A huge planting operation is currently going on in the so-called New World, chiefly Australia, California, Chile and Argentina. Very little of it involves the choosiness shown by Alban, Jensen and Haas. The criteria have changed since the Côte d'Or in Burgundy was planted some 2,000 years ago. Speaking in 1999 at a debate, *Nature versus Nurture*[1], Mike Paul, European director of Southcorp, dismissed the focus on place as an Old World marketing ploy. He is right, to the extent that bad growers often exploit a famous vineyard name to demand excessive prices for thin, over-cropped wines. But all farmers know that crops grow differently on different sites. You can't spend long writing about wine without realizing that the claims made by Patrice Rion for his different vineyards are true; finding the proof is simply a matter of going into the cellar and tasting from the barrels. And they are not small variations, but on a scale that even an inexperienced taster would recognize.

Terroir differences even show up under the microscope – or rather, under the modern analytical chemist's favourite tool, gas chromatography-mass spectrometry (GC-MS). This technique splits up wine into a range of peaks representing esters, flavour components, terpenes, aldehydes, higher alcohols, polyphenols and so on. A printout for wine looks quite different from one for, say, fruit juice, and fine wine produces many more peaks than the cheap stuff. Fascinating as this analysis is, it does not do justice to wine's complexity: a substance that shows in a peak on a printout may taste of nothing on its own, but spring to life when combined with other elements. It is misleading, too, to believe that gas chromatography contains a kind of recipe for fine wine. About 30 years ago, chemists working for Suntory, the giant Japanese drinks company, tried to reproduce Château Lafite using synthetic chemicals. They served it blind to a group of top Japanese wine waiters, and the sommeliers' verdict was that the wine tasted of mud – quite the wrong kind of terroir.[2]

In 1996 a paper in an American learned journal attempted to identify the chemical differences in wine that corresponded to terroir.[3] The research team comprised a microbiologist-turned-winemaker, a chemist and a statistician from the University of California, Santa Cruz. The winemaker Leo McCloskey defined terroir for the purpose of this exercise as "the unique ecotypic expression of regional grapes which causes differences in the secondary chemical flavorants detected in bottled wines which are defect-free." The team surveyed Californian Chardonnays and tried to establish whether the wines varied consistently between regions. They backed up gas chromatography with tastings – 26 members of the wine industry tasted samples made from similar clones from four Californian regions: Carneros, the Central Coast (south of San Luis Obispo), Napa Valley and Sonoma.

Sure enough, some recognizable traits emerged. Wines from Carneros, the fashionable little region that skirts the southern boundaries of Napa and Sonoma, were consistently identified for their distinctive fruity, citrous flavours, and which correlated analytically with the chemical 3-methylbutyl acetate. Was it the cool, dry microclimate of Carneros or its low fertility soils that made its wines stand out? Leo McCloskey says that there is no verifiable way of separating the two factors. "There's no scientific proof that soils alone do the trick – if there was, big corporations such as Gallo and Southcorp would be shifting topsoil onto their vineyards until they had exactly what they wanted."

However, there have been Californians willing to maintain that soil type makes a difference for at least a quarter of a century. The Chalone vineyard was planted in 1919 by an expatriate Frenchman, Curtis Tamm, in a remote location in the Gavilan Mountains, which – unlike much of California – had an outcrop of limestone soil. Dick Graff, who bought the property in 1965 (and who died in 1998 when his light aircraft crashed) wanted to return to Burgundian attitudes and techniques.

In the mid-1970s Robert Benson interviewed Graff for his book, *Great Winemakers of California* (Capra Press, 1977). Graff claimed that after drinking Chalone for a year or two, a wine drinker will come to recognize the unique *gout de terroir* of the Chalone vineyards. Benson reminded Graff that while most American winemakers acknowledged the role of climate, few felt that soil was so important. Graff replied that the whole notion of soil versus climate had been decided in favour of climate many years ago by professors Amerine and Winkler, for the simple reason that climate produced differences in grapes which were measurable in the laboratory. Any idiosyncrasies which resulted from soil could not be measured in the lab. But some scientists now believe they can explain the role of soil.

Meanwhile, marketing is eclipsing both soil and climate as a reason to favour "regionality". The Australians find that this concept gives them a useful point of difference to beat off the competition from Chile and South Africa, in terms of Cabernet and Chardonnay at rock-bottom prices. Southcorp, like other big Australian companies, has installed computer systems to keep track of the crops from individual vineyards as they are processed in their vast gleaming wineries. One Australian region, Coonawarra, is seen as synonymous with a particular soil type – the famous terra rossa. A less positive example of the influence of soil can be detected in some of the irrigated regions of Australia where a build-up of soil salinity is often perceptible in the wine. "It tastes like Badoit water" (a mineral water), complained one disillusioned taster.

But traditionally, wine farming elevates soil from dirt into a rare, precious and magical prize – the worthy goal of Bob Haas, John Alban and Josh Jensen on their respective expeditions across California. And this is where wine joins league with the theorists of organic agriculture.

For advice on the health of their soils, many of the most celebrated French estates are turning to the soil scientist Claude Bourguignon. This former head of department at the *Institut Nationale de la Recherche Agronomique* (INRA) has lectured for two consecutive years to seminars organized by the *Académie Internationale du Vin*. When he isn't acting as a consultant to French wine growers, Bourguignon spends much of his time in the Third World, advising on problems like erosion, compaction and loss of fertility.

Claude Bourguignon lives with his wife, another ex-INRA scientist, in a big old stone house in the lovely village of Marey-sur-Tille, an hour's drive north from the vineyards of the Côte d'Or. When I met him he'd just got back from Tunisia, where he had been getting to grips with the consequence of a long drought. His soil analysis business has full order books, and the Bourguignons are not taking on new clients. They work not with the subsistence farmers of the Third World, but with the bigger proprietors – the reason they seek him out is that chemical agriculture is just too expensive. One example he gives is that "dead" soils cost more to plough, that European arable land now needs ten times higher energy inputs than just after the Second World War. Bourguignon promises that by looking after the life of the soil, his clients can make dramatic cuts in their expenditure on fertilizers, weed killers and pesticides.

It was his experience of Third World poverty that made Bourguignon want to be an agronomist. He grew up in Paris, in the area of St Germain-des-Prés, a doctor's son. By the age of 14 he had become a fanatical bird-watcher and in his teens he formed Paris's first ornithological society, which surveyed the city's birds of prey. During his holidays he did voluntary work for the World Wildlife Fund, with Dian Fossey, the champion of Africa's gorillas, and in the Himalayan habitats of Indian mountain tigers. "In 1970 I found people in Old Delhi in starvation. It was then I realised that it is impossible to protect nature if people are hungry." He later studied biochemistry at university and won a place at France's elite *Institut National de l'Agronomie*.

In *Le Sol, La Terre et Les Champs* (Sang de la Terre, 1991) Bourguignon sketches the origins of his science – pedology, or the study of the earth's skin. This became a separate discipline from geology when scientists began to recognize soils as something alive, dynamic and infinitely varied. The word "ecology" was coined in the 1870s, the decade in which the Russian researchers Dokuchaiev and Sibertsev began developing approaches to understanding soils. Earlier analysts had viewed soil as an inert reservoir for storing plant nutrients, a school of hydroponics writ large. In its place, says Bourguignon, the Russians offered a holistic vision of a special environment; somewhere "very complex, constantly in the course of formation, that was born, that grew and that could die."

The Russians now saw soil as more than the sum of the various processes that created it – erosion, oxidization, bacterial action – and each soil as having a distinct combination of properties. (In fact soil, in taking on a new life independent of its origins, can be seen as undergoing processes rather like the fermentation and maturation of wine.) The old, chemists' approach continued to dominate soil science until the 1920s, and has an echo in the basic geological classification still used in discussing vineyard areas. What Bourguignon has to say is not news to soil scientists, but is an original and important message for wine growers. This is that soils are defined and formed by the life they harbour, as well as by their mineral composition. It is for this reason, as we'll see later, that organic and biodynamic growers claim that, without a respect for life the idea of terroir (wines being true to a specific location) becomes meaningless.

Tasters often talk about wines tasting "mineral". Bourguignon shows how micro-organisms transmit this quality from the soil to the wine, transforming minerals into compounds that can be absorbed by the vines' roots. Jacques Néauport, organic guru of an influential circle of Beaujolais growers, relies on Bourguignon's work to explain the distinct characters of wines from the different Beaujolais villages. He says the reason agronomists have never been able to offer a scientific explanation for terroir and typicity is because they have always neglected the fundamental role played by microbes in plant nutrition.

One example is the way in which micro-organisms transform raw elements into a form usable by plants. Bourguignon cites the chemical process called chelation. Doctors know chelation as the treatment for heavy metal poisoning. A chelating agent binds with the toxin to create large, ring-shaped molecules that the body is able to flush out via the kidneys. Chelated metals are easily absorbed by plants: farmers who want to correct alkaline soil find that the standard treatment, iron, is absorbed three times more easily as a chelate than as iron sulphate. (The drawback is that iron chelate costs 15 times as much as iron sulphate.)

However, soil micro-organisms do the job free. The wines from the Beaujolais village of Morgon, for example, grow on manganese-rich granite. Bourguignon's analyses found that the soil bacteria there were busy forming manganese chelates which also appear in the wine, and that exactly the same process goes on in neighbouring Brouilly, where the soil is rich in copper.

The vines don't simply serve as a passive conduit for the chelated metal compounds, according to Bourguignon. They also actively draw helpful bacteria deep into the bedrock: his analyses show that the soil surrounding a vine's extensive root system has the same characteristics as the surface soil.

A traditional vineyard is a place where big ancient vines and tiny bacteria cooperate in a dynamic process to produce wine that tastes of a unique soil. Modern agriculture hinders the process with its use of chemical treatments which kill the life in the soil. Bourguignon frequently observes that "there is less microbial life in some Burgundian vineyards than in the Sahara desert." If you take away the bacteria, you lose the mechanism to mobilize soil nutrients and make them available to the vines. This means losing not just trace elements but naturally produced nitrates and phosphates, which are created by bugs from otherwise inaccessible nitrogen and phosphorus. The alternative, chemical fertilizers, causes pollution in soil run-off.

Another problem is that vines are becoming shorter-lived, which Bourguignon attributes to a combination of the overuse of fertilizers and pesticides, and the effects of compacting soil. The result is that vines get torn out just at the point that their roots reach deep-lying rocks, which is where they would start to give the best expression of terroir.

This is analysis at a sophisticated level, and it's no surprise that it is France's top estates that are funding it by employing Bourguignon. The result is a version of organic production which is as much about connoisseurship as environmentalism.

Soil has only recently begun to interest New World growers, because the favourable climate distracts their attention. As Anthony Hanson comments in *Burgundy* (Faber and Faber, 1995), you can grow a vine virtually anywhere, so long as it is not actually standing in water. This holds true especially in California and Australia; vines planted in the wrong place, by European standards, still make drinkable wine under the endless summer sun – they will be deep coloured, alcoholic and fruity.

A minority, however, do look for the subtleties they find in the best European wines. Josh Jensen, who's created one of California's most unusual wine estates, says that: "When you move up the quality scale, it isn't that the wines are more powerful or riper tasting or more oaky. It's that they have more levels, more nuances. It's really all about complexity of flavour."

John Alban grew up in LA with wine-drinking parents: "I was very fond of wines that don't show any or much oak, and given that this was a time when California was going through a major love affair with oak, I tended to drink a lot more European wines." Alban was studying viticulture at Fresno State University when a single bottle of wine, bought by a friend for his birthday, changed the course of his life. It was a Condrieu, a white from the Northern Rhône made from the Viognier grape, which was then hardly known outside the Rhône: "It was the texture. I'd never drunk anything so velvety, so viscous. The incredible aromas sucked me in, but it was the texture that finished me off."

Alban had been told, wrongly, that Condrieu was a cheap wine, and he thought he had stumbled on a discovery that would make him world famous, as the first Californian winemaker to reconcile quality and quantity – equivalent to the philosopher's stone, or perpetual motion, or cold fusion. His excitement kept him awake all night. Though he would never overturn the laws of wine economics, Alban did become a pioneer on two fronts. He showed that Rhône grapes could make great wines in California, and he was one of the first to plant new vineyards in the hills around the little university town of San Luis Obispo, roughly halfway between San Francisco and Los Angeles. It was here, thousands of miles from Burgundy and the Rhône, that I was given the most fluent account yet of how different soils make different wines.

John Alban is an engaging example of the Francophile Anglo-Saxon wine enthusiast, a type that's quite common in California.

(The way you recognize them is by the way French slips into their conversation, not as actual French words, but as English words that aren't real English. Robert Parker told me about his professional "formation", meaning his training. David Ramey asked if I wanted his "coordinates", meaning his contact details.) John Alban's reactions were very Gallic when I congratulated him on his articulation, quoting Patrice Rion, who had said of the Americans: "*Ils decortiquent les choses*" – they analyze, or unravel, or get to the bottom of things. But John was worried that this phrase could be taken pejoratively, and imply that the Americans could pick phenomena apart but miss the big picture, the interconnectedness of things.

This, anyway, was the John Alban soil seminar. It involved tasting from three barrels, each containing a wine made from Syrah grapes, but from different vineyards, with the relevant soil samples in glass bottles for visual reference. The first soil sample (from his Seymour vineyard) was chalky: a handful of white and densely compacted powdery lumps. The second (from his Lorraine vineyard) was darker, more lumpy and less homogenous. John called it a mix of river rock, a lot of sand and a very small amount of clay. The third was the darkest, full of fine gravel.

The two crucial variants were the speed with which the soils heated up and the amount of water they retained. John explained that all three samples came from vineyards on the far side of the Edna River: those on the near side held too much water to make top-class red wine. "Here we have a tremendous variation of soil types. Everything on the far side of the stream is erosion from that mountain range, and everything on this side has rotted out of these hills. They are a completely different geological form.

"That side is all red and this side is all white, because of the soil composition and the way it drains. On this side of the stream the soil holds too much water to make great reds, because they stay in a vegetal cycle longer. They are all well-drained soils, but if you get enough clay with enough rock the vines continue to suck moisture far into the summer. They just keep on growing."

The preoccupation with this aspect of soils is shared with Professor Gérard Seguin of Bordeaux University, who has spent his career investigating the world's most famous vineyards and trying to establish what they have in common. His conclusion is that great wine grows in places that start drying out at precisely the right stage of the vines' annual growth cycle. The idea is that the vines begin to feel slightly under threat and start to put their resources into the next generation – the grapes – rather than into luxuriant growth. But it is also important that the roots find enough moisture to allow the grapes to ripen.

John Alban compares the process to the struggles of ambitious parents. If you want your children to have a university education, you have to start budgeting early. If you then have lots of children and try to fund them all, you go bankrupt. That's what happens to a vine when there are too many grapes and not enough water: it runs out of resources, shuts down and stops ripening.

It is easy – too easy in Alban's view – to get Californian grapes to ripen. His Lorraine vineyard, with its sand and rock, is a hot zone. He explains that it warms up like a brick but doesn't hold much water. "To the extent that I make a Californian wine, this is a Californian wine. It's unctuous and full with a smell of brown sugar, not quite as fruity as the black-cherry-scented wine from the gravel soil, but particularly Californian because of the sweet impression it gives in the mouth."

The first wine I tasted was from the chalky Seymour vineyard, which is the most inhibited in the ripening process. The white chalk reflects the sun, which stops the soil overheating, and as it is light and porous it is a natural insulator. Because the soil is free-draining there's also a strain on water resources. The result is a wine that, year in year out, is the most French-tasting of all the vats. It smells more spicy than fruity, especially of white pepper – with notes of violets – and it is fine, neither insipid nor rough. A visiting French grower, Jean-Luc Colombo from the village of Cornas in the Rhône, told Alban that this wine wasn't Syrah but Côte Rôtie. As he told me, John was still glowing with pleasure at this comparison with the great Rhône appellation. "It's my personal taste: I prefer elegance to power."

John Alban learned about soils when he travelled to France, meeting the people he'd learned to idolize through tasting their wines; while a stream of French growers have been heading in the other direction. Around 30 kilometres to the north of John Alban, in the Paso Robles district, John Munch was set on a new career after a group of French growers turned up on his doorstep, eager to invest substantial sums of cash without necessarily troubling their country's tax officials with the details. They were from the Côte des Blancs district of Champagne, where the soils are white with chalk, and they were looking, with ebbing confidence, for somewhere in California that could offer equally suitable soils for making sparkling wine.

"In my naivety I made the mistake of trying to do the research for them, by getting in touch with the wine university", recalls Munch. "When I started talking about calcareous soils to anyone connected with the wine industry, I received the two standard replies: one, 'it doesn't matter' and two, 'it doesn't exist anyway'. Even though here in Paso Robles we're sitting on a mountain of limestone, we were told that limestone doesn't exist in the west. I hadn't thought to go downtown to the soils conservation office, who would have shown me all the limestone here."

John Munch looks more like an ex-member of The Grateful Dead than a wine type, and this first impression is right. His best school buddy was "Pigpen" Ron McKernan, one of the founder members of the Dead, who died in 1973. "My main experience of wine had been drinking with Pigpen," John told me. "We used to mix up Thunderbird and Ripple. We called it Thundernipple."

I suggested that Thundernipple sounded an ideal accompaniment for another well-known Californian intoxicant that flourishes in the northern terroir of Humboldt County. Munch chuckled in confirmation.

Before meeting the Champagne party in 1979 Munch had worked at restoring Victorian houses, first in San Francisco and then along the Central Coast. Next he became involved with wine, first researching sources of grapes for the French group, and later making wine for them. When one of his wines won a gold medal at the International Wine Challenge in London, he felt established in his new career, despite a lack of formal training.

A few years later he met another group from France who were looking for limestone soils to start a Californian vineyard. It was led by the Perrin brothers, proprietors of Château Beaucastel in Châteauneuf-du-Pape, in the Southern Rhône, and friends of the importer Bob Haas, with whom they were planning this new venture. The party was sent to John Munch by Randall Grahm, the quirky, highly literate philosophy graduate who has become unofficial spokesman for the handful of Californians trying to emulate Rhône wines – the "Rhône Rangers".

By now, Munch had moved on from sparkling wines and was trying his hand with Rhône grape varieties, on vines that grew on the region's limestone soils. However, the winery was surrounded by sandy loams. "They were all disappointed when they saw the terrain," Munch told me. "But when they tasted the wine, they all said: 'This didn't grow here!' At that point I understood what they were looking for and I took them out to Peachy Canyon Road, where you can see the white soil everywhere. They were literally jumping out of the car with excitement." That trip down to Paso Robles marked the end of their three-year search across California for the right site for the Haas-Perrin project: their new vineyard at Tablas Creek, just up the road from Munch's Adelaida winery, began making wine in 1997.

Every wine region in the world has at some time seen the arrival of pioneers carrying vine cuttings. Some vineyards, like the Hunter Valley in New South Wales, were created by trial and error; here the first planters made the elementary mistake of trying to put vines on waterlogged soils. Whether the Celts or Romans who planted the Côte d'Or had prior knowledge of the virtue of limestone soils is unknown, but their roaring success has inspired growers to look for similar soils to Burgundy's.

The most quixotic search for terroir in modern times has been that undertaken by Josh Jensen. The story of his quest from 1972-1974 in a Volkswagen campervan has been told elsewhere (*The Heartbreak Grape: A California Winemaker's Search for the Perfect Pinot Noir*, HarperCollins West, 1994). Jensen ended up in San Benito County, where he built a unique hillside winery on the site of an old rock-crushing plant in the isolation of Mount Harlan, in the Gavilan mountain range. At that time, Jensen told me, apart from the Martin Ray property that was all but abandoned, there was no exciting Pinot Noir from California. "I said to myself, if I'm going to make world class wine, which was and is my goal and my mission, then I've got to find limestone. It was frustrating, because it was like looking for a needle in a haystack. Sometimes I'd find one little speck on the geological map and then just not be able to find it at all on the ground."

Eventually Jensen ended up far from what is considered wine country, ten miles from a little 1950s timewarp market town called Hollister, where, along with neighbouring Gilroy, they grow most of America's garlic. And somewhere along the way his marriage came unstuck. "I once suggested to *The Wine Spectator* that they should do a story on divorces in the wine business," he says, "but they didn't bite. Actually, I think I'd have been divorced even if I'd been in the computer business."

What motivated Jensen was his time in Burgundy, working in the vineyards and cellars of the Domaine de la Romanée-Conti and Domaine Dujac. When he tried to find out why Burgundy was unique, he always received the same answer: the limestone.

But was he right? James Halliday is the Australian writer and founder of the Coldstream Estate in Victoria, which specializes – like Jensen – in Pinot Noir. He disagrees with Jensen. In his *Wine Atlas of California* (Viking, 1993) Halliday argues that soil type is relatively unimportant compared to soil structure; and that the preoccupation with mineral content and organic composition is unscientific propaganda, trotted out by PR apparitchiks on both sides of the Atlantic. If soil acidity is too high it can be adjusted, and Halliday quotes a number of unnamed authorities quick to dismiss the relationship between soil minerals and grape flavour. Limestone makes for superior wine in Burgundy, he argues, because it is free-draining, which counters the effects of the region's abundant rain. "Why on earth should limestone be critical in the bone-dry summer hillsides of Mount Harlan, where Josh Jensen has his vineyards?" Halliday asks. "I strongly suspect any other mountain soils could do the job as well."

Halliday is a genial man who makes good wine, but he argues like a scientific reductionist – someone who will only admit the existence of what current technology allows him to measure. In any case, Claude Bourguignon believes he is on the way to explaining why limestone has such an effect on the flavour of Pinot Noir, and plans to publish a paper on the subject in the near future. In the meantime, he explained the gist of it to me, based on a chemical formula describing the action of bacteria on limestone ($CaCO_3$). The essence was that limestone is a unique rock, with its origins in life, made from the remains of tiny sea creatures. It is also, because of its high alkalinity, an extremely inhospitable growing medium for most plants, though vines – over the course of several millennia – have developed a unique symbiosis with limestone. Very few other plants can adapt. To make this adaptation the vines produce a layer of clay around their roots, clay that has a very high exchange capacity. In other words, the roots transform the limestone by producing an acid that neutralizes its alkalinity.

With their marine origin, calcareous soils are more abundant round the Mediterranean than anywhere else in the world. Bourguignon suggests that this is why Mediterranean civilizations have been founded on the grape, from the Lebanon to the Côtes du Rhône. Generally acidic soils don't make very good wine, he observed, although today it is possible through good oenology. Wine makers in Oregon observe that acidic soils tend to make wines with low acidity. Their answer is to add lime to the soil and tartaric acid to the finished wine.

Such an approach is anathema to someone like Jensen, whose heart is still in Burgundy. He took me to see the Calera vineyards, (named after the Spanish for a lime kiln – there are two ancient-looking structures among the vines). Because they are so remote, even from the parent winery, this journey meant him losing the best part of a morning's work. On our way up in a four-wheel drive, we met a party of Mexican vineyard workers on their way down. They had given up pruning for the day as rain had made it unsafe for their non-four-wheel drive car to negotiate the steep and slippery tracks. There's no flat ground: the vines grow in contour lines up and around slopes, swellings and hillocks.

On the basis of this single winery, 3,000 hectares (ha) of Mount Harlan are registered with the Bureau of Alcohol, Firearms and Tobacco as an American Viticultural Area (AVA).

Calera owns 324ha, of which Jensen has so far planted 31ha with Pinot Noir, Chardonnay and Viognier. The wines are regularly rated as among the best California produces, and fetch prices to match, trading at $50-$80 for a single bottle. He was the first president of the growers group, Pinot Noir America, and the Burgundians he once laboured for as a cellar-hand are now good friends and regular visitors.

So why, as we drive through this mountain kingdom under sheets of rain, does Jensen keep telling me about tough times and catastrophe? Put simply, the estate is making very little wine. Yields from the limestone ridge that constitutes the Côte d'Or in Burgundy average around 45 hectolitres per hectare (hl/ha) of vineyard. Many think that this is too much and would prefer to see a return to the 30 hl/ha mark reached earlier in the 20th century, before the advent of chemical fertilizers. But in 1998, Jensen's Pinot Noir vines produced just ten hectolitres per hectare, a pathetically small harvest, he says. In 1999 the crop level was barely higher, at just under three-quarters of a tonne.

Proprietors learn to balance years of dearth with years of plenty, and Calera's cellars in early 2000 were full of wine from a plentiful 1997 crop. But 1998 and 1999 were not freak years: since the first crop in 1978 there was an uninterrupted succession of drought years from 1987-1991. "It was just a nightmare," said Josh. Even when there was normal rainfall in 1992, the year a reservoir was first dug, the land was so dry that the rain that did fall just percolated in and didn't run off the land to fill Calera's reservoir. It was a very wet 1993 that ended the drought.

But the underlying problem in this part of San Benito County is revealed by the annual rainfall statistics. California's wine country, Napa and Sonoma, gets on average 1,000mm per year. Santa Cruz mountains, the home of Ridge Vineyards and the old Martin Ray estate, get a little more. But Hollister has only 380mm of rain per year, so Jensen was profoundly grateful for the downpour that was keeping his workers from their seasonal tasks. "Four or five weeks ago everybody was talking about the possibility of this being another drought year. In Calera, drought years are catastrophes." In other Californian vineyards farmers complain that if the rains don't come they'll be forced to start drawing on their reservoirs: here, the danger is that the 15 million-litre reservoir that Calera has recently created will simply be dry.

And on Mount Harlan, as tends to happen in arid regions, the distribution of water supplies is becoming a source of conflict. The round recently-dug pond is now the focus of a row with a woman living further down the mountain, who claims that it is interfering with her water supply. Jensen blames outsiders, with their own agenda for developing the mountain, for stirring up trouble. In any case, the water authority has insisted on an overflow pipe so that the reservoir drains when it reaches a certain level; and as I cowered beneath the deluge that marked my visit, it seemed likely that the half empty reservoir would reach capacity. It seems a gruelling way to make a living, but the Calera project does work, despite the droughts and wrangles. It's never been a crime at the elite end of the market to make too little wine. The estate is funded by what in France would be called a *négociant* business, through which Jensen buys in more than twice as many grapes as he grows on the estate, in order to make wines simply labelled as "Calera Pinot Noir" and "Calera Chardonnay" at his innovative, gravity-fed winery. The project has been expensive, with a starting cost of $1.5 million, but what mainstream growers would regard as a quirky choice of site meant that the land cost a fraction of what it would have in Napa and Sonoma, even in the mid-Seventies. It must be nice, too, to own your own mountain.

The difficulties arose partly because Josh Jensen broke with established practice in California and looked at soil before he looked at climate. Virtually everyone else does it the other way round, even a worshipper of French wines like John Alban. Alban spent even longer than Jensen traipsing through California in his search for possible sites, but his main research tools were tables of climate data, not geological maps. This is the method prescribed by the department of viticulture and oenology at the University of California, Davis, although Alban will have used more precise measurements than the tool that UC Davis bequeathed to the industry: the system of climate zones.

These were mapped in the late 1930s by professors Maynard

Amerine and Albert Winkler and range from Region I, the coolest and considered most suitable for quality wine production, to the hottest, Region V. They use a formula based on the number of days when the temperature reaches over 11°C, multiplied by the number of degrees in excess of 11°C on each such day. Calera is in region I and so, in theory, should have an ideal climate for Burgundy varieties. But it doesn't have this reputation, thanks to the opinion of the world's best-selling wine writer. "For some reason Hugh Johnson says this is too hot," says Jensen, wincing at the finality of the verdict. "But he doesn't know; he's never been up here and he's dead wrong."

However French its inspiration, there is something very Californian about the decision to turn a mountain into a wine estate and hillocks into vineyards, each separately named and vinified on the model of the Burgundy *grands crus*. Even standing apart from the mass of proprietors who huddle together in the Napa Valley is a Californian tradition in itself. Jensen follows in the footsteps of Curtis Tamm, the French-born founder (in 1919) of Chalone, another isolated winery in the Gavilan Mountains, 30 kilometres south of Calera; or Martin Ray and Chafee Hall in the 1940s, up in the Santa Cruz Mountains; or Dr Stanley Hoffman in Paso Robles, 20 years later. The solitary winery belongs in the Hearst or Getty tradition of withdrawing into a realm of European splendour. And Calera's wines are as weirdly individual, in their way, as the architectural fantasies of Hearst

Castle, built by newspaper magnate William Randolph Hearst at San Simeon. Jensen's decision to make wine in a drought region has resulted in a tannic, chewy, slow-maturing version of Pinot Noir that is the opposite of the fruity, early-drinking New World stereotype. It became so chiefly because of Jensen's determination not to do things in the conventional style.

John Alban takes a less combative attitude to mainstream winemaking than Jensen. On the day I visited, he had taken the trouble to put on a UC Davis T-shirt, a signal that he was not about to indulge in the usual Davis-bashing (he's an alumnus). Alban believes soils are of crucial importance, but he doesn't think they are the starting point. "When choosing a location," he told me, "the single biggest factor is climate. I took 40 years of climate data from the Northern Rhône and from that I took great vintages, to figure out what was going on. A lot of people think that great vintages are unusually warm years. But what they are is unusually warm at the end of the vintage – September and October." Alban found the equivalent to the hot, late summers of the Rhône in a Californian weather condition called Santa Anna, which boosts summer temperatures from an average 23°C to over 35°C. "We have to have it here to ripen and you almost certainly get them in September and October. In ten years we've never failed to have one."

But why are there these different senses of what matters in deciding where to grow grapes? John Alban points to the weight of wine history that has already enabled the French to decide what regions are suitable for viticulture, and to work out where different varieties of grapes can ripen optimally: "They've had 2,000 years to do what we are trying to do in 50 years. If you go to France they talk incessantly about soil, while here in California the big discussion is always about climate. You have to understand that with the appellation system, climate has been addressed. There's no change in climate across the Côte d'Or, but there's a tremendous variation in soil types, and that's why one vineyard can taste different from another just 200 metres away. If you're foolish enough to talk to a Burgundian about Cabernet, they'll say 'Go to Bordeaux'. They don't have a climate that can grow Cabernet. Nobody buys land there and wonders what variety to grow; climate isn't an issue."

Even if Josh Jensen may sometimes rue his quixotic decision not to consult rainfall data before settling on Mount Harlan, he would have done worse had he put his faith in Davis's climate guidance. The degree-day measurement system persuaded many of the biggest names in the industry to move to Jensen's home county, San Benito; only, without the lure of limestone, they went for the cooler areas and even nearer the coast, further west in Monterey County near Salinas. In the fourth edition of his *World Atlas of Wine* (Mitchell Beazley, 1994), Hugh Johnson entertainingly describes the Salinas valley as: "a highly efficient funnel for a regular afternoon visitation of cold sea air.

Unfortunately, the funnel proved all too efficient. On a hot day inland, clammy coastal air comes rushing up the valley with such force that it actually tears off vine shoots." The growers, writes Johnson, explained the green, unripe flavours in their wines by suggesting they were inherited from the lettuces that had previously grown in the same fields.

Wente Brothers was one of the producers that made a big commitment to the new region. This historic firm arrived in the mid-Sixties and bought no fewer than 400 ha of the Arroyo Seco sub-district. It was among the pioneers who at the peak of the wine boom planted more than 12,000 ha, a figure that is now reduced considerably. "We thought it was going to be a bit warmer, closer to what we get at Livermore," explains Eric Wente. But he looks on the positive side: "It forced us to grow some quite interesting grape varieties."

Wente finds the degree day system "a good general indicator, but when you start to get into the detail of things it can break down." The analytic tool of "degree days" was simply too blunt. Revealing that the temperature exceeded 11°C – the minimum for photosynthesis – does not tell you how long it stayed above 11°C, and measuring the number of hot days did not reveal the Salinas wine funnel effect. Not only were too few readings taken during a 24-hour period, there weren't enough recording sites. Growers throughout the state will tell you that the microclimate of their valley or hillside has little to do with that of the local town from where the Davis professors took their temperature data. If the system of calculating mean temperatures failed to reveal problems, it also overlooked some opportunities: grapes can keep fresh acidity even after the hottest days, if night-time temperatures fall sufficiently.

Great wine is the result of the infinite attention to detail that is required when an almost unmanageable number of variables are in play, starting with the complex and cyclical forces that create and sustain the soil. The difficulties at Salinas in the 1960s and 1970s resulted from the urge to oversimplify, but the Davis experts' most damaging error was still to be revealed.

(1) *Nature versus Nurture – will technology replace terroir?* Debate organized by Harpers magazine, London, 16 March 1999.

(2) Paul Draper anecdote to author.

(3) Chemical markers for Aroma of Vitis vinifera var. Chardonnay Regional Wines. SP Arrhenius, LP McCloskey and M Sylvan. *J Agric. Food Chem.* Vol 44 Mo 4 1996, pp1085-1090.

2
PLANTING THE VINEYARD

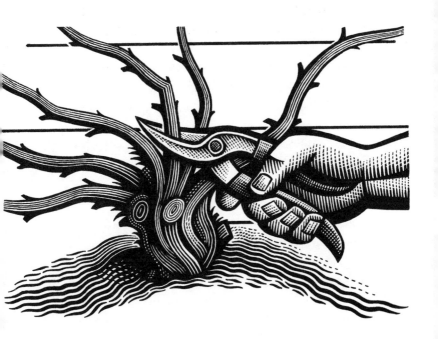

So far I've looked at the contribution made to wine by land, soil, water and climate. Soon I want to discuss the choice of a grape variety and its clones and how the vines are planted and trained. This means meeting a cast of people: the proprietors, growers and consultants who take all these decisions. And before plunging in among the vines I'd like to pull back for a moment and survey the human landscape. Who are these people and what do they want?

One reason to pause is that it's easy to start using misleading language. If you say that a retired American cardiologist or a supermarket magnate in Bordeaux planted a vineyard, it's very unlikely that he did any such thing in person. On the other hand, small-scale growers in Europe really are likely to spend time out on the land clearing trees, breaking up soil, or digging holes for the young plants when they arrive as grafted cuttings from the nursery. The international success in the 1980s of Henri Jayer, a septuagenarian grower in the village of Vosne-Romanée in Burgundy, didn't take place overnight – it was built on decades of his wife's meticulous work in their holdings.

Most estates in France, Germany and Austria are owned by families who have been on the land for generations, whether as peasant farmers or landed gentry. Such people are capable of making astonishing wine, while remaining quite unworldly. The Cotat estate at Chavignol, near Sancerre on the Loire, was founded in the 1920s by a relative of the Cotats, Ferdinand

Thomas, shortly after he returned from the war. His photograph still hangs in the cellar, dashingly moustached with the plumed *casque* of a cavalryman. The Cotats have gone on making wine the same way ever since, from ancient hill-grown Sauvignon Blanc vines, producing something that has little in common with regular Sancerre. Their wine is concentrated, not thin, and improves out of recognition – rather than collapses – when aged. François Cotat is 37 years old and is taking over the wine making. "Have you been to Paris?", he asks me. (Paris is little more than 160 kilometres to the north.) "Have you seen the prices the restaurants charge for our wines? It's a completely crazy place."

But some visitors feel equally lost in the back woods of *la France profonde*. The winemaker Gary Farr, whose estate is in Geelong, near Melbourne, is obsessed with Burgundy and its wines, but he never loses the sense of being somewhere strange: "It's amazing how many of the peasants living in some of these little towns have hardly been outside them," he reflects. "You go into the Hautes-Côtes de Nuits and they haven't been down even to Nuits-St-Georges twice in the year. I went there first in 1983, then again in 1987 and 1988 and when I went back there was a phone box – the first one they'd had. They're not that far from anything, but they don't want anything to do with other people."

Another major difference between Europe and the New World is that there's so much family-owned property. François Cotat doesn't need to succeed in a professional career in order to afford to buy his own estate, nor does he need to take an oenology degree and then seek a rich patron to hire him to make wine. Paul Draper, the presiding genius of Ridge Vineyards, high up in the Santa Cruz mountains, finds something uncomfortable in the spectacle of celebrity winemakers looking for rich benefactors; he compares them to con artists eyeing up their next mark, and says he's heard some discuss their employers in very cynical terms. The deal is that the winemaker undertakes to manipulate the grapes into a super-concentrated oaky concoction in order to impress the show judges and massage his employer's ego.

But happier partnerships exist, particularly when proprietor and winemaker have a common passion and philosophy. Gary Farr's love for Burgundy came through tasting with the owner of his Bannockburn winery, Stuart Hooper. The Adelaida Estate, where John Munch worked until recently, was born out of a creative partnership with the Van Steenwyck family (who built their fortune from offshore oil-exploration equipment). The Peter Michael winery is a partnership between the British entrepreneur who invented Quantel – the equipment that first enabled broadcasters to flip, squeeze and freeze TV images – and winemakers, first Helen Turley and then the Burgundy fanatic, Mark Aubert.

In Australia, young graduates tend to work for those big corporations that dominate their country's wine industry, which may be one reason why the Australian winemaking philosophy is highly geared to the requirements of agribusiness. The youngsters streaming out of Roseworthy College recognize that they won't make a living by biting the hands that feed.

In Europe the proliferation of family estates has a liberating effect. If you are heir to some hectares of vines in a well-known wine village, you can afford a certain independence of mind. Of course California is also full of heirs, some with indulgent parents who are willing to launch their children into business before their own demise. Another form of freedom is enjoyed by a group in Northern California – in sequoia country, beyond the range where vines are usually planted. These are marijuana growers, financially secure – if at some risk in respect of their liberty. To pass the time, they each tend a few rows of Pinot Noir and taste each other's barrels in a spirit of friendly rivalry. Indeed, these outlaws probably enjoy a greater sense of security than the Mexican labourers in California who prune, tie, spray and pick. If, as Burgundians and their admirers claim, 90 per cent of a wine's quality is determined in the vineyard, then these Mexicans could claim to be the real winemakers.

One of the pleasures of driving in California is the Mexican pop radio, with its passionate voices and flamboyant rhythms. As I drove up to Jim Clendenen's winery in the Santa Maria valley the song on the car radio faded into the winery radio. The Mexican Indians ate at the same table as the white guys, but didn't share the food or wine (they drank Coke and ate burritos). Few have all the necessary papers: John Munch witnessed a raid by US Immigration and Naturalization that sent staff diving into empty barrels for cover. Perhaps I should be less ready to curl my lip at the Australians' mechanized vineyards.

Vineyard work is hard and unpleasant. It gives you backache, and if chemicals are used can cause chronic health problems. People I know in Burgundy would stoop to labouring in a vineyard only if desperate for funds (unless, of course, they owned it). French vineyards are especially uncomfortable places to work. In America, Australia and New Zealand the vines are tall and wide-spaced, and don't require the agonising stooping involved in training or picking fruit from a conventional French metre-high vine. So when the New World growers visit their counterparts in Burgundy they see an unfamiliar landscape. It bristles with vines, up to ten times as many on a given piece of land as you might find in California: there must, by law, be no fewer than 11,000 plants per hectare in Burgundy.

Not all the differences are visible: like other shrubs and climbers, as much of the vine is hidden beneath the earth as appears above the ground. In fact, in a traditional form of French vineyard culture called *provignage*, the plants were hardly visible during the winter. "Beneath the earth's surface", wrote Richard Olney (the American food and wine writer), "lay a dense web of roots and chains of layered vinestocks; the gradual disappearance of the oldest wood permitting the system of *provignage* to eternalize, the process of perpetual renewal and decomposition going hand-in-hand."[1] Above ground vines grew at a density of up to 32,000 per hectare, higgledy-piggledy rather than in rows, as little as a foot apart. Horses and ploughs were out of the question. "The vineyards could only be cultivated by hand, with hoe and pickaxe. It was called plantation *en foule* – in a mob." Three of these ancient vineyards still exist, owned by Champagne Bollinger. Everywhere else they have been replaced with orderly rows of vines, usually trained on a wire trellis. This was done throughout France at the end of the 1875-87 phylloxera epidemic which destroyed one third of the country's vineyards, together with the livelihoods of hundreds of thousands of growers.

Phylloxera vitifoliae was an unwelcome American visitor which arrived on imported vines, along with the two forms of mildew, oidium and downy mildew. The Americas have so many species of *vitis* (the vine family) that Viking explorers named the "new" country Vinland. But the classic European grape *Vitis vinifera* is not one of them, and native grapes were not considered suitable for fine wines.

American species such as *labrusca*, *riparia* and *rotundifolia* were able to coexist with the tiny green insects that fed on their sap. But European vinifera vines had no resistance to this pest and succumbed to infections after the phylloxera lice had gnawed through their thin skins. The French deployed various chemical treatments against phylloxera before deciding to capitalize on the resistance of the American species. As the roots rather than the stems were vulnerable, all vines were now grafted onto American rootstock. This meant the end of provignage, as the whole point of the old system was to make new vines by burying the stem and letting it send out its own new roots: similar to the technique which gardeners call "layering".

The great expansion of the Californian vineyards took place during the 1960s and 1970s, and resulted, as we've seen, in a landscape that bore little resemblance to Bordeaux or Burgundy. Things were different below the ground's surface as well. The French, scarred by the disaster of the previous century, shunned rootstocks containing vinifera parentage. In particular the University of Montpellier warned against a rootstock that had been developed from crossing the American vine *Vitis rupestris* with Aramon, a high-yielding, low-quality vinifera that was used to make the most basic southern French red. The French had developed the Aramon-*rupestris* cross – AxR1 – at the height of the phylloxera epidemic, but it had been repeatedly found to lack resistance to the bug. This message was picked up across the Atlantic. The authors of a standard textbook *General Viticulture* (University of California Press, 1974) wrote: "That its resistance to phylloxera is not high has been demonstrated in other countries."

This did not prevent AxR1 from being overwhelmingly the most popular rootstock in California. In 1982 Sir Peter Michael began sinking his Quantel fortune into new vineyards on virgin land above Knights Valley, in Sonoma County, and he turned without hesitation to AxR1. His neighbours in the region reported great results. Bernard Portet, who had arrived a decade earlier from Bordeaux, was enthusiastic following his experiences creating Clos du Val in Napa: "AxR1 was terrific – perfect for California, not over-cropping and maturing earlier than St George: it was the mother of all rootstocks. When we started I was looking for other rootstocks; I hadn't wanted it because everyone knew about the recommendation from the University of Montpellier – that it was subject to phylloxera. But when I came here there were no other rootstocks; there was no choice."

There was no choice because UC Davis had put its reputation on the line in the debate, arguing against Montpellier's pleas for caution. Mark Aubert of the Peter Michael winery describes the hype when it replaced its non-vinifera predecessor, St George, in the early 1970s. "It was being touted as the vignerons' dream for producing uniform cropping." Reports of collapsing vineyards in South Africa reinforced Montpellier's objections, but the Davis viticulture department doubted that the lice were present in California. Then in 1980 four diseased vines were discovered in Napa. It took a decade for the insects to travel up into the Myacamas Mountains and to Sir Peter Michael's new vines on the slopes of Mount St Helena. Aubert saw his first case in 1990: "The vine looks like it's being stunted and you'll find the root-louse breeding and living on the sap. They're very small, about two millimetres, and you need a magnifying lens to see them. But their feeding produces these little tumours. Once you find these you know you've got phylloxera, so you look for the tumours." Yet only in 1989 had Davis finally retracted its support for AxR1, and the university's viticulturalists continued to endorse the tainted rootstocks even when their own experimental plantings had become heavily infested. "I think it was a kind of cover up," says Aubert. "Who knows?"

Replanting cost Sir Peter a million dollars – more than the original cost of creating the vineyard. Bernard Portet had to find many times that sum at Clos du Val. The story was repeated across California, and one victim was the Davis viticulture and oenology department, as the industry slashed its financial support.

The San Francisco novelist Lynn Steger has analyzed this tale of the blind leading the blind, and looked for explanations and a moral. In her article *The Siren Song of Aramon* (Global Vintage Quarterly, July-September 1999) she watches the tragedy unfold through the careers of three generations of Davis professors: Frederic Bioletti, who conducted rootstock trials from the turn of the century until Prohibition; Harry Jacob, who resumed the trials after repeal in 1933; and Jacob's graduate student, later associate professor, Lloyd Lider. The key factor, Lider told an interviewee, was yield – an extra five kilos of grapes per vine. "Growers were dazzled by the crop potential," wrote Steger, who argues that a combination of greed and arrogance blinkered the industry to the coming disaster.

When UC Davis experts were called in to see the damaged vines, they first reported that another rootstock, thinner-skinned than AxR1, must inadvertently have been brought in to the vineyard. When this was disproved a Davis entomologist blamed a uniquely destructive sub-strain of the insect, the so-called Phylloxera Type B. This theory may have got Davis off the hook, but as Lynn Steger points out, it is irrelevant – phylloxera will adapt to any susceptible rootstock, so the only answer is to use a resistant strain.

Why did Davis not respond to the warnings coming in from around the world, and especially Montpellier? Steger concludes: "In addition to being science junkies, American viticulture was too young to have evolved its own traditions, and it wasn't about to borrow from the French. Indeed, it was often dismissive of French methods." Steger's description of California in the 1970s and 1980s sounds like Australia today. With some distinguished exceptions, Australian winemakers and viticulturalists dismiss the classic French approach of low yields in the vineyard and minimal intervention in the winery as unscientific dogma. But phylloxera has meant the Americans are more willing to learn. "Australia is where we were 30 years ago", observe some Californians.

One sign of the new mood is that California's vineyards are starting to look more French. The first Peter Michael vineyard, named *Les Pavots* (The Poppies, after the bright orange Californian poppies, *Eschscholtzia californica*, that grow virtually everywhere), was planted at the then-standard density of 1,235 plants per ha, with the vines two metres apart in four metre wine rows. Replanting has halved the width of the rows and the space between individual vines, meaning that there are now upwards of four times as many vines per hectare. The new rootstocks make less extensive root networks and are less efficient than AxR1 at setting large quantities of fruit. The result, says Mark Aubert, is that the fruit has started to express the terroir characteristics of Californian Cabernet Sauvignon: liquorice, aniseed and what the French call *réglisse* – black cherries, black skinned fruit. "Beforehand the wines were OK; now they're highly collectable."

The before and after comparison sounds decisive, but it also reminds us how difficult it is to know which decision contributes what to the finished product – there are so many variables. A common mistake can be to suppose that flavours that derive from winemaking are the expression of terroir. Two examples of this are the sweaty, leathery aromas of the Syrah grape grown in the Hunter Valley in New South Wales, which have been shown to come from a wild yeast infection rather than the soil, and the Chardonnay wines from the adjacent villages of Meursault and Puligny in the Côte d'Or. Meursault is traditionally described as having an oatmeal flavour, while Puligny is like toasted bread.

There were three new innovations in Les Pavots vineyards: new rootstocks, new planting densities and new Cabernet Sauvignon clones. How much did each change contribute to the makeover of the wine? Mark Aubert guesses 60 per cent of the change is down to new rootstocks, 30 per cent is due to the new clones and 10 per cent to the tighter planting.

The case for tighter planting distances was explained to me by Patrice Rion in his cellars in the village of Prémeaux, a few kilometres west of Nuits-St-Georges. The more grape clusters that an individual vine has to ripen, the more dilute the wine is likely to taste. It therefore makes sense to get the same yield per hectare from a larger number of vines, each producing, say, three or four rather than fifteen clusters. The theory is also that roots jostling for space will be forced downwards, both making them drought-resistant and encouraging them to pick up minerals from the bedrock. Patrice Rion has spent some time overseeing replanting in the Chehalem Mountain Vineyard in Oregon with his friend Harry Peterson, a chemist formerly employed in the aerospace and computer industries. In Oregon especially, many growers have wanted to follow the lead of Drouhin, the Burgundy house which planted high density vineyards there in the mid-1980s.

The wider spacings recommended by UC Davis were not so much chosen as imposed on growers by the equipment available. In 1972 the newly-arrived Bernard Portet found that big tractors were all that was locally available. No-one used the specialist vineyard tractors that had been invented by Robert-Jean de Vogüé, the aristocratic head of Moët & Chandon. In California, grapes were just another crop, grown on the same sites that would otherwise be filled with fruit trees rather than on slopes – as in the classic European regions. "Rule number one of the farming business," says Portet, "is make sure you buy a tractor from a firm whose representative is no further away than your nearest town."

But could it be that tight plantings are undertaken simply because that's what the French do, rather than because of a rational appraisal of the potential benefits? This charge is brought by those who don't have tightly-planted vineyards themselves.

Jim Clendenen of Au Bon Climat, who is another honorary Burgundian, looks sceptical when I start talking about Patrice Rion's work with Peterson at Chehalem. Much of Au Bon Climat's production is with grapes bought in from wide-planted vineyards, planted in Santa Barbara county in the 1970s to make sparkling wine. "I don't believe that Chehalem is especially close planted," he demurs. "Gary Farr planted close together. It just leads the predators to get closer. The red spider mite population gets huge." Like many Californians, Clendenen favours tight but not-too-tight plantings on soils that tend to be much richer than those of Burgundy. "In Geelong, Gary's vines grow faster and much more vigorously, and that's our problem here as well. I want very close spacing so we can have fewer clusters per vine, but I still want to get equipment through the rows. So that means three-metres-by-one instead of one-metre-by-one."

The last time I had spoken to Gary Farr was just after a freak hailstorm had battered his vineyard, wiping out the whole of the

1998 harvest. When I telephoned him for news of his one-metre-by-one vineyard he said: "There's no more pressure of disease problems in that vineyard, and because of our climate – we get so much wind – we probably do far less spraying than anybody else." What's more, the five per cent of the Bannockburn vines that are tightly planted survived the hailstones better than the more conventionally-spaced remainder. Gary Farr has a special affection for this little corner of Burgundy and makes a separate cuvée from it, with a French name of course – Serrée, meaning tightly packed. "It's the wine I make for myself, the way I like it: 18 months in 100 per cent new oak. I know this vineyard produces so much more character, so many layers of flavour, a great earthiness." It sells for $110 Australian a bottle.

Not everyone has been in favour of California's vineyards becoming more like French ones. One sceptic is the influential Australian consultant, Dr Richard Smart. He thinks proprietors should think twice about whether a system that has evolved on low-fertility French soils is necessarily right for rich Californian ones. He accuses some Americans of imitating the detail of French vineyards without understanding how they work.

Smart's life's work has been to get the old wide-spaced vines to produce better fruit. He has studied the way in which French farmers manage traditional, close-planted vineyards and has used the same principles to devise methods of training and pruning big vines that will produce comparable results. His mission is to rewrite the hallowed equations – low yield equals high quality, and high yield equals low quality – by designing vineyards where high yield can equal high quality.

Of course, if you redesign a vineyard containing 1,235 vines per hectare to make room for five times as many plants, the total crop will rise. There will now be so many vines as to compensate for their drop in productivity taken as individuals. It's this simple fact, rather than blind imitation of the French, that seems to me to have inspired the new, denser plantings.

But some New World vineyards are on such rich soil that if the vines are close-planted they will immediately smother each other with foliage and stop sunlight getting to the grapes and ripening them. The classic answer would be that vines are simply the wrong crop and that the land would be better utilized for fruit trees or arable crops. Dr Smart's techniques, however, can make the best of a bad situation, provided there's access to irrigation water that helps to build the vines' woody skeleton.

His theories stand or fall by their usefulness to grape growers – but they have a wider implication. It is hard today to find many in his profession who will stand up for the idea that viticulture should be about increasing the quantity of grapes. Smart's first challenge was to tackle the paradox that vigorous vines in fertile soils produced low yields. The explanation was that the vines got locked into the vegetative stage of their growth cycle: in the deep shade cast by mounds of leaves and tendrils small quantities of fruit set, and tended not to ripen. In Smart's book *Sunlight into Wine: A Manual of Viticultural Practice* (Winetitles, 1992) Australian vineyard manager David Lowe, of the Rothbury Estate in the Hunter Valley, writes that what attracted him to Richard Smart's techniques of canopy management were the yield increase and the improvement in quality. But Dr Smart is more circumspect in linking quality and quantity. He writes, also in *Sunlight into Wine*, that he may have created some confusion by associating increased quality with increased yield. "We are not saying that high yield always leads to higher quality, or that the world's best wines will come from high-yielding vineyards." He is simply arguing against the idea that there is a direct causal link between high yields and low quality. Very productive vines often have shaded canopies, and it is this, he claims, rather than high yields that are to blame for unripe, under-flavoured fruit.

Dr Smart's rhetorical question "Does high yield reduce quality, or does it have little or no effect?" contains its own implied answer. But one Australian grower, Don Lewis of Mitchelton in Victoria, distinguishes between simple ripeness (meaning sugar levels) and intensity of flavours. Lewis agrees that it's possible to have physiologically mature grapes at high yields, provided they are not shaded; but above a certain level there won't be enough of the anthocyanins and the other phenolic compounds that are needed to give wine its flavour and character.

I wrote my last wine book, *The Wild Bunch: Great Wines from Small Producers* (Faber and Faber, 1997), when it was fashionable to contrast European growers – who were seen as dogma-ridden, unhygienic and strangled by red tape and regulations – with the glamorous young English-speaking winemakers who were then breezing through the wine world, bringing their refreshing blend of common sense and scientific rigour. Endless column inches were devoted to the flying winemakers employed by supermarkets in Britain to raise the standard of wine made by impoverished cooperatives in Eastern Europe and the Third World. At that time the darling of the wine writers was a flying winemaker – now with somewhat clipped wings – called Hugh Ryman, who first told me (on Richard Smart's authority) that yields didn't matter.

Although I had discussed his arguments, I had not spoken to Dr Smart before I began researching the planting-densities debate for this book. Our chat on the phone got off to a sticky start. He'd been upset by the section in *The Wild Bunch* that was based on conversations with Prue Henschke, who with her husband Stephen is proprietor of Australia's greatest vineyard, Hill of Grace. Prue had told me that she had declined Smart's offer to retrellis her historic collection of 19th century dry-farmed Shiraz vines. She also told me that she felt his emphasis was wrong in countries with scarce water resources, because of the irrigation requirements of big vines. "You're the bloke who's been writing nasty things about me," Smart said on the phone. "You made me out to be an enemy of wine quality. It's quite unfair. I contacted Prue Henschke and she claims she never made those statements."

My problem with Richard Smart has been that he seems, like many Australian winemakers, to be a reductionist. And his questioning of the importance of low yields means he can appear something of a vandal. If wine quality in Burgundy is related to the balance of leaves to fruit, and isn't intrinsically related to low yields, then growers might as well replant at wider densities, irrigate, fertilize and push up yields, mechanize, make a lot more wine and a lot more money. Fortunately no-one is tempted, although Smart might observe that French law would prohibit them. On his home ground, as I've noted elsewhere, when Penfolds are looking for the best possible grapes for Grange, Australia's first growth wine, they pay over the odds to the owners of low-yielding ancient vines. These low-yielding vines seem fairly economically viable.

But perhaps Smart has earned the right to be an iconoclast. The Californian winemaker Zelma Long recalls his eruption onto her home turf in the early 1980s. "I remember Richard driving through Napa and saying, 'In ten years all these vineyards will look different.' That's about what happened. The new vineyards were planted with more canopy management and the whole standard of Cabernet went up."

Smart's prescription was usually the implementation of one or other of a range of training systems: the Scott Henry (devised by a grower of that name in Oregon, a former NASA rocket scientist); Smart Dyson; Te Kauwhata Two Tier (TK2T) and several others. These may seem to symbolize the coming of the machine, displacing artisan labour. But actually, Smart admits, he doesn't get many calls from peasants tending a few hectares on stony hillsides.

It's really an exercise in damage limitation. As he writes with winning modesty on the flyleaf of his book: "To Patrick Matthews – a guide to improving wine quality when poor decisions have been made in advance, esp. [sic] choosing the soil."

It is pretty sophisticated to regard rich soils as a poor choice. The wine industry in general has chosen productive soils – in California, Australia, New Zealand and the Mediterranean – because they satisfy demand at low cost. Wine was once only for the well-off; even members of the English professional classes, like my parents, couldn't afford to drink it every day. Smart's work has helped make high-volume inexpensive wine taste better, and to this extent vindicates the scientific approach. The irony is that his method is based on close observation of the way that French peasants manage their vines.

But his legacy of elaborate trellis systems does seem to be threatened by the fashion for closer planting. He faxed me a reasoned if strident attack on this trend, from the pages of *Practical Winery & Vineyard*.[2] His point is that close spacings only do the intended job of devigorating vines when the soils are poor. On rich soils the roots go down and down; the plants' hormonal signalling system then balances the underground growth with a matching profusion of leaves and tendrils. [He's on weaker ground when he claims that wider spacings are used in the Entre-Deux-Mers region in Bordeaux just because of the richness of the soils. Big vines – *vignes hautes* – were planted to a model developed by Lenz Moser in Austria, as they were more suitable for mechanized vineyards and thus cheaper to maintain. This was important because of the lowish prices fetched by the wines from this sub-region. There is, anyway, now a trend in Entre-Deux-Mers to revert to closer planting.]

Not even all the wine producers who contribute essays to *Sunlight into Wine* are on message. The Robert Mondavi winery in the Napa Valley uses the tightest possible spacings of one-metre-by-one-metre in its vineyards for the ultra-premium Cabernet Sauvignon-based Opus One (made in partnership with the Rothschilds of Château Mouton). This is despite the fact that this vineyard is on the richer soils nearer the Napa River. In another historic Napa vineyard, To-Kalon, Mondavi say they've found that a 1.4 x 1.4 metre spacing works best. Clay Gregory, Mondavi's general manager, denies that his employers are just chasing the latest viticultural fad.

"A block of the vineyard is called H Block, which is experimental, that we started years ago. We have some vines planted a metre-by-a-metre, some four-foot-by-four-foot, others two metres-by-two-metres and eight-foot-by-ten-foot as well. So every year we'd do blind tastings of all the different spacings, and of different rootstocks and clones as well. Our sensory evaluation led us to decide that four-foot-by-four-foot was the best planting in terms of the balance of the vines and the quality of the wines."

I doubt if everyone using close spacings is as rigorous as this. There must be many mistaken attempts on inappropriate sites. It's a fashion thing, just as it was fashionable until recently to dismiss the Old World's preoccupation with low yields. Zelma Long regrets the sheep-like tendencies of her colleagues: "I think the best thing is to look at each individual wine and each individual vineyard and see what's best." But she is still inclined to stay with close-spaced, shorter, single-canopy vines because they are more easily managed. "A lot of Richard's work was done on already established vineyards. But starting from scratch, a single canopy is a simpler farming system."

Even in California, though, hardly anything begins from scratch. Before the arrival of the broad rows of vines that have now been a feature of the landscape for half a century, Italian wine growers worked with equidistant vines about two or three metres apart, leaving enough room for a horse and cart. You can still see ancient pre-Prohibition Zinfandel vines, for example, at Ridge's Lytton Springs vineyard in Dry Creek Valley, Sonoma County. And more than a decade before Richard Smart first drove through the Napa Valley, another pioneer was trying to adapt European viticulture to local conditions.

Joe Swan died in 1988, but his legacy tends to materialize in unexpected places. (I found some mature bottles of his distinctive cherry and eucalyptus-scented Pinot Noir in a corner shop at a giveaway price.) While travelling in Burgundy, Swan discovered that red wines could lose their character by being filtered, and he was one of the first in California not to filter – and to advertize this on the bottle. The importer Kermit Lynch was alerted to the fact by tasting one of Joe Swan's wines – a Zinfandel – and raised the issue with his suppliers in Burgundy and elsewhere. Swan's wines were one of the reasons that Zinfandel became the hot Californian grape. Joel Peterson, who learned his craft alongside Swan, is now one of the state's Zinfandel kings and his winery, Ravenswood, has recently grown out of all recognition into a high-volume producer, with bottles on every supermarket shelf.

I went to the winery Swan built near Forestville in Sonoma to meet Joe's son-in-law and heir, Rod Berglund. Rod continued another Swan tradition in 1978 when he and three partners founded La Crema in Petaluma, aiming to make the most Burgundian wines that they could. La Crema used grapes from Carneros, and helped build the reputation for Carneros Pinot Noir that had been created by Andre Tchelitscheff.

The small tasting room often throws visitors, according to Rod, by being so obviously a workplace, not a hospitality area.

The handwritten descriptions of the wines follow suit: "If you're looking for a toasty, buttery Chardonnay with gobs of ripe melon fruit, this isn't it." When Berglund took over the vineyards during Joe Swan's final illness, what he found had more in common with a work of art than with a conventional vineyard. Tending it was a process of self-education, like everything else he had done before.

"Where Joe grew up in the Dakotas there was wasn't much to do when he was young," said Rod. "But he was an avid reader, and read about someone making rhubarb wine. Although his parents were teetotallers his mother had a clothes wringer and he wrung some rhubarb and put it in the attic. His sister saw him popping up to the attic once too often and soon threatened to tell their parents, so he warned her that she did so on pain of death. But that wasn't his first real winemaking. That came later, when he lived in Salt Lake City and found some Zinfandel vines in Bountiful Utah, near an old cherry orchard, and made a wine he called José's Rosé."

Joe Swan had wanted to be a painter and studied art, but the course of his life was mapped by World War Two. He joined the army as an aviation instructor and after demobilization went into civil aviation. Rod Berglund, who himself has a navy background, identifies a link between flying and winemaking. "Most of Joe's winemaking came from observation. He used to keep a log book, recording cloud cover, temperature and so on. He was a general observer as well. He'd put down how much a cab fare cost, what the meals were. It's fun to read about his travels in Burgundy as it's very detailed. He was an amazing traveller. His interest in wine spurred him to visit the wine regions; he'd visit people, ask questions; he picked up some French along the way."

It wasn't until he retired in 1969 that Swan went from being a home winemaker to a vineyard owner, with a plot in what is now the Russian River viticultural area. After his travels in Europe he wasn't impressed with the way most Californian vineyards were kept. "People used the same equipment as for their orchards. They weren't farming wine, they were growing grapes. They would plant 12 different grape varieties because they wanted to hedge their bets. There was no notion of matching vines to a place. Those vineyards were jungles, and the wines were vegetal and lacking in character compared to what he tasted in France. And so he did certain things that most people found appalling.

"Instead of a system of a trellis and wires, Joe decided that the best way to mimic the open, unshaded vines he'd seen in France was to support each vine with a single tall pole – rather like Riesling in Alsace or the Mosel. These were pruned so that the new year's shoots would grow from three short spurs that he called stations, at different heights up the stem. Each one was a unique entity: it was a real case of sculpting the vine. You had to look at each vine to determine its potential vigour; decide how many buds to divide between three stations and then balance them so they wouldn't shade each other.

"He said nobody else could figure out his pruning system. Only I could because I didn't have a lot of preconceived notions." So when Swan became ill, Berglund hand-pruned all the vines. "I don't think anyone else could have done it. You had to look at every vine and think like Joe Swan. It drove the picking crew nuts. They'd scratch their heads before every vine."

Today, some winemakers claim the status of artist, comparing their wine to creations like music or paintings. The eccentric Joe Swan vineyard might have become a place of pilgrimage, like the visionary Watts Towers in LA. But in the end Berglund decided he could make better wine using a more conventional system. "We started the conversion and began to see positive results almost immediately," he told me. Dr Richard Smart would be irritated to know that Rod has moved from Joe Swan's broad spacings to tight plantings – one-metre-by-two-metres in places. And now, on the poor sandy loam of the vineyard, he says he's getting great results.

(1) Olney, Richard, *Romanée-Conti: the World's Most Fabled Wine*. Rizzoli International Publications, New York, 1995.

(2) *Practical Winery & Vineyard*, November-December 1995.

(3) Winkler, Albert J et al, *General Viticulture*. University of California Press, Berkeley, 1974.

3
SOURCING THE
VINES

Soon after I started writing this book I encountered a vine smuggler, a type of offender I'd never met before. He initially hinted that he would be willing to talk at length, but as I quizzed him he became increasingly uncomfortable and cut short the interview, regretting that he had agreed to it in the first place: "The more attention this subject gets the more impossible it becomes for me ever to pass through customs without getting stopped."

He wasn't a professional; instead he was one of scores, if not hundreds, of Americans who have brought in vines from Europe rather than going to an approved source – such as UC Davis – or abiding by quarantine rules (two years in California, three years in New York State, where the plants grow more slowly). Many smugglers have been caught and fined. The best way to ensure that plants survive the flight is to transport them in hand baggage. If a smuggler is stopped there's little chance that customs officers will miss the precious bundle, each cutting being as thick as a pencil and 15 inches long.

It may seem like a fuss about nothing, as indeed the smugglers like to argue. But the spread of plants and micro-organisms has been hardly less potent in world history than actual movements of peoples. Staple foods from the New World such as cassava and sweet potato gave rise to a population explosion in 19th-century Africa that exceeded the losses caused by the slave trade. Infectious diseases brought to Central America by the Spanish in the 16th century killed not just some but most of their new subjects. On a different order of catastrophe, rural Europe was economically devastated by the phylloxera and mildew that arrived in the 19th century with American vine species. Pests can be devastating at shorter range as well; the vine growers of Napa and Sonoma are currently putting Northern California into a state of alert against the glassy-winged sharp-shooter, a tiny insect that's native to Florida (*see* Chapter Five).

Ever since the dawn of agriculture, people have had a greater dependency on an increasingly narrow range of plants (genetic engineering being the latest extension of this trend). This carries the risk of devastating failure, as witnessed in the Irish potato famine during the 1840s.

Wine grapes matter in a different way. The vine is a plant whose importance is cultural rather than staple, or an ingredient of survival. "Modernity" in the wine business, as in other forms of agriculture, has meant standardization and the loss of a host of local interactions between people, plants and places. Today's vine smugglers, however misguidedly, believe they are in the vanguard of a cultural resistance.

Wine growing arrived in the New World amid the destruction of local cultures. Ken Boek, of the pinkish, environmentalist Fetzer Vineyards, reserves special vitriol for the so-called "father of Californian wine", the Hungarian-born Agoston Haraszthy who, as city marshal of San Diego, provoked and then repressed an Indian rising. According to Boek, Haraszthy liked to brag that the best soil for a new vineyard was created by burning an Indian village. Native America had its revenge, however, in the shape of a Nicaraguan alligator reputed to have devoured this "swashbuckling" figure in 1862.

In narrowly viticultural terms the so-called "count" was a force for diversity. When he toured Europe in 1861 on behalf of the governor of California, he returned with 100,000 different cuttings, which represented no fewer than 1,400 different grape varieties. Until then, California had relied on the Mission grape brought from Mexico by the Franciscans. Australian viticulture owes a similar debt to James Busby, who toured European vineyards in 1831, and amassed a huge collection that he handed over for propagation to the Royal Botanic Gardens in Sydney.

Busby and Haraszthy were spoilt for choice. In the *Oxford Companion to Wine* (OUP, 1999) Jancis Robinson and Richard Smart estimate that there are about 10,000 cultivated varieties of *Vitis vinifera*; all are hermaphrodite, or self-fertilizing, selections from the wild grape, *Vitis vinifera sylvestris*. Because wild vines reproduce from seed, each is genetically distinct, although wild grapes – like wild flowers – tend to be much more similar than cultivars. People select and propagate plants with exceptional and desirable features, and also raise new seedlings. New varieties can result from a cross between two cultivated varieties, or even between two parent plants that are the same variety.

We don't know precisely when farmers started to create grape varieties by taking cuttings from promising-looking wild vines. Roman authors, especially Pliny the Elder and Columella, offer their opinions as to which grape varieties are the best, but there's no way of knowing how long these grapes had been established, or which of the names that are now familiar to us might be hiding behind a Roman alias.

What we do know is that generations of growers have done much more than simply preserve the varieties down the centuries. French peasant farmers in Burgundy, for example, traditionally renewed their Pinot Noir vines by a technique called *sélection massale*, known as "field selection" in the US. This involved going round the vineyard in late summer and marking the most promising looking plants to use for cuttings in winter, once they became dormant. As each grower had slightly different criteria for making this selection, each vineyard's population of Pinot Noir vines took on distinct characteristics, creating, in effect, the beginnings of a host of new sub-varieties.

What's more, *sélection massale* by definition uses a group of plants as the parents, rather than just one plant. Lalou Bize-Leroy, then the co-proprietor of Domaine de la Romanée-Conti, told Richard Olney in the 1980s that its vineyard was like a village made up of many individuals with their own personality traits, all of which were important to the local community. The Domaine continues to use a modified form of *sélection massale*, although they no longer use the whole vineyard as source material – only a certain number of parent vines which have been laboratory-certified as virus-free.

Sélection massale is no guarantee that the grape quality will improve. When Bob Haas was searching for a source of Rhône varietal vines for Tablas Creek he looked at what was on offer in California. Mourvèdre was quite widely grown under the name of Mataro and there was an abundance of Grenache, but he wasn't impressed. "None of what we tasted in the three or four years that we were looking seemed to be as good as it ought to be. California was the same kind of economy as the Midi of France, where it was just making mixed reds and mixed whites, and when they did field selections in the course of 120 years they selected the plants that were the most productive."

Haraszthy's legacy may have been devalued over the years, but there was also an intermittent flow of high-quality vines from France that created local reputations. One valued source of Chardonnay is the "Wente Clone", from the Livermore vineyards of the famous old family firm, which is believed to have come from the To-Kalon vineyard, which was planted in Napa in the 1870s. Another collection was created the following decade in the Inglenook vineyard, a few kilometres to the north.

When the expatriate Frenchman Paul Masson founded his sparkling wine business in the 1890s, he went back to Louis Latour's Burgundy vineyards for his Pinot Noir and Chardonnay.

In 1936 Martin Ray bought Masson's La Cresta vineyard in the Santa Cruz mountains; the Ray vineyards in turn became the source for California's Burgundy pioneers, Joe Swan and James Zellerbach's Hanzell, both in Sonoma.

In the late 1940s Dr Harold Olmo, UC Davis's chief authority on grape varieties, made several trips to France, Germany and Switzerland, returning with a collection of Pinot Noir cuttings. When the Champagne house Louis Roederer set up in Mendocino in the 1980s, it imported its Pinot Noir and Chardonnay vines from France, and is still the only Champagne outpost in California to use fruit only from its own vineyards.

Since the 1960s America's West Coast has witnessed a burgeoning interest in quality wines and a boom in new wineries. But there hasn't been a simultaneous wave of vine imports in the fashion of Haraszthy. Fear of virus infection has led to extreme caution: the United States Department of Agriculture (USDA) insists on a slow and laborious quarantine programme at a limited number of institutions, such as UC Davis. The bottleneck was tightened further in the 1980s when the USDA's scientist in charge of the Davis programme ruled against importing any more new material from Europe, on the breathtaking grounds that it was all basically the same anyway[1].

Like phylloxera, viruses are an unforeseen and undesired by-product of the traffic in vines across the Atlantic. Debbie Golino runs Davis's Foundation Plant Material Service, which supplies certified plant material to commercial nurseries and manages the university's quarantine programme. She believes that viruses were endemic in Europe and more or less harmless before phylloxera. The insects (an American import) gnawed into the plants' stems and weakened them; the plants then succumbed to opportunistic infections such as fan-leaf virus, a condition which stunts the vines, deforms the leaves and limits sugar concentrations in the grapes. Golino suggests that grafting onto American rootstocks solved the acute crisis but left vinifera vines with a chronic lack of resistance to viruses. Her experience is that the AxR1 rootstock, which is half vinifera, is relatively good at coping with viruses, but that American vines have much less immunity than their European counterparts.

Few people agree on the scale of the problem, and it is difficult to speculate on its historical scope, since these tiny organisms were only identified and made visible quite recently. Only through studying the infection caused by Tobacco Mosaic Virus at the end of the 19th century did researchers discover a class of disease-carrying micro-organisms that were smaller than bacteria, and too small to be seen through a conventional microscope. With the development of the electron microscope in Britain and Germany in 1935, virologists could see and describe the enemy.

The campaign against viral vine infections took off after the World War Two as a manifestation of Franco-German cooperation.

The French viticultural institutes developed genetically identical plants (or clones) propagated from disease-free vines. Meanwhile their German counterparts developed a method of heat-treating vines, maintaining them at a little over body-heat for a period of 50 or 60 days. At UC Davis, a USDA scientist, Dr Austin Goheen, adopted both approaches.[2]

The problem was the quality of clones offered by the research institutions. Those issued by the French government's *Service Viticole* in Beaune and Mâcon during the 1970s were healthy and productive, but their grapes were big, thin-skinned and didn't make good wine. One of the first to sound the alarm was Michel Bettane, a former classics teacher who now occupies a place in France roughly on a par with Robert Parker in America.

Bettane dismissed most Chardonnay clones, with their large berries and high ratio of juice to skin, as "*une catastrophe*". He not only denounced the new selections, he also organized counter-measures. There was a conference to alert Burgundy growers, with Olivier Leflaive of the famous family of proprietors from Puligny-Montrachet, and Jean Delmas from Château Haut-Brion, the Bordeaux first growth. The delegates claimed that the new clonal selections favoured high-yielding vines that produced grapes with high sugar levels, but at the expense of flavour and individuality. Bettane also learnt all he could about possible alternatives, so he was able to direct growers to those nurserymen willing to offer traditionally selected and genetically diverse young vines.

The agitation was effective. In 1992 the *Chambre d'Agriculture de Saône et Loire* admitted: "The urgency of the problem compelled us to act fast, and different types of clones were authorized. Certain of these are perhaps not compatible with the production of great red wines, nor of white wines with complex aromatic character. This is why a second wave of clonal selection has begun."[3] Bettane accepts that the newer Pinot Noir clones are better than the older ones, but regards the clonal selections of Syrah, Mourvèdre and Chenin Blanc as almost as disastrous as the Chardonnay. Above all he regrets the undoing of the work of generations of small growers, each competing to create their own best selections from the vines on their own small parcels of land. "What's the point of having 500 vines in a vineyard that all mature at exactly the same time, that all taste the same, that all have exactly the same levels of acidity?"

The Davis clones also acquired a mixed reputation. Mark Aubert, formerly of the Peter Michael winery in Knights Valley, is not a fan of heat treatment. "They basically cook them in an oven. It kills off the virus and it almost kills the plant – sort of like chemotherapy in medicine. It makes the vines strong – too strong." James Olney, nephew of the late writer Richard Olney, makes wine with Paul Draper of Ridge, with special responsibility for the label's Sonoma Zinfandels. Olney contrasts Davis's clones with those from French institutes which, unlike Bettane, he is willing to credit with an interest in flavour. "Davis have done enormous things to improve the health of vineyards around California," he says, "but they've done absolutely nothing about the quality of fruit. Maybe they can't or maybe they don't want to. I've sat in on many of their conferences where it's one of their points and they are very proud of it: 'We don't develop a clone and then make wine from it and decide if it's great wine or not great wine.' Davis puts out a Zinfandel clone and it has huge berries that are two times as dilute as they should be and that's just fine by them." Zelma Long, who made her name with Mondavi and Simi, thinks the picture is more complicated, with Davis supplying good quality clones for Cabernet Sauvignon, less good for Zinfandel, and frankly poor material for Chardonnay.

Pinot Noir is the variety that seems most sensitive to clonal variation, and it was the growers of the then-virgin territory of Oregon that took the initiative in searching out the best forms. The father of Oregon Pinot Noir, David Lett, planted the first section of his Eyrie Vineyard in the Willamette Valley with a clone that Dr Olmo had brought back from Switzerland named Wädenswil, or Davis 2a. To Lett, though, in 1970, it was just "Pinot Noir"; no-one at that time had heard that different forms could give different results.

But three years later people began passing on news about European work on clonal selection. In 1973 David Adelsheim, who worked with Lett before setting up on his own, responded by organizing a tasting of the different clones planted in Oregon, which revealed dramatic differences. Adelsheim describes the Wädenswil Pinot Noir as being at the opposite end of a spectrum of flavour and concentration from Pommard, a selection Harold Olmo had made from the Château de Pommard in Burgundy in 1945. Adelsheim responded by becoming an active plant hunter.

The following autumn David Adelsheim left for Burgundy. His destination was Beaune, where he was booked in at the *Lycée Viticole* for a short placement. However, he also made time for a detour to the south of France, on the recommendation of Dr Austin Goheen, the USDA scientist who was UC Davis's expert on plant importation. There he called in at ENTAV (*Etablissement National Technique pour l'Amélioration de la Viticulture*) which – with its unique vineyard at L'Espiguette on the Mediterranean shoreline – houses a collection of ungrafted vines that grows on sandy and, hence, phylloxera-free soil.

"I walked in out of the blue and asked if there was any way that they might ship a range of clones of Pinot Noir and Chardonnay to Oregon State University. It took them two years, but they finally did it. But then we realised that what they'd sent were the most common clones. We got some wrong ones at that time." There was a fresh wave of imports from France in the mid 1980s. A new professor arrived at the State University from New Zealand in 1984, and on his way he stopped in France and met Raymond Bernard, of the *Office National Interprofessional des Vins* (ONIVINS). Bernard managed the clonal research station at

Echevronne in the hills above the Côte de Nuits and he was keen to help. After first sending a selection of plant material to Oregon, he turned up in person.

"He came for the first cool climate conference held in Eugene and talked about the clonal selection programme, and which clones he thought would make the best wine," recalls David Adelsheim. The new Dijon clones caused a buzz of excitement, and many found their way south to California. However some of Bettane's reservations were justified, in Adelsheim's experience. "Most of the clones Bernard sent were too productive and weren't going to result in the kind of fine wine we were looking for. They didn't compare with the Pommard clone we already had planted."

There was another disappointment in the form of the man who was running the Davis import programme. Dr Austin Goheen "sort of wanted to believe that the only difference between clones was the result of the degree of virus infection. It was partly a turf war – also he felt that it was expensive and that his job was to get virus-free versions of as many varieties as possible, and that he had no mandate to clean up a whole range of clones." To circumvent Dr Goheen, Adelsheim and his fellow growers persuaded Oregon State University to obtain a federal import permit.

The Oregon collection might have addressed the lack of Pinot Noir material, but it did not solve the problem faced by Bob Haas and the Perrin brothers, François and Jean-Pierre, when they tried to establish a Californian counterpart to the Perrins' Rhône estate, Château de Beaucastel in Châteauneuf-du-Pape.

Tablas Creek, the winery they established in 1989, is possibly the most "terroirist" estate yet created outside France. Haas was dissatisfied with the Grenache and Mourvèdre on offer from Davis. Even now, with the dynamic and open-minded regime that is now responsible for the Foundation Plant Material Service, there is still a dearth of Rhône varieties. Although nurseries can now choose from 25 Cabernet clones and no fewer than 50 Chardonnays, there are only 7 versions of Syrah and just 2 of Grenache. And white Rhône varieties are simply non-existent – neither Viognier nor Roussanne are on offer.

The Tablas Creek team is convinced, like the other "Rhône Rangers" – Randall Grahm, John Alban, Doug Danielak, Sean Thackrey, Steve Edmunds and Cornelia St John – that California belongs with the Mediterranean rather than with central France. This means that the grapes that will make the best wine, with minimum intervention in the winery, will be southern French varieties. Haas and the Perrins found that local vines were either not good enough, or that the varieties they wanted to use were not available at all. But there is also an ideological reason, that can only be appreciated with a rather Jesuitical cast of mind. The team has used French vines because without them it would be harder to detect the vineyards' distinctively American terroir.

Without using exactly the same grape varieties as are planted at Beaucastel, how could you tell whether the differences in the Californian wine came from the soil and climate, or were caused by genetic differences in the vines?

Winemaking in California has often been led and directed by Frenchmen, from Charles Lefranc, who founded Almadén in 1852, to André Tchelitscheff (1901-1994), who described the hills west of Paso Robles as "a jewel of ecological elements"[4]. (He oversaw the planting in 1965 of the HMR vineyard, which is now the jewel in Adelaida Cellars' crown.) But it's rarely been as consistently French in spirit as Bob Haas's project. This isn't that surprising in the light of Haas's career. As this short, genial, crinkly-haired man drove me the short distance from the winery to the plant nursery I mentioned my interest in the legendary wine importer and wine writer Frank Schoonmaker. "I worked with Frank for ten years," he said, "from 1955 to 1965, in the importing business." I must have registered my excitement at finding myself seated beside a witness to history: "Aw," said Bob. "I feel like the thousand-year-old man."

Haas, like Schoonmaker, was a follower of Raymond Baudoin, founder of the *Revue du Vin de France*, champion of France's system of *Appellations d'Origine Contrôlées* and – though Haas was never aware of this – briefly a Nazi sympathizer. Haas was a follower in a more literal sense than Schoonmaker. His father had owned a smart grocers called Lehmann in New York, which was one of the first retailers to be awarded a liquor licence when Prohibition ended in 1933, because it was known not to have been involved in bootlegging.

Haas senior had employed Baudoin as his agent in France, and young Bob had met him in the early Fifties. When Baudoin died in 1953 Bob Jr had recently left Yale, and was soon sent out to France to replace Baudoin. "I went to France – just like that, you know. It took forever before jets came in. Going took 12 hours, back 14 hours. This was pre-de Gaulle and France was recovering from the war. Prices were really cheap, as the dollar was frightfully overvalued. You'd go to the finest three-star restaurant and it would come out at $30. But I loved the whole experience.

"I started with d'Angerville, Gouges, Ponsot, Etienne Sauzet. I was the one who stole Domaine Matrot from [Alexis] Lichine. Lots of the time I just knocked on doors. I was 24 – I didn't see being young as a problem, it was just about convincing people that it would be a good thing to sell in the United States. Sometimes one of the proprietors would say, 'Why don't you try so and so?' The Burgundians were politically pretty conservative. They had an ideological leaning to the United States: they admired it. They certainly weren't prickly or antagonistic."[4]

Quite soon Bob Haas ventured outside Burgundy. The great postwar cult wine was Château Pétrus, after Raymond Baudoin bought the 1945 vintage and Schoonmaker sold it to Le Pavillon restaurant in New York. "It was the first really authentic three-star-type French restaurant in the US. It was opened by a man called Henri Gould, who had run the French restaurant at the New York World Fair of 1939."

Haas visited the co-owners of Pétrus, the Moueix family in Libourne, east of Bordeaux, and acquired exclusive importation rights. This connection led the heir to the family business, Christian Moueix, to choose to study oenology at UC Davis rather than at Bordeaux. And it was at Davis in the 1960s that Christian got a taste for the great Californian wines of the era, particularly the Cabernets made by André Tchelitscheff at Beaulieu in the Napa Valley, and Martin Ray's Pinot Noirs from Santa Cruz.

Ten years later the wine boom was at its height, but Christian Moueix felt that the wines weren't as good any more – something he attributes to the fashion for "adjusting" their acidity with tartaric acid powder. In response Moueix bought the historic Napanook vineyard and began making "Dominus", his Californian counterpart to Pétrus back home in Bordeaux.

From Bordeaux, Haas travelled south and discovered the Banyuls appellation. Here, some of the world's most beautiful vineyards overlook the Mediterranean, the ancient vines clinging to narrow terraces dug centuries ago into the foothills of the Pyrenees. The grower he imported from Banyuls, Dr André Parcé, gave him a lead to the greatest domaine in Alsace, near the German border, but warned that the proprietor was implacably anti-American. Haas wrote to the proprietor, and was told that Domaine Weinbach was not at all interested in selling to the United States, but that he was welcome to visit. Theo Faller, the proprietor, had died, but his widow seemed equally unreceptive.

"Weinbach is a really good-looking domaine with a courtyard and climbing roses", says Bob. "Colette [Faller] said: 'Don't you need special labels?' Well we did; and at that time Alsace used 70 not 75 cl bottles. She asked: 'Don't you need 75 cl? Oh no! It's impossible.' Anyway we continued to talk, and we talked and talked and finally she said: 'The 1979 hasn't all been bottled yet. Let's go into the cellar and taste some wine,' and we emerged two hours later having tasted every cask in the cellar. I ended up with 2,000 cases of wine and I've become very good friends with her and her daughter. I consider Colette, Jacques d'Angerville and the Perrins as real friends."

The question is whether Haas and the Perrins will be able to achieve success comparable to that of Dominus in Napa. After all, Christian Moueix had insurance: the fact that his Dominus vineyard had been part of one of California's top estates a century earlier, with the quality of fruit that goes with mature vines. And even so, it wasn't until the 1990s and the arrival of David Ramey (formerly of Chalk Hill vineyards) that Christian's wines were widely acknowledged to have hit the spot.

So far, the wines made from the Beaucastel cuttings are big, alcoholic and fruity – more American tasting than European, although the blend put together for the 1998 vintage is restrained by Californian standards. There are teething problems. It's a matter of principle not to add laboratory strains of bacteria to trigger secondary "malolactic" fermentation, which stabilizes the wine and blunts the rawness of the acidity. However, the 1999 wines, like the 1998s before them, are nerve-wrackingly slow to get going spontaneously. And the four red varieties selected from the 13 that go to make Beaucastel Châteauneuf are behaving unpredictably in the terroir of Paso Robles.

The joker in the pack is the Counoise, which had been intended to add a bit of delicacy and finesse to balance out the heavyweight Syrah and Mourvèdre. "It wasn't supposed to be dark coloured or to have high alcohol levels," Haas says, looking at the inky liquid he's just drawn from a barrel of Counoise. He suspects one factor is the richness of his virgin soils, and another is that their plans had been based on virus-affected vines at Beaucastel, whereas these are virus-free. "The problem is that things just don't do what you expect."

Not only the upper parts of the vines (the "scions") but also the rootstocks have been imported from ENTAV at L'Espiguette. Bob Haas is delighted with the quality of the material and was unworried by my account of Michel Bettane's criticism of France's Syrah and Mourvèdre clones. "I think I have more experience of Mourvèdre than he does," Haas tells me, though he does concede that using a single clone might reduce the complexity of a wine. Haas has imported ten clones to date.

At the moment, with only three full-scale vintages under their belt, Tablas Creek has the atmosphere that you associate with the first night at a theatre, when the cast are waiting for the press notices to come in. Like Randall Grahm, one of the Rhône pioneers, they are growing a lot of different grapes, but unlike Grahm they're putting all their eggs in one basket and producing just two wines, a red and a white. "The worry about doing it that way is that the wines have really got to kick ass," says Randall.

While they wait to find out if they've made one of the world's great wines, the Haas-Perrin team can take short-term pride in a spin-off from the main business. The Davis Foundation Plant Material Service not only failed to ensure that California had good commercial stocks of Rhône varieties; it also emerged that the system of heat treatment was not even producing virus-free vines. When Tablas Creek needed to import cuttings from France the service was out of business, and its new head Deborah Golino was rebuilding it from scratch. This meant that Haas and his greenhouse manager, a former Catholic priest called Dick Hoenisch, had to learn the job from the bottom up.

In October 1996 Bob Haas, as a temporary commissioner of marriage, married Dick Hoenisch to Deborah Golina in the white garden at Tablas Creek, that Hoenisch created in imitation of Vita Sackville-West's at Sissinghurst, in Kent. The couple had met at Davis in the late Eighties where Hoenisch, who was then still in the priesthood, was studying for a masters degree in plant pathology. Now the couple are both back at Davis: Hoenisch runs the vineyard, while Golino continues as head of the reinvigorated Foundation Plant Material Service.

Haas and Hoenisch found another quarantine and certification agency – Cornell University's Geneva research station in New York State – and while they were sitting out the quarantine period, built a 500-square-foot greenhouse on their new estate. Hoenisch describes the high point as the moment when, after three years, "we took the vines out of the pots and washed the soil off them and air-freighted them to Tablas Creek." Now, Tablas Creek has become a vine nursery as well as a vineyard, with the state's would-be Rhône Rangers for customers. Randall Grahm complains that they can't sell him all the Roussanne he needs.

UC Davis no longer uses heat treatment for vines: these days the preferred technique is "meristem" culture. In this procedure the vines are grown under artificial heat – "so fast that they out-grow the virus", as Haas puts it – and a tiny virus-free portion is removed from an emerging shoot. A whole new plant is then grown from this collection of cells.

Even now there is little consensus about what James Halliday and Hugh Johnson term "The viral menace"[5]. Francis Mahoney of Carneros Creek winery carried out systematic trails of different

Pinot clones between 1974 and 1985. Mahoney told *Practical Winery & Vineyard* magazine in 1989 that "if a vine achieves ripeness and reasonable yields I think a little virus is OK." Randall Grahm of Bonny Doon vineyards has observed that tests give inconsistent results as to whether a given vine is or isn't affected. Mark Aubert thinks that at low levels – or "titer", to use the term used in measuring the degree of infection – a virus can even improve wine, and has observed its presence in Burgundy.

"Some of the old vineyards in the *premiers crus* and the *grands crus* have some viral infection; not at a high level at which they stop the grapes ripening, but at a low level at which it just makes the vines work a bit harder, so the grapes hang on the vines a little longer. A badly affected vine might have a titer of 100. A low titer vine, of say ten, makes great wine."

When carrying out his own *sélection massale* to extend the Peter Michael vineyards, Mark Aubert happily tolerated a little suspected infection. "If we saw the virus expressing itself – and the tell-tale signs are vines that had a terrible colour, or leaves rolling away from the sun – we'd never take cuttings from that plant, but we would take cutting from plants that we knew had low titer of virus, even if there were no visible signs of it."

But Bob Haas is pleased with his clones and proud that they are virus-free. Some of the worst effects, he observes, have been with smuggled vines – or "suitcase importations", as they are more tactfully described. "I've seen people who have suitcased-in vines from Europe, where the vines have lived with a particular virus and are reasonably resistant to it. But you bring that in and stick it in the ground in California and the virus is suddenly rampant. It may be the grafting, it may be the stress. Probably when you put a plant under stress its resistance is lowered."

The vine selections are only part of Bob Haas's vision for Tablas Creek. There was his search the length and breadth of California for the right terroir; the planting distances are fairly Old World (at 4,216 vines per hectare); then there is his spirited refusal to bow down to the cult of unblended single varietal wines; the winemaking is as natural and non-interventionist as you could wish. The estate is more or less organic and it generates topsoil through composting. [Much of the agriculture on which we depend destroys topsoil in a "spending spree" of this slowly-accumulated capital. The United States has lost one-third of its topsoil; much of the rest is degraded. The environmentalist Paul Hawken writes that nearly three-quarters of the productivity of the soil of the Great Plains was lost in just 29 years of agriculture.] Haas's vineyards will be dry-farmed, something that may be routine in France but which is extraordinary in California – a state whose agriculture has depended historically on profligacy with water resources.

I do not believe that the ecological stuff is simply a by-product of the pursuit of terroir: they are two sides of the one coin. When

Americans started learning about wine from the French, they also imported an ethical stance – although, like environmentalism itself, this acquired sinister allies in the late 1930s. Since then, wine has become imbued with the more everyday vices of elitism and social snobbery. But modern wine culture began in France as a straightforward consumer revolt against fraud.

(1) Clonal Selections: obstacles and opportunities with Pinot Noir. Hock, Stan, *Practical Winery & Vineyard*, May-June 1989.

(2) There is something rather American about this approach to zapping the opponent, like the "War on Drugs" or the mentality that led federal inspectors to seize "nobly-rotted" grapes intended for sweet wine at the Louis Martini winery in 1967 and order them destroyed as unfit for human consumption. (See p333 Brook, Stephen, *The Wines of California*. Faber and Faber, London, 1999.)

(3) Hanson, Anthony, *Burgundy*. Faber and Faber, London, 1995.

(4) Blue, Anthony Dias, *American Wines*. Doubleday, New York, 1985.

(5) Halliday, James and Johnson, Hugh, *The Art and Science of Wine*. Mitchell Beazley, London, 1995.

4
CHOOSING GRAPE VARIETIES

Supermarkets aren't the same everywhere. As well as the ubiquitous Cornflakes, Nescafé and Colgate, there is almost always some local colour. Supermarkets in the US tend to be empty of shoppers, by British standards, to have bright clinical lighting and an unfamiliar regularity in the way the fruit and vegetables are stacked. Another thing you don't find in the UK (along with appeals to Report Underage Tobacco Sales and displays of embarrassingly intimate products) are wines called "Mountain Rhine", "Golden Chablis" or "Mellow Burgundy": in the European Union, these labels would be illegal.

Since 1997 these lines have been joined by "Chardonnay with natural flavors", "Merlot with natural flavors" and – especially outrageous if you're Italian – "Chianti with natural flavors". All these are marketed by Almadén, California's oldest wine brand, founded in 1852 by an expatriate Frenchman, Charles Lefranc.

Of course, neither the Chablis nor Burgundy come from within five thousand kilometres of these classic wine regions, and the Mountain Rhine has no connection at all with riverside German vineyards. And although the "wines with natural flavors" are on the wine shelves in conventional bottles, they aren't wines and the flavours aren't especially natural. The "Chardonnay with Natural Flavors" is legally required to contain all of 3.75 per cent Chardonnay by volume. Other ingredients include water, sugar, neutral alcohol and chemical flavourings, but the exact recipes are not disclosed. When I asked

Canandaigua, America's second biggest wine producer, how they made the "natural flavor" wines that sold with the Almadén tag, their spokesperson told me that this was commercially sensitive information. However, she pointed out that alcohol, water and sugar are all found in conventionally made wine.

These bogus names are not unique to California. The American David Ramey told me about helping to make "Rhine Riesling" for one of Australia's most respected names. Obviously it didn't come from the Rhine – nor did it have even a glancing connection with Riesling. The grapes were grown in the irrigated, semi-desert flatlands of South Australia, and mostly they weren't even white grapes, but red Shiraz. These were decolourized with absorbent carbon and blended with Thompson's Seedless (which is not a wine grape variety) and a little Muscat for an aromatic lift that might conceivably be associated with Riesling.

The hot growing conditions and high yields of South Australia create wine that lacks acidity, so to prevent it being insipid or flabby the winemakers used an Ion Exchanger. This device raises acidity by replacing potassium ions with a mixture of sodium ions and hydrogen ions. There are health concerns about this procedure, especially for people on low salt diets, as the raised sodium levels cannot be tasted. It is banned in the EU.

A case like this undermines the Australian mockery of European regulation. Dr Richard Smart, for example, told an American journalist in 1994 that: "The Old World approach is to lob its energy into what's written on the label, with all the bloody laws and legislation that prop up the appellation contrôlée." But there is nothing particularly New World about wines with misleading labels sold by hard-headed businessmen. It was a familiar story in France at the start of the 20th century, when over-cropped wine was bought at knock-down prices and corrected, or "knocked into shape", even if it meant using chemicals that posed a health risk. It was the very progress of science, according to many observers, that made fraud commonplace and dangerous.[1] And there is no natural dividing line between Anglo-Saxons and Europeans on issues such as pure ingredients and honest labelling. Although the French were the first to create a system that gives consumers a level of information that accompanies few other foodstuffs, they have been greatly helped by American allies.

Since time immemorial wine has been an expensive drink. Among medieval Arabs its costliness made it a status symbol. From the period before Islam a poet wrote: "She has grown angry with me because I financed my drinking by selling my woollen cloak; if she carries on I will drink by selling my sheep."[2] Unlike cannabis, which sold for a fraction of the price, wine required vinification and long storage to become, in the words of another poet, "A drink saved for Adam before his creation, preceding him by a step in time."[3] So in parallel, there has been a tradition of cheap imitation. The historian Theodore Zeldin describes how until well into the 19th century, real wine was drunk only by the well-off; the working classes settled for *piquette*, which was made by adding sufficient sugar to the crushed skins and pips left over after the winemaking, to enable them to re-ferment.

Piquette was made in industrial quantities and was sold and labelled as wine, and it filled the gap created in France by the impact of phylloxera. In *Burgundy*, Anthony Hanson describes the artificial wine industry: "Concentrated must (grape juice) was imported from abroad, water, sugar and colouring matter were added, and the result sold as wine; then other ingredients such as animal blood, chemicals and industrial alcohol appeared."

The fight-back began with the law of August 1 1905. This set up the wine industry's *Service de la Répression des Fraudes* and gave legal protection to regional wine names. At first, the French system resembled its US counterpart, the American Viticultural Areas (AVAs), in that it made no claim to a wine's quality, only that it came from the specified region. A later law, passed in May 1919, gave local courts the power to ban appellations in response to any petition that the wine was not made authentically and in accordance with the traditional local practice – "*contrairement des usages locaux, loyaux et constants*". M. Capus, who was elected as a parliamentary deputy for the Bordeaux region that November, then began a national campaign against the law. He said it was ineffective in guaranteeing that a wine actually had the qualities associated with the region from which it originated.

Capus had been horrified by an encounter in one of the water-logged clay fields near the village of Barsac. Some time earlier, local growers had planted these with red varieties in order to make *vin ordinaire*, as well as the great sweet wine that had made Barsac famous, and which had to be grown on free-draining gravel soils. Capus came across a vigneron cutting away the red wine vines from the rootstock so as to attach white grape vines, an operation called field grafting. The point was that only white grapes were entitled to the Sauternes or Barsac appellation, and by replacing the red variety the grower could make considerably more money. Capus tried to explain to the grower that if he sold the rubbish that these soils would produce as Sauternes he would discredit the whole appellation. The grower simply replied that everyone else was doing the same, and that it was perfectly legal. "I raise this case", wrote Capus, "to demonstrate that if morality influences law making, laws can in their turn have their influence on public morals and can corrupt them. It's reasonable to say that bad laws make bad citizens."

Another disastrous effect of the new law was that growers began tearing up traditional French grape varieties and substituting vines created by crossing *Vitis vinifera* with non-vinifera American grape varieties. The wines bore no relation to real Bordeaux, but they were easy to grow, disease resistant and equally entitled to the appellation. In response, Capus introduced the laws of 1927 and 1934, which created the modern appellation system, specifying permitted varieties, yields and minimum alcohol levels. The earliest laws had been designed to deal with the specific problem of the pseudo-wines – the ancestors of the modern American "wines with natural flavors". They were not framed to protect consumers but producers, who found it difficult to compete with alcoholic sugar-water cooked up in a factory. The result gave winemakers the opportunity to fleece the public, which some gratefully took.

Interestingly, when appellation systems were introduced in post-war Germany, and in Australia during the 1990s, there were similar developments. In each case there was a rush to plant new vineyards in famous name sites – around Bernkastel in Germany, and in Coonawarra and around Langhorne Creek in Australia, for example – irrespective of whether these new vineyards showed the potential of the traditional sites.

Capus' successful battle plan was to use the press to mobilize French public opinion, and involve parliamentarians and growers' organizations. As we have seen, the 1919 law decentralized the process of deciding who was or was not entitled to an appellation. Instead of the Paris-based commission that was set up 14 years earlier, the onus was placed on interested parties in the regions to challenge abuses in court. It proved a divisive exercise.

Unlike Bordeaux, which is famous for châteaux, Burgundy is dominated by the old merchant houses or *négociants* of Beaune and Nuits-St-Georges – names like Drouhin, Bouchard, Chanson and Jadot. Both in Bordeaux and in Burgundy, blending was a long-established practice. It was traditional for Château Lafite to beef up its wine with a little Hermitage from the Rhône, and equally accepted in Burgundy to use wines from the Midi or Algeria for the same purpose. The resulting blend was known disparagingly as *soupe*.

The merchants dealt in wines from the great vineyards of the Côte d'Or that had been named and enclosed centuries earlier by the Cistercians of the Abbey of Cluny. The wine might be fine but it wouldn't necessarily come from the named vineyard. The father of the current Marquis d'Angerville and another grower, Henri Gouges, led an action committee, the sonorous-sounding *Union Générale des Syndicats pour la Défence des Producteurs de Grands Vins de Bourgogne*.

During the 1920s the appellation system for the Côte d'Or was hammered into shape in the courts of Beaune and Dijon. In his history of Romanée-Conti, Richard Olney describes the litigation that defined the appellation for the La Tâche vineyard. The original owners wanted to exclude a section called Les Gaudichots, which was owned by the de Villaine family. But after the judge and his assessors visited the vineyard and took part in a tasting they concluded that Les Gaudichots did belong alongside La Tâche.

But the most resounding ruction was caused by the actions brought by members of the *Union Générale* against the *négociants*, to limit their misappropriation of vineyard names. Often the growers were suing their own customers who, not surprisingly, subsequently refused to deal with them. Throughout France most aristocratic growers had had a tradition of bottling a little wine themselves for direct sales. Now they had to look to this market for most of their income. Raymond Baudoin's *Revue du Vin de France* was a useful ally and source of publicity, but with the crash of 1929 it seemed a dreadful time to launch a new kind of wine business. To sell their wine in 1934 the Volnay proprietor Michel Lafarge and his son Frédéric were obliged to make a trip to Paris, where they went round to personal contacts, organizing tastings where they could take orders in what sounds like a foreshadowing of a Tupperware party. Then, from a country where the sale of alcohol was prohibited, came an unexpected source of salvation.

The future of both the American and French wine industries was radically altered by the initiative of a waiter at the restaurant Le Roy Gourmet, where Baudoin regularly dined. For several days a young American journalist had been eating there and picking the waiters' brains on the subject of wine. The waiter thought that the two men might be interested in meeting each other. Decades later, the old Marquis d'Angerville's son, Jacques, was to deliver the funeral eulogy to this American, Frank Schoonmaker.

At the time of the meeting at Le Roy Gourmet, Schoonmaker was already the author of two successful travel guides: *Through Europe on Two Dollars a Day* and *Come with me to France*. According to d'Angerville, Schoonmaker had discovered wine during a trip through Provence, where he had taken lodgings with a small-scale grower. His host had taught him to taste, making him assess bottles blind and depriving him of wine with his meals to punish him for mistakes.

As the end of Prohibition approached it was obvious to Schoonmaker that Americans would want to rediscover wine. At the time of his trip to Paris he was researching a series of articles for *The New Yorker* that would provide the basis for the *Complete Wine Book* (Simon and Schuster, 1934). This appeared with a dedication "to M. Raymond Baudoin, founder and editor of the Revue du Vin de France, who is not only one of the outstanding oenological authorities of Europe, but who has, for more than a decade, waged unrelenting warfare upon fraudulent practices in the wine business, and through whose kindness the author found all doors open in the wine-producing regions of France."

Schoonmaker quickly realized that there was a huge thirst in the United States not just for knowledge about wine, but for the actual stuff. Baudoin took his new friend on a series of trips through the wine regions to meet independent-minded growers who were looking for fresh markets. *The Complete Wine Book* gives a flavour of the contemporary politics of Burgundy.

"The merchants, needing to market wines that are consistent – whether good or great – blend the wines they have bought. It thus happens that in a single bottle of Chambertin, for example, sold by a merchant who is the soul of honesty, there will be wine from half a dozen plots in the Chambertin vineyard. Each one of these plots may well have been cultivated and tended in a different manner, some of the grapes may have been picked when ripe and some when not entirely ripe, some of the wine may have been fermented with the greatest care and some carelessly. Human frailty and human honesty being what they are, one should buy Burgundy only from the most trustworthy dealers, and should regard every brand as suspect until it proves its worth."

To bypass these dealers Schoonmaker went straight to Baudoin's grower friends. Jacques d'Angerville made me a photo-copy of the first ever consignment of wine his father sold to the newly-created New York importing firm of Bates and Schoonmaker in 1932. Ten weeks later I met the importer Bob Haas, who showed me a copy of the first Bates and Schoonmaker retail list. Sure enough, there was the Marquis' wine – a Volnay of the highest class, described as: "Fruity, perfect in color, with a fine bouquet and a magnificent aftertaste, it is unquestionably one of the best Côte de Beaune wines in existence." It retailed at $27 a case.

It's usual today to think of wine as divided into two semi-hostile camps: the Old World and the New World; one defined by classic regions, small growers and traditional wine making, the other associated with wines sold by the name of the grape variety and by "star" winemakers. It's extraordinary to reflect that one man defined both these propositions, in collaboration with his mentor, Raymond Baudoin. So, what was Schoonmaker like?

Four men who knew him are Jacques d'Angerville, the son of the Marquis who played such a major role in the campaign for the appellations and estate-bottle; Peter Sichel, the former head of the German branch of the great wine dynasty and a colleague of Schoonmaker in the Organization of the Secret Service (OSS), the wartime predecessor of the CIA; Bob Haas, who worked with him in the wine business between 1955-1965; and Ken Onish, the sales director of Bates and Schoonmaker, the New York-based wine importing company. Two written memoirs, by Sichel and d'Angerville, are given in an appendix.

The first surprise is Schoonmaker's lack of geniality, the wine merchant's basic stock-in-trade. He had a mastery of French, Spanish and German and in his obituary Jacques d'Angerville spoke of his friend's "strange and scintillating intelligence". Ken Onish recalls that "Frank knew his own worth, his own value. I don't think he liked dealing with people who were ignorant. The 1960s was a time in the US when we were just learning about wine. He'd flare up a bit when people weren't familiar with names or would mispronounce them. He wasn't a consumer-friendly guy; you wouldn't want Frank on the sales crew."

Bob Haas describes Schoonmaker as "not cosy, but he was fun to be with. He was very opinionated." Haas was the first person to see one of Schoonmaker's most acclaimed books, on German wines, written with help and advice from his wartime colleague Peter Sichel. "We were riding on the train from Bordeaux to

Paris. He had the galley proofs and gave them to me to read, and the first page was all one sentence, which must have been 30 lines long. I said, 'Frank, isn't this a little long?' And he said: 'That's the way I write', and that was that. He didn't really want to hear criticism: he only wanted 'that's wonderful'."

Schoonmaker may have been arrogant but at least he did not follow the political direction taken by his friend and mentor. According to Michel Bettane, the wine critic and leading light of the *Revue du Vin de France* (RVF), Baudoin had long been torn between admiration of America and of Hitler's New Order in Germany. In 1939, shortly before the outbreak of hostilities, he wrote what Bettane describes as a "very very bad" article in the RVF, denouncing Jewish influence in the wine trade and calling for the expropriation of Jewish wine merchants. The magazine didn't publish during the war, but Baudoin was kept out of its editorial chair between the liberation of France and 1949. His eventual rehabilitation was due, Bettane says, to his American contacts – Alexis Lichine, Ken Onish's predecessor, who had been Eisenhower's personal secretary, and Schoonmaker, who had spent the war undercover with OSS in Spain, smuggling shot-down Allied aircrews to safety, and in North Africa and France.

Both Sichel and Schoonmaker came ashore in France with the invading American forces in the Côte d'Azur in August 1944. Soon afterwards Schoonmaker was in a bad car crash, for which he always credited Sichel with saving his life. Sichel remained a close friend. "He had been a heavy drinker and was extremely argumentative – at times aggressively so. But I had always had a wonderful relationship with him, maybe because he really thought I had saved his life (he would tell everyone), or because we had a common interest and love of German wine. Frank had a loyal following among the wine growers, particularly in Burgundy and Germany. Bordeaux was not his stick. He liked the small, individual growers, had an eye for personality and quality and was really a romantic."

Jacques d'Angerville saw less of the irritability and inability to suffer fools gladly. In contrast to the *négociants* of the 1930s, Schoonmaker showed real respect for and appreciation of the growers of the Côte d'Or. Although d'Angerville concedes that Schoonmaker could be brusque with his fellow Americans, "this aspect of his character disappeared when he was mellowed by a good tasting. However unassuming the producer, Schoonmaker would recognize dedication and hard work, and show the respect that's owed to the creator of any artistic masterpiece."

It's hard to exaggerate how innovative he was. For the first time in history, the previously anonymous wine maker was an artist: "Schoonmaker never wanted to remove the creator from his work. Being an artist himself, he saw the face, the character, the temperament of the winemaker in each bottle, and he had the knowledge and ability to convey this vision." d'Angerville compares Schoonmaker with Paul Durand-Ruel, the art dealer who championed the Impressionists and who, after opening a New York office in 1887, was able to generate sufficient sales for them to live in comfort.

In a way he did much more than Durand-Ruel. Schoonmaker was the first person to denounce the bogus nomenclature that has become part of American popular culture. (When Bob Dylan sings "I started out on Burgundy but soon hit the harder stuff"[4] you don't assume that he's a customer of Kermit Lynch.) In the process Schoonmaker created the notion that the definition of authentic wine is that it comes from a single grape variety rather than a blend.

A clue to the direction of his new career is given in the letter he wrote Baudoin from New York on July 23 1934. "So here I am back home, but I hardly recognize the place. It's legal to drink everywhere, and you're allowed wine if you can find something drinkable, which isn't so easy. The average American continues to knock back his gin, whiskey or other spirits just like during Prohibition – and I must say it's a sensible choice. As someone who tastes good wine every day, you can have no conception of the terrible quality of what gets sold over here as wine."

To begin with he concentrated on importing producers he'd met with Baudoin. Then as war loomed in Europe he began to turn his attention to California. As well as finding wines to sell he also worked with individual wineries on product development – Wente brothers in Livermore, Louis Martini in St Helena and

Almadén in San Jose. His idea in each case was that they should make and sell wines under the name of the main grape variety, rather than call them "Chablis" or "Claret". In 1940 Schoonmaker anticipated the success 40 years later of "white Zinfandel", by overseeing Almadén's launch of the first Californian rosé wine, a pink Grenache. The proposition is now so familiar it's difficult to appreciate its impact at the time.

But it wasn't Schoonmaker who invented the emphasis on grape varieties. The theme comes straight from Baudoin, with his campaign on behalf of Capus and his efforts to prevent growers in Bordeaux replacing Cabernet and Merlot with American hybrid vines. Or you could trace it even further back, to the late 14th century when Philippe-le-Hardi, Duke of Burgundy, ordered the uprooting of the "bad and dishonest" Gamay vines. It's the notion that there are noble and ignoble grape varieties, and that you can only make great wine from great grapes.

Schoonmaker wrote in *American Wine* (Duell, Sloan and Pearce, 1941): "There are only 30 or 40 superior grape varieties in the world and only about a dozen capable of producing great wine. No really distinguished wine has ever been made from an inferior grape." He believed that by using these grapes – and by naming them on the label – American wine was coming of age, something he celebrated as being of "tremendous sociological significance", representing a casting aside of the national inferiority complex in the face of Europe.

There's a welcome element of subversion in this, an attack on the freedom of companies to say what they like in support of their brands. The companies naturally resent this, not wishing to be reduced to selling generic commodities that attract no mark-up: for example, Lever Bros want to sell Persil, not "Washing Powder". However, the wine firms would soon learn to appreciate the marketing potential of varietal names (as in the case of the so-called Australian "Rhine Riesling"), which they could offer alongside their established brands.

The other champion of varietals in the 1930s and 1940s was Martin Ray, former stockbroker and admirer of the French-born Paul Masson. In 1936 Ray had bought Masson's hilltop vineyard La Cresta, in the Santa Cruz mountains, concealing his identity in the process – Masson was unwilling to sell to him. Witnesses disagree over whether Ray should be remembered as a colourful, larger-than-life character or as a nasty megalomaniac. His most staunch defender is his widow Eleanor, co-author of his biography *Vineyards in the Sky: The Life of Legendary Vintner Martin Ray* (Heritage West Books, 1993). This is a gripping read, both when we are disbelieving – there are pages of supposedly verbatim dialogue between the infant Ray and his childhood hero, the portly, boater-wearing Paul Masson – and when it rings true.

Eleanor describes a visit by a group of winemakers, "graciously conducted" through the winery by their host, who "explained the crucial importance of vintaging the fine varietals separately, rather than blending everything together in one vat. That way, he said, a distinctive wine could be made to reflect fully a fine wine grape's merits." Later, Ray gave a tasting for his guests but observed, sadly, "that none of them possessed sensitive palates." However, the wine companies picked up varietal labelling as a marketing gimmick, especially after Schoonmaker "latched onto the idea." Eleanor Ray accuses them of retrospectively labelling their stocks of blended wine as Cabernet or Pinot. There was, after all, no legal protection for varieties, which even today need only make up 75 per cent of a generic named varietal wine.

His opponents were wrong, but was Martin Ray right? After a quarter of a century of trying to find the right grapes to grow in California, Randall Grahm is only prepared to admit that Ray and Schoonmaker had half a good idea. He thinks that the emphasis on noble varieties has more to do with snobbery than a proper evaluation of whether they are suited to the state's quasi-Mediterranean climate. "Everyone's thinking about value and prestige. If you want to make a premium product you think, what's the most expensive wine? Chardonnay caught on because it makes the most prestigious white wine in the world. But have you tasted Chardonnay grown in the San Joaquin valley, or Pinot Noir from Fresno? They're poor, to say the least."

Randall Grahm began his career by trying to grow Pinot Noir. He caught the Burgundian faith from Kermit Lynch and later lost it, and when he talks about this grape variety it's tempting to think he's being deliberately provocative. "In modern Burgundy I think it would be as well to mix some other variety with Pinot. Maybe I'm not drinking enough Burgundy, but I think people pretend to discern qualities that I wonder whether are there any more. I'm often disappointed with it. Perhaps I've just got fussier."

More than any other Californian I've met, Grahm is living out the vision of winemaking outside Europe as a quest. He conveys a sense of the Old World as a lost Eden, where growers could get on with their work in the knowledge that they were growing the right grapes in the right place. He seems to belong to another tribe, one condemned to restless wandering. For Josh Jensen or Bob Haas the quest was for the right vineyard – they had already decided what grapes they should grow. Randall Grahm doesn't even have this certainty. "We don't have the European *a priori* knowledge of what the great sites are and where this grape or this grape does well. Until we do it's trial and error, and unfortunately you need many lifetimes and generations to get it worked out. I think the significant varieties of the future are still unknown. Forty years ago there were just a hundred acres [40 hectares] of Chardonnay in California. Now we can't imagine white wine without thinking of Chardonnay.

"So the question is: 'What is the most interesting wine you can hope to make in your lifetime?' What I've come up with – and I'm just working this out – is you make your best guess, you try it, and if it fails horribly you abandon it and regroup. If it seems promising you stick with it, and maybe add bits to polish it up. Maybe you don't get exactly what you had in mind."

This quest will be familiar to many of Randall's generation or anyone who's seen *2001: A Space Odyssey*. Perhaps you could guess it from his ponytail or his interest in philosophy (a popular discipline with winemakers: Paul Draper also studied philosophy at university). "I believe in the Tao of wine making," Randall says. It's the journey of discovery which ends at the point you started from, where you return enriched by adventures and discoveries.

For many Californians this means the rediscovery of Zinfandel. According to its chronicler, David Darlington, this grape variety of obscure European origin was the star of the 1880s planting boom and survived Prohibition simply because home winemakers liked it. In his book *Angels' Visits: An Inquiry into the Mystery of Zinfandel*, Darlington comments on the lack of consensus over what sort of wine Zinfandel is supposed to make; a quality, he says, which makes it "a purely American wine. Like the country in which the vine found a home, the wine had no precedent and had to invent itself. Unlike Californian Cabernet or Riesling, that live in the shadow of Bordeaux and Germany respectively, Zinfandel has been California's contribution to the world of wine.

Zinfandel enjoys increasingly respectful attention, at home and abroad, but Randall Grahm thinks the expensive versions are wildly overpriced. "I think it's a lovely grape, but it's lost its purpose. I see it as a good fruity-drinking wine." (This is close to Schoonmaker's view that Zin is "among the most pleasant table wines in the world".) Instead Grahm has returned to another Californian tradition, one for which Ray and Schoonmaker had little regard – blending. Many old vineyards were planted with a mix of varieties – as in Portugal – to create vineyard blends, in which different varieties were picked together and vinified together. Today these blends are still made, even by someone as grand as Paul Draper of Ridge.

"I don't necessarily believe that single varietal wines are the best idea for California," argues Grahm. "One of the things you get is a wine that sort of works but is missing something. Rather than just pitch the whole thing out you could say: this could be a great wine but it lacks acidity, or it's aromatic and has great texture but it needs something to fill out the mid-palate." As the original Rhône Ranger he is a fan of the underrated Grenache, a grape I think of as Pinot Noir's southern cousin, making wine that's not aggressive but is often lovely. He doesn't believe that Grenache has sufficient tannin to age properly, so, along with most Châteauneuf growers, he blends, following the Perrins in their enthusiasm for the beefy Mourvèdre.

His dream is to find the grape that turns the key of a particular piece of terroir, as Riesling does beside the Rhine or Syrah on the banks of the Rhône. He claims to have had an unlikely degree of success with Nebbiolo, the dense, acidic grape that makes Barolo and Barbaresco in Piedmont in Northwest Italy. Instead of the chalky foothills of the Alps, Grahm grows it on a plain near Soledad, halfway between San Francisco and LA. The way he describes it makes it sound like an act of cruelty. "The only thing it has going for it is the exquisitely long growing season, but the soil is total crap. It's sandy, not very interesting." Somehow, though, Nebbiolo works on this drab terrain, so Randall's next step is to find something obscure to blend it with. His friendship with Alfredo Currado of the Vietti estate has led him to Rouchet, a light-coloured, acidic, aromatic grape variety that's too obscure to get a mention in Jancis Robinson's exhaustive *Vines, Grapes and Wines* (Mitchell Beazley, 1986). "Rouchet could be a complete disaster," says Grahm, "but I'm looking for more complexity. I find out about these sorts of varieties really just by hanging around and asking if there are any strange old antique grapes that I should know about." When he strikes gold he has the cuttings legally quarantined at a Missouri university institute.

When looking for blending material, Randall travels a long way from the purist ideas of most terroirists. One of his blends is Riesling from Washington State with wine from Mosel Riesling, in Germany. "Washington State Riesling is good: it's got texture, it's got length but it doesn't have fragrance. Mosel has that and acidity, so by blending we don't have to add tartaric acid. Mosel tends not to be fully ripened and it doesn't make a balanced dry wine, but with the American wine we have enough extract to make it complete."

A Beaune merchant of the sort that Baudoin and d'Angerville fought in the 1920s would have reasoned in exactly the same way when putting together a *soupe* of Burgundian Pinot, Algerian Carignan and Alicante Bouschet. So why do we distinguish between old-fashioned dishonesty and modern creative blending? The difference is that Grahm is open about the process. Indeed, he bombards his customers with information, not just technical notes but his famous newsletters, and not merely upbeat mood music but his reservations, uncertainties and second thoughts.

"I think I do more to confuse the customer than anything else," he tells me. "Someone often jokes that my job at Bonny Doon is Director of Sales Prevention." But Grahm recoils from the single headline approach to marketing taken by Joel Peterson at Ravenswood. "I think their phrase 'No Wimpy Wines' is appalling. I think it's appalling to reduce wine quality to lack of wimpishness." He may not believe in noble unblended grape varieties, but by offering himself and his wine to public gaze Randall Grahm shows that he is the heir and beneficiary of Ray and Schoonmaker. As Jacques d'Angerville wrote in his obituary, Schoonmaker never wanted to remove the creator from his work.

Randall views wine as an expressive medium, unlike academic philosophy, from which there is a notable exodus into the world of wine. He observes that "philosophers don't make any money and don't make any women. Philosophy graduates who don't become winemakers become chefs; it's the same impulse.

"In winemaking the primary gain is to make good wine," he says, but you have also to look at the secondary gain. In our culture we are starved for authenticity and for creativity and we are also starved for connection with other people. And it's an absurd function that chefs and winemakers have become superstars. Maybe it's an aspect of American culture that we are exporting. In Europe, the winemaker isn't a rock star, but in the States winemakers spend a tremendous amount of time pressing the flesh, being raconteurs. One's personality sells the wine as well as the wine itself. It is truly bizarre."

(1) Capus, J (the former agriculture minister who introduced France's system of appellation controls), *L'Evolution de la Législation sur les Appellations d'Origine*. Paris, 1947.

(2) al-Qāli, al-Amālī, quoted in Kennedy, Philip, *The Wine Song in Classical Arabic Poetry*. Oxford University Press, 1997.

(3) Abu Nuwus, from Kāna l-Šabābu Matiyyata I, Jahl, quoted in Kennedy, Philip, *The Wine Song in Classical Arabic Poetry*. Oxford University Press, 1997.

(4) Bob Dylan, Just like Tom Thumb's Blues, from *Highway 61 Revisited*. CBS (1965).

5
GROWING THE
GRAPES

Near where I live is an all-organic supermarket. Not surprisingly, it isn't much like a Walmart or a Tesco, but then it isn't much like a health food shop either. Instead it slots into the bohemian inner city, serving sit-down breakfasts, and offering a juice bar and a busy alcoholic drinks section. One of the leaflets on display is about organic wine and it's dominated by a big quote that says: "It is estimated that conventional vineyards account for over 75 per cent of all the agricultural herbicides and nearly half of all pesticides used."

This is not the sort of fact you tend to see in specialist wine magazines or newspaper wine columns. When such stories emerge it will be on the general news pages – as for example, in April 1988, when *The Sunday Times* reported on working conditions in the Chilean fruit and wine industry. The report, headed "Children pay the price of cheap Chilean wine" [1], claimed that workers as young as 12 were required to apply toxic sprays without protective clothing. While *The Guardian*'s wine writer Malcolm Gluck was indignant at this affront to the industry's good name, Richard Neill of *The Daily Telegraph*, who has worked in Chile's vineyards, conceded that the allegation was perfectly plausible.

Within the industry, the mainstream view is that put by Russell Johnstone, who contributed the article on agrochemicals to Jancis Robinson's *Oxford Companion to Wine* (OUP, 1999), in which he said that "viticulture requires fewer agrochemicals than many other field crops."

Both the alarmist and the reassuring generalizations are vague to the point of being meaningless. *Who* is offering these estimates for the share of pesticides used in conventional vineyards? And does Mr Johnstone mean to say that viticulture has low requirements for chemicals compared to most other crops? If this is what he means, then why doesn't he say so? If it isn't, why does he use a phrase that gives this impression?

A different picture is painted by a report published in 1999 on the impact of pesticides on California's two-and-a-half million farm workers.[2] The core of this study, compiled by trade union and environmental activists, is county-by-county statistics for acute poisoning cases. The authors acknowledge that the data is incomplete: in many cases there is no reference to the type of pesticide or the crop in question. They also claim that the mainly Mexican workers, many of whom are illegal immigrants, are often dissuaded from reporting such incidents by threats of dismissal.

Between 1991 and 1996 there were 539 reported cases of acute poisoning in California's vineyards. This compared to 399 in cotton, the next highest category – and an industry notorious for its heavy use of pesticides. Third was broccoli, with 307 cases. There is no breakdown of figures between wine grapes and table grapes and raisins. The trend was downwards in grape growing, and it is likely that many of the cases involved dusting with sulphur as a fungicide. Sulphur is unpleasant, but it is far from the most toxic product used on modern farms or vineyards.

Tony Coturri makes organic wine that gets high scores from the mainstream American wine media. He believes the wine business would be killed stone dead if customers saw how most wine was grown and manufactured. "They're making it out to be this beautiful thing, with this guy riding a horse through the vineyards. They use this notion of it as agricultural, whereas it's industrial. If you drove round Sonoma you'd see the results of the explosive growth of wineries and vineyards, the complete disregard for basic ecological principles, the herbicides, the absence of cover crops."

Across California pastures, orchards and woodlands are being turned over to vines. Tom Piper, the manager of Fetzer's organic vineyards, estimates the expansion at 30,000 acres (around 12,000 hectares [ha]) a year. The woodlands are home to mice, rats, squirrels, possums, skunks, bobcats, hawks and owls. "It's a very big media issue," says Piper. "There's very obvious measurable damage." In Santa Barbara county voters approved an initiative to prohibit the removal of oak trees over a certain size. Piper regards his business as "pretty ecologically minded. We could show you where we left the vegetation and we work around the big oaks. But there are cases where a huge field of large trees is just erased."

Sonoma is at the centre of the controversy because the state's appellation system gives companies an incentive to site their vineyards there. There was an outcry after Gallo bought the 202 ha Twin Valley Ranch, felled trees and used earth-moving equipment to sculpt new vineyards. One correspondent to the

Santa Rosa Press-Democrat in October 1997 wrote: "If any good comes from Gallo's plans to chop up Sonoma County land, pulling up every tree and bush in the path of its behemoth monocrop, it will be that finally people are waking up to protest." Another resident, who had moved to Oregon, said she was shocked at what had happened to the old ranch. "It's amazing to see what a powerful corporation with political power can do. In this case the Gallo corporation can literally move mountains. It looks like the beauty of Sonoma County is being levelled to approximate Modesto" [Gallo's corporate home in San Joaquin valley]. Two concerns were soil erosion and the effect on the breeding grounds of indigenous fish: coho salmon and steelhead. Not even the environmentally aware Fetzer has had an easy ride. In April 2000 the firm agreed to review its plans for a newly-acquired 305 ha ranch south of Ukiah, in Mendocino County, in the light of local protests. The company plans for vineyards involved the destruction of historic cherry orchards.

Wine critics like to stress the positive aspects of their subject. For many, the rise of organic viticulture is a sign that all is well. It's when you talk to industry insiders that you realize that it is not a refinement, but a response to a real problem. Both Gallo and Fetzer now make extensive use of "grey" waste water to irrigate their vineyards; demands placed on the local Russian River have imperilled fish stocks, and a radical rethink is now underway at UC Davis, where the college's 20 ha of vineyards were, until recently, managed traditionally. In his analysis of the problem, written as part of an in-house document for UC Davis in 2000, Dick Hoenisch, the new vineyard manager, wrote:

"For many years, the UC Davis Department of Viticulture and Enology was committed to 'old school' management of vineyards. The old school dictated heavy use of tillage and pre-emergence herbicides to provide an image of 'clean farming'. There was a policy of not tolerating or encouraging native or even selected non-native vegetation on vineyard edges. Such an approach runs the environmental risks of contaminating ground and surface waters with pesticides, of contributing to increased sediment loads in nearby Putah Creek, and of failing to harbor desirable wildlife species, such as various raptors."

Hoenisch has begun to convert the vineyard to what he calls "bio-responsible management". The main move has been away from monoculture to the sort of diversity that once characterized the Old World. Cover crops have been sown between the rows of vines; a programme of planting culinary and medicinal herbs and ornamental plants began in spring 2000. This last move recalls the traditional practice of putting a rose at the end of a row of vines: because roses are even more susceptible to mildew than vines, they give the grower early warning of a problem.

The University's standard text book *Grape Pest Management* (Oakland: University of California, 1992) makes it clear that the change in approach is motivated by necessity rather than sentiment. Time and again chemical warfare has failed to work. The book describes two post-war insect infestations caused by the population explosions of grape leafhoppers in the San Joaquin valley, which had developed immunity to spraying despite a "vast increase in the use of insecticides". These leafhoppers stripped the leaves off vines and spread two serious infections: flavescence dorée and Pierce's disease.

Californian farmers in 2000 are being mobilized against the glassy-winged sharpshooter from Florida. This pest was detected only in 1997, and is the most effective vector yet known for Pierce's disease. This kills plants by blocking their water-conducting tissues, which are overwhelmed by a bacterium, *xyella fastidiosa*, secreted by feeding insects. Pierce's disease is endemic in America's hottest states and, wine quality apart, is the reason that the European grapevine can only be planted in relatively cool regions.

So far the glassy-winged sharpshooter has appeared in the hottest, southernmost grape growing areas, and is just starting to spread into the Central Valley. At the Callaway vineyard in Temecula, south of LA, 16 ha had been lost by September 1999. Four months later the figure was up to 50 ha: nearly a fifth of the estate. Almost every vineyard in Temecula has been hit and the damage in this one county alone is estimated at $40 million. The Federal government has so far committed $7 million in emergency aid, and the northern counties like Napa, Sonoma, Santa Cruz and Mendocino are holding their breath.

But unlike with previous leafhopper plagues, chemicals will not be the grape growers' first line of defence. In December 1999 the state set aside $200,000 for researching biological controls. It's difficult to kill glassy-winged sharpshooters with insecticide, although one systemic product – the insecticide imidacloprid, or "Admire" – is being used. But the University of California's main emphasis is on natural methods. These build on the controls used against other leafhoppers. It was found that vineyards near streams and rivers suffered far less because wild grapes and wild blackberries on the riverbanks harboured a minute wasp that ate the eggs of the leafhoppers. Later, French prune trees were found to be an even better host plant for the wasp, *Anagrus epos*. Now another small wasp, *Gonatocerus ashmeadi*, is the chief candidate to prey on the glassy-winged sharpshooter.

The catchphrase is Integrated Pest Management – an approach which often means, quite simply, going back to mixing vines with other plants. The illustrations in *Grape Pest Management* show how far California has parted company with this ideal. This book uses aerial photography as a tool to diagnose the health of vineyards: it's odd and depressing to imagine people doing hand labour in such an endless prairie of vines.

Grape Pest Management reveals why workers are so likely to be poisoned. The catalogue of offenders starts with the herbicides used in the interests of "clean farming": Diuron, Simazine, 2,4-D, Dicholbenil, Sulphumeturon and Glyphosate ("Roundup").

There's a description of how to keep these out of the irrigation water – a particular risk if flood irrigation is being used. Then there are the major fungal diseases. Powdery mildew or *Uncinular necator* sends out chains of white spores in the spring, after over-wintering in black fruiting bodies. The choice is a pre-emptive strike with one of the sterol biosynthesis-inhibiting fungicides, or fortnightly spraying if mildew has become established with Bayleton, Rally and Rubigan, or sulphur in either case. You use different sprays for bunch rot caused by *Botrytis cinerea*: there's Benomyl as a systemic treatment which is taken up and circulated in the plant, or the dicarboximide contact sprays such as Iprodione and Vinclozolin. So before you reach the insecticides – the most toxic group of pesticides – you have already encountered several of the 36 carcinogens that the US government agreed in 1994 to phase out, in response to anxiety over residues in foods.

It is also striking how many conditions can be helped or avoided by practising good traditional viticulture. Hand pruning and removing old clusters removes the habitat in which many fungi overwinter. Leaf removal – once dismissed as a French superstition – has been shown to be as effective against botrytis bunch rot as a triple application of fungicide. An open-leaf canopy ensures good ventilation, which makes it harder for spores to build up. The sharpshooters that spread Pierce's disease thrive in waterlogged pastures – although in the Old World such a site would never even be considered for a vineyard.

But Europe had no prejudice against chemicals. After all, Sinox, the first modern herbicide, was invented in France in 1896. The organochlorines, far more toxic than their predecessors, came into use after the Second World War. They were a spin-off of wartime research and would prove devastating in the Vietnam War, in destroying the Vietcong's food crops and jungle cover. (Claude Bourguignon points out the origins of nitrogen fertilizer as a spin-off from mass-produced nitro-glycerine explosives in the First World War.)

In *Le Vin du Ciel à la Terre* (Sang de la Terre, 1997) Nicholas Joly gives a vivid description of the coming of herbicides to La Coulée du Serrant in the 1960s. This ancient monastic vineyard on the Loire was bought by his father. It makes a dry white wine from Chenin Blanc which Curnonsky (France's top gastronome in the early years of the century) listed as one of France's five great white wines, although as Curnonsky came from nearby Angers, he may have been biased. Joly recalls the "technical consultants and other white-coated salesmen" arriving at his father's estate. The older generation were sceptical about abandoning ploughing, but were won over by the promised savings on labour costs.

Similar arguments will have taken place at the 22-hectare Domaine Leflaive in Puligny-Montrachet, in the Côte de Beaune. This great domaine was created by a retired marine engineer, Joseph Leflaive, who began bottling his own wine in the 1930s. After the war sales to America became increasingly important, through the agency of Schoonmaker's rival and contemporary, Colonel Frederick Wiseman. In 1975 the domaine stopped ploughing and went over to herbicide. Joseph's grand-daughter Anne-Claude, who now runs the domaine, remembers the persuasive influence of an agrochemicals salesman who doubled up as a viticultural consultant. He would react with horror at the sight of a spider in the vineyard and recommend another dose of chemical warfare, administered in what Anne-Claude describes as "cosmonaut outfits". The sprays had been expensive, had caused skin eruptions and hadn't even worked.

Joly, however, writes that when ploughing and herbicide were compared, the section treated with weedkiller looked more attractive. He attributes this to the death of the invertebrates and micro-organisms in the soil, which gave the vines a one-off fertility boost. This would expire, typically after five to ten years, and signal a new sales opportunity for the consultant, who would then recommended chemical fertilizers to compensate for the sterile soil. "The foundations had been laid for a new desert. Viticulture was now not about feeding soils but feeding vines… Our proud consultants, champions of their young branch of science, tried to persuade us that soils were irrelevant in the appellation."

Anne-Claude uses the analogy of a patient on life support: "The vines were on a drip." The fertilizers used by the domaine created an excess of potassium, mopped up by the roots which, without ploughing to drive them downwards, rose to the surface in search of moisture and nutrients. Consequently the wines became "flabby" and needed treating with manufactured tartaric acid. Deficiency diseases began to appear, which in turn needed correcting with additions of trace elements. If the domaine hoped that winemaking would disguise these problems with New World techniques such as acidification and single yeast strains, they were wrong: by the late 1980s word was going round that Leflaive was not what it used to be.

When Anne-Claude took over from her father in 1990 she had already decided on a change of direction. In 1989 she had seen a poster advertising a conference on organic agriculture, to be addressed by the soil scientist Claude Bourguignon. She went along and was swept off her feet. Like many others before her, Anne-Claude was transfixed by his prophecy that, on current trends, the soil of Burgundy's vineyards would end up more lifeless than the Sahara. There was one grower in the region who had already sworn off agrochemicals: Jean-Claude Rateau of the Clos des Mariages in Beaune had begun cultivating organically and, more recently, biodynamically. Thus inspired, Anne-Claude organized a second conference specifically for wine growers, and invited as speakers Bourguignon, Rateau and François Bouchet, a consultant who had worked with Aubert de Villaine and Nicholas Joly. Joly had switched to biodynamic agriculture after picking up a book on biodynamic farming in a Paris bookshop, one winter's day in 1981.

Biodynamics has spread through a mixture of proselytizing and historical accident. Anne-Claude Leflaive works to spread the word: since converting Domaine Leflaive in 1995 she has thrown open the doors to her neighbours, and claims Dominique Lafon as a convert, with strong interest from Jacques Lardière, the wine-maker at the American-owned Maison Louis Jadot.

Biodynamics was the earliest form of organic farming. It has its origins in lectures on agriculture given by Rudolph Steiner in 1924, at the estate of Koberwitz in Silesia, which has been part of Poland since 1945. The message filtered through to vineyard owners via indirect routes. Christine and Nikolaus Saahs own Nikolaihof, Austria's leading biodynamic estate and producer of some of the country's best Riesling and Grüner Veltliner wines. Christine discovered Steiner through meeting Dr Jutte Schae, a Munich homeopath who was married to her husband's best friend, the year before her marriage in 1971. (She calls Dr Schae her "ghost mother", which translates as "spiritual mother".) Jutte is also godmother to Christine's daughter Elizabeth, and has the responsibility of remembering birthdays: "The first present was the calendar from Maria Thun. She was disappointed: she expected a nice present…"

Maria Thun's planting calendar is one of the essential tools of biodynamic agriculture. It tells growers which days are best for different farm operations, as well as seasonal tasks such as washing down trunks of fruit trees with a solution of lime, water and manure. It works on the premise that phases of the moon and alignments of planets affect the way plants grow, and sounds to some like the organic movement's lunatic fringe. Yet the Maria Thun calendar is used even by such growers as Jean-Gérard and Jacqueline Guillot in the Mâconnais, who are not even registered biodynamic growers. The phases of the moon have always had a role in traditional winemaking, governing the timing of pruning vines and "racking" wine from barrel to barrel: the waxing moon normally corresponds with a period of high atmospheric pressure, which keeps the sediment from rising up and clouding the wine.

Steiner believed in an oral and uncodified tradition of peasant farming. His wish to identify himself as "a small peasant farmer" derived from his childhood in what is now Slovenia, and from his friendship with a gatherer of medicinal herbs that began with a chance meeting on a Viennese train. Discussing the influence of the heavenly bodies, he concluded: "There is not yet a science about these things; no-one wants to make the effort to develop it." (3)

Soon, though, his followers took up this challenge. Maria Thun's work continues a tradition begun by Lili Kolisko who, in the late 1920s, began sowing wheat at different phases of the moon and comparing the results. In *The Moon and The Growth of Plants* (Kolisko Archive Publications) she wrote that sowing at the full moon produced the highest yields. (This is not so far from the conclusions of Steiner's followers in California today, who try to ensure that seedlings emerge at the time of the new moon. So, celery, tomatoes and peppers are sown at the full moon, but lettuce, which germinates much faster, is sown three days before.)

This approach has been taken further by Frau Thun at her home in Dexbach, a village in the Rheinhessen, in southern Germany. She had wondered why successive sowings of radishes in the first ten days of April 1952 had behaved so differently, when there were no appreciable differences in the soil or weather. To find out, she began a programme of daily sowings of radishes, recording the outcome and relating it to the positions of the moon and stars. In the 1960s and again in the 1980s she looked at yields of potatoes, cucumbers, dwarf beans and soya beans. In each case she found three annual peak periods and three annual lows. All the crops, apart from the potatoes, did best from sowings in April, August and February (or, as she would put it, in Aries, Leo and Aquarius). Sowings in July (Cancer), September (Virgo) and March (Pisces) produced the lowest yields. In the case of potatoes everything happened a month later.

Some wine growers find her work very helpful. James Millton in New Zealand ploughs a lonely furrow among colleagues who regard the heavy use of fungicides as indispensable in a cool, damp climate. He compares biodynamics to a bus timetable that tells him what will happen and when.

Since the 1990s wine has given biodynamics a high profile; else-where amid the organic food boom it has remained relatively obscure. The word "organic" comes from a separate foray into chemical-free farming associated with the Rodale family in Pennsylvania in the 1940s. JI Rodale championed the work of Sir Albert Howard, who emphasized composting as a means to repair the fertility of soils in India. Howard was dismissive of Steiner's followers and claimed they hadn't backed up their theories with evidence. His research spawned the Soil Association in Britain and the Rodale Press in the US, which publishes *Organic Gardening*, with a circulation of three-and-a-half million.

There are still many more organic than biodynamic wine-growers, but the second group is making the running. Nicholas Joly was in California in March 2000, lecturing to a group that included representatives from Mondavi and Joseph Phelps. Aubert de Villaine in late 1999 was hesitating over whether to go from organic to full biodynamic cultivation, while Anne-Claude Leflaive has helped transform the Côte d'Or. Jean-Claude Rateau says that a majority of the region's small growers are now at least turning to the semi-organic approach of *lutte raisonée*. (The growers of Vosne-Romanée have got together to use pheromones rather than sprays against red spider mite, the technique the French call *la confusion sexuelle*.)

During the early 1990s Anne-Claude Leflaive maintained organic and biodynamic parcels of land side by side and compared the wines; she made her final choice through comparative tasting. Jean-Claude Rateau, by contrast, plunged straight in. What he liked was that biodynamics was a "finer" system, that took note of small details and constantly strove for improvement. Nicholas Joly makes a similar argument when he writes that wine growing and raising flowers for perfume are the two branches of agriculture in which the quality of the crop is of supreme importance.

Chance played a part in bringing biodynamics to the American West Coast. The bridgehead was the University of California, Santa Cruz, the coastal town 130 kilometres south of San Francisco. In 1965 the first phase of the university opened on the site of an old ranch amid redwood forest. "There was quite a lot of disruption to the landscape and the students wanted to do something positive for the land," according to a university spokesperson. Two years later the new university welcomed a distinguished European visitor, who took an interest in the idea of creating a student garden. This was Freya von Moltke; whose anti-Nazi husband Helmuth had been hanged in 1944 for his role in the Kreisau Council (named after his family estate in Prussia, where the group used to meet).

Freya admired England and had an English friend whom she thought would be ideal to lead this project. Alan Chadwick was 58, a former Shakespearean actor, an ex-wartime minesweeper commander and a keen gardener. Rudolph Steiner had even acted as tutor to the young Alan at his parents' country house in Hampshire. Chadwick worked at Santa Cruz for six years, but left in 1973 after the university declined to fund what it describes as "a Roman road effect with quarried limestone." The original plot has grown to a ten hectare farm, managed organically and run by Santa Cruz university's Center for Agro-ecology. Its spokesperson, Martha Brown, says that the farming has never been strictly bio-dynamic, although Chadwick learned about biodynamics from Steiner and described his work as Biodynamic-French-Intensive. "But we use a lot of principles like high rates of organic matter, lots of compost, intensive planted beds. It grew out of the French market garden system around the edges of Paris. They'd compost the horse manure from the city and build very rich beds with the plants very close together.

"The garden that Chadwick started is only about two acres and had a view of Monterey Bay. It's just a riot of plants, and it went to being this from somewhere with almost no topsoil, which was covered with brush and poison ivy."

Chadwick's early garden became the nucleus of the organic movement in California and beyond, developing techniques used by many suppliers of the state's farmers' markets, patronized by the new wave of chefs and restaurateurs. But the project was not aimed at the middle classes. One claim of chemical agriculture is that it's the only way to feed the world's growing population; but the organic movement makes the same claim. The Soil Association grew out of Albert Howard's work in India and Chadwick wanted to demonstrate that composting could give high and sustainable yields, even from unpromising soil. Today, apprentices at the Center for Agro-ecology include a number of Kenyans and Zimbabweans.

Wine growers also responded: it is in response to Chadwick's message that Fetzer Vineyards, the sixth largest wine producer in the US, now has a high proportion of organic production. The Fetzers followed a path trodden by their friends and neighbours the Frey family, also of Mendocino County, where California starts to merge into the Pacific Northwest. There are 12 Frey children and 11 Fetzer siblings. Jonathon Frey worked with Chadwick both at Santa Cruz and then again in the mid 1970s at Covelo, in a small valley in the northeast corner of Mendocino County. Here a farmer called Richard Wilson had invited Chadwick to create the Round Valley School for the Study of Man and Nature; like Santa Cruz, this involved making a garden and offering training to apprentices. Jonathon's younger brother Paul describes Chadwick as "the organic pioneer, an eccentric."

Frey Vineyards feels some way from the mainstream. When you finally reach the Freys' place in Redwood Valley it's hard to believe that you're at a modern winery – it looks like something out of a Grimm tale, and the travel writer Jan Morris described its appearance as "Japanese Bavarian". The Frey parents, who were both doctors, built it in 1980 from the timbers of the disused Garret Winery in Ukiah. For the past four years they've been accredited by Demeter, the biodynamic certification group, and Paul thinks they were America's first-ever organic winemaker.

The even less technological Coturri winery in Sonoma opened a year earlier. However, the Freys had been growing grapes as early as the late 1950s – originally as a scam to increase the value of land that was threatened with compulsory purchase for a dam – and Paul Frey says that, like their neighbours, they were *de facto* organic. "The old Italians always grew their crops organically. All the time they'd have these chemical salesmen coming to their door and saying 'you've got to use this or that' and they'd kind of look at them and laugh."

At the local school from the 1960s onwards there were Fetzer and Frey children in most classes. Barney Fetzer, an executive with the hardboard manufacturer Masonite, had begun growing grapes from the late 1950s, selling them to home winemakers. Then in 1968 he started making wine, initially on a modest scale. In 1992 the family sold the winery, enabling the younger Fetzer generation to set up as grape farmers with a commitment to organic and biodynamic methods. Dr Beba Frey smiles as she remembers the original scepticism of the Fetzer family about the enthusiasms of "those hippie-dippie Freys."

Now Jimmy, the eldest Fetzer son, former company president and Jonathon's school contemporary, has created an estate that tries to go beyond vineyards – even biodynamically managed ones – to a vision of polyculture, in which decorative plants, local wild species and herbs for cooking and medicine are grown beside and between the vines, and where sheep roam, grazing on the cover crops and fertilizing the soil with their droppings. The result is as much gardening as agriculture. There is a return to a human-scale landscape more reminiscent of Europe or the Third World than of America, home of prairies and monoculture. One typical detail is the way cat-tails, a local kind of rush, are grown to make a biodegradable material with which to tie up the vines.

As part of the deal when the Fetzers sold up, Jimmy and the rest of his family were barred for ten years from making or selling wine under the Fetzer family name. Instead they sold grapes, often to make Fetzer Vineyards' organic wines. But from 2000 the estate has started to make a little red wine (Petite Syrah and Merlot) and sell it under the name Ceago. Ceago is the old McNab ranch, renamed after the Pomo Indian word for "shady meadows" and converted from mixed use (including substantial marijuana plantations). In its current form it was planned and planted by Alan York, who, like Jonathon Frey, worked with Chadwick at Covelo. He found it gruelling at times.

"Like most people that make a contribution to the world, he was a really complicated person and he had many different sides to him. He ranged from being one of the most charming people you'd ever met to the biggest asshole you could possibly imagine. The guy could be so brutal with his tongue that he could just destroy someone. It's like a buddy of ours said: 'Jesus Christ man, he just scorched my ass.'" Sometimes Chadwick could be provoked by an apparently innocent remark:

"The thing that totally set him off, that pushed his button, is if you were doing something and he'd ask why you were doing it like that. If you said 'I thought that...' he'd go ballistic. His whole thing was that gardening was not a thought process. If you were really out there working with the plants and in the right frame of mind you would be an extension of what was going on, and in that condition there's no way you're going to do something wrong."

From appearances you wouldn't suspect Chadwick of such a philosophy. In the most widely reproduced photograph of the man he's wearing shorts and has a haircut that looks unchanged since the 1930s. "He was typically English," according to York: a description that, when pressed, he elaborates as formal and uptight. "One time I went to the Garden Project and it was early in the morning, like 4.45, and I walked by his house and he was with an ironing board ironing white shirts with this big can of Niagara Starch; and he was bearing down so hard on the iron I could see the veins popping out of his arm, and when he came out of the house those shirts were so-o-o stiff."

Chadwick was not just a living link with Rudolph Steiner: he also brought with him the traditions of the Edwardian country house, with its virtual self-sufficiency in fruit and vegetables. The formal gardens of the four hectare estate where he grew up had also been influential. According to Alan York: "Wherever he went he built the same garden over again, a British estate garden with big herbaceous borders and intensive vegetable gardens."

Alan York sees biodynamic grape growing as closer to horticulture than agriculture. "Conventional agriculture is about the management of a single species and you tend to think that everything is in competition with it. So all other plants are taking away the nutrients, water and sunlight. In biodynamics, on the other hand, your whole management system is organized for the maximum number of species." But York thinks he's been more successful than his mentor at finding the right plants for places where there's no rain during most summers. At Ceago, the vines grow alongside olives and Mediterranean herbs, and horticulture frequently shades off into a kind of managed wilderness. This is reminiscent of certain French properties, where a patchwork of vines grow in and among the wild *forêt*. Wild and native plants are ecologically important, as they are home to the insects and spiders that keep down vine pests.

An important trend in German gardening recently has been ecological: instead of choosing decorative plants and modifying the landscape to suit them, designers analyze the site and choose plants that will thrive and multiply themselves in these specific conditions. Tom Piper, who manages Fetzer's organic vineyards, is professionally qualified in this kind of landscape gardening. He worked for the University of Arizona, advising on converting from old-style landscaping – which used non-native plants with a high demand for water – to new-style gardening, using plants adapted to low rainfall.

Alan York is also keen on the ecological approach. "That's my personal interest," he says, "working with plant communities on large pieces of property. It's just the economics of planting. Here at Ceago we have a couple of ditches, 2,000 feet long and 1,000 feet long. You have to develop these along ecological lines, of what plants are going to thrive with a minimum of care. You look at what can be achieved in five years, ten years, twenty years of actively doing something every single year. What you're doing is for generations to come. That's the stuff that's exciting."

The day-to-day management is now in the hands of Javier Meza, a Chilean who joined Alan York in 1997 with a degree in (conventional) vineyard management. As is usual on California's organic vineyards, there is a big emphasis on growing cover crops between the rows of vines. There's also a trend to do this in the south of France, but in more traditional regions such as Burgundy, the Rhône or the Loire, the vines are close-planted and there simply isn't room. Instead, ploughing is the favoured means of reducing competition from weeds; on some estates, such as Nicholas Joly's, there's even a return to horse ploughing.

At Ceago alternate rows get different treatments. One is sown with a winter cover crop of oats and nitrogen-fixing plants, such as mustard and red clover. These are ploughed back into the soil in the spring, the cooler areas a month before the rest. "You want to take some of the water out of the ground," Javier Meza explains. "It gets really cold in the winter. In the spring you still have a lot of cold, so you want to evaporate off some of the water and permit the soil to warm up faster." The other rows are mown but not ploughed and contain a mix of native flowers – California poppies, blue bachelors, tizzy tips – that self-sow after their annual cutting in June. These are home to a mixture of little creatures that prey on vine parasites, and Meza is especially pleased with the appetite of the larger spiders. In addition there are anagrus wasps and persimilis spider mites, and a population of lacewings hatched from eggs that Meza and Alan York bought and applied with something called a "biosprayer". Not all spider mites are helpful: red spider mites eat vine leaves and delay the ripening of the grape bunches. But Meza uses the irrigation system to exercise a form of biological control over these.

"They like to reproduce when it's really high temperatures. So in July and August, when it gets really hot here, we wait until the temperature gets up to 110°F (40°C) and then turn the system on for an hour. They like to breed where it's hot and dry and dusty, so we make it very humid and bring the temperature down." This technique doesn't get rid of the pests, but it stops the population from exploding, a symptom that takes effect, Meza has noticed, in the dry-farmed vineyards.

At Ceago insecticides are banned, but the team uses sulphur against powdery mildew. Growers sceptical about biodynamics occasionally point to their rivals' use of copper sulphate or "Bordeaux mixture" and sulphur dust. The suggestion is that they splurge on these old-fashioned fungicides to compensate for the absence of more modern alternatives. Perhaps it's human nature to suspect that those who claim to be pure have skeletons in their closets, but I've found that biodynamic growers are willing to admit losses, and are convincing when they claim that their use of sulphur has gone down, not up. Anne-Claude Leflaive, for example, says she now uses only a fifth of the amount that was applied in the 1980s.

Javier Meza is a reluctant convert to Alan York's theories. "For me it was really new. Organic was new for me, biodynamics was new and in the beginning I was complaining about it. But since I started doing it I started seeing the effects, and then you start to believe. Everything that makes you pay attention to your plants makes things better." I feel the same sort of discomfort as Javier Meza. Like many people, I've wondered what the apparently anti-rational elements in biodynamics contribute to ordinary organic farming. Isn't it enough to use compost instead of chemicals? This scepticism is shared by many growers who have adopted certain biodynamic approaches, and even to some extent by those like Noël Pinguet, of Le Huet-Lieu in Vouvray, who have embraced the philosophy lock, stock and barrel.

The most cynical way to explain the success of biodynamic viticulture is that it isn't a very efficient way of growing grapes. If you lose part of your crop to parasites and predators then you are subjecting it to a form of crop thinning, which might well make the grapes tastier and the wine more concentrated. Javier would agree that low yields are vital, but he would argue that an over-cropped vine is out of balance and more prone to disease.

Some organic purists enjoy biodynamics precisely because it is difficult. It's not so hard to change from nitrogen fertilizer to imported guano, for example; but for biodynamic accreditation you have to turn your farm into a self-sufficient unit, capable of producing the necessary composts and preparations on the spot. This insistence reflects Steiner's desire to see the revival of the peasantry; a desire he shared with a wide range of contemporary opinion, from Eamon de Valera, to Adolf Hitler, to Mahatma Gandhi... Wine is today one of the few agricultural products (apart from illegal drugs) that is sufficiently profitable to make this faded ideal a reality.

John Williams runs Frog's Leap, the best-known organic estate in the Napa Valley, with 28 hectares of land and contracts with many other growers. He says that he's spent a lot of time reading Steiner's Kobervitz lectures and trying to apply their principles: "I've tried to think about what Steiner would be thinking out in the Napa Valley today, instead of in Germany in 1924. I find more inspiration in Eastern thinking than in anything written anywhere else. That's finding the natural way, the harmonious way, the sense that the farm is a harmonious organism; that the cosmos, homeopathy and the farm animals and the crops are all integrated into the same system. This to me is the exciting part."

But Williams doesn't think that everything in biodynamics is relevant to grape farmers: "Grapes are quite a different crop from most of the things Steiner was talking about. Planting calendars are the hardest thing to apply, because they're written for annual crops as opposed to perennial plants, like vines."

The link between farming and celestial bodies predates Steiner. People have used the sky as their calendar for centuries – it's as natural for Chaucer to talk about "The Ram" as to say "Aprille". At Covelo Alan Chadwick used the moon as his cue to sow seeds; Alan York points out that this made it very easy to keep track of operations in the greenhouse – you only had to look at the current phase of the moon to know the age of a batch of seedlings. There is no mystery about the effect of the moon on atmospheric pressure, and hence on the clarity of wine in casks. The idea that the constellations affect plants is not a matter of dogma: Rudolph Steiner did no more than suggest that it was something worth looking at.

At Ceago they believe they get the best results by pruning weaker vines on so-called "root days" and stronger vines on "leaf days", as determined in biodynamic calendars. This sounds quite like the regime at the non-biodynamic Bodegas Remelluri in Rioja, where they prune young vines while the moon is waxing and old vines when it's waning. Maria Thun has gone beyond observations about the relative position of the sun (in other words, the seasons) and the phases of the moon to create a detailed system involving the other planets. Since she has reached this through observation and experimentation it seems churlish to dismiss it out of hand as "unscientific".

The most notorious aspect of biodynamics is the various "preparations" – Number 500, for example, in which a cow's horn is filled with manure, buried during the autumn equinox, then disinterred and used to make a water infusion. This is diluted to homeopathic levels and "energized" by being whirred round in a chestnut barrel. In a similar preparation, the horn is filled not with manure but with silica (quartz crystals). Alan York says of preparation 500, "there's no question that it makes a difference." Aubert de Villaine, who has recently been conducting controlled trials of biodynamism, says that the silica preparation is, if anything, too effective in spurring vine growth.

Aubert de Villaine and Anne-Claude Leflaive have come closest to a scientific evaluation as to whether biodynamics makes a difference over and above simple organic farming, but their conclusions differ. Leflaive is convinced the wine is different, and has many tasters on her side; while de Villaine doesn't see any qualitative difference in Romanée-Conti's wines. In each case Claude Bourguignon has analyzed the different parcels of soils for microbial activity, comparing the different regimes.

"We observed the same degree of biological activity in the topsoil," Bourguignon told me, "but in the deep soil we had a greater activity in the biodynamic parcel. We also observed a higher concentration of nutrition elements such as magnesium, potassium and boron. We can explain this because if you increase the biological activity you also increase the available elements."

Bourguignon credits this to preparation 500. He says the manure-filled cow's horn is extraordinarily rich in microbial life, with concentrations in the trillion per millilitre – "something very difficult to obtain in a normal laboratory." And he finds the dilution very similar to the level appropriate in a mainstream agricultural practice – of inoculating fields of alfalfa with bacteria that enable the crop to "fix" atmospheric nitrogen and make it available to plant roots. "For me it's probably through a microbial inoculation of the soil that we get a fantastic diversity of species."

(1) Children pay the price of cheap Chilean wine. *The Sunday Times,* April 12, 1988.

(2) *Fields of Poison: California Farmworkers and Pesticides.* The United Farm Workers Pesticide Action Network, and California Rural Legal Assistance Foundation, 1999.

(3) From Thun, Maria, *Work on the Land and the Constellations.* Landthorn Press, East Grinstead, 1990.

6
MAKING THE WINE

There was a time in the 1990s when Britain swarmed with "winemakers". Typically, they were young or youngish Australian men, casually-dressed, sometimes "larger-than-life" personalities – but more often nice, modest guys. They gave interviews, generated press coverage and worked in PR, either as "flying winemakers" on contract to supermarket chains or as the in-house stars of big corporations. Some had an air of not knowing quite what the fuss was about, a diffidence that only seemed to increase the turmoil in the breasts of their female admirers. But the young women who worked with European wine growers were less susceptible. Lucy Faulkner of Morris and Verdin says that in her experience French growers do far more hands-on work but refuse to call themselves "winemakers". And Charlie Allen, then of Richards Walford, grumbled: "What's the fuss about? You just squish some grapes up and it turns into wine."

It isn't unknown in California to hype fermentation technologists like pop-stars. But since the mid-1970s there has also been a reaction against what Tim Mondavi calls the post-war cult of the man in the white coat: "That GI Joe, 'we're going to move the earth around,' technologically-based orientation." There is a vivid expression of the change in aspirations in the *Book of California Wine* brought out by the University of California in 1984. One of its editors, Doris Muscatine, writes in the foreword about meeting Bernard Portet, the Bordeaux-raised proprietor of Clos du Val in Napa, when she had a carload of Zinfandel grapes.

Portet wanted to know how she and her partner planned to crush them. When they joked "by foot" he told them, in all seriousness, that it was the best way. Portet then demonstrated the technique of making a loose sieve, with chicken wire and a wooden frame, to shake the grapes free from the stems. Later that day the couple trod the grapes in two plastic garbage cans. The wine that finally resulted was, she wrote, "the best we had ever made. Savouring it, we realized that what Bernard had given us that day was more than hints about how to improve our winemaking technique. He had shared with us a tradition of pleasure in and veneration for the grape that has endured for over 4,000 years."

I've seen people doing something similar in a shed at the bottom of the garden of a small terraced house in Harringay, in London. They were Italian home winemakers, first-generation immigrants from Emilia-Romagna. They trod the grapes then fermented the pulp in plastic barrels and matured the wine in glass demi-johns. They did it partly so they could afford to drink in heroic quantities, and also because they believed supermarket wine was full of additives. "This is a real grape wine," the younger of the two men, Luigi, told me. "Two glasses of the wine you buy in the shop and I'm already drunk. There's got to be something wrong with that." The friends' previous year's vintage was made without sulphur to kill off bacteria and wasn't at all bad, though wine professionals might have noted volatile alcohol and oxidation. For these guys the trickiest part of the job was finding good grapes; they had spent weeks rejecting plausible-looking box-loads in different London greengrocers before finding a batch they could agree was "really beautiful". But unless there was a tradition in the family of making this kind of wine, I think most people would risk the additives.

Tim Mondavi, winemaker and heir apparent at the Robert Mondavi winery, says that hygiene and consistency have been the main reason for the New World's success. "Californian wines may not have shown their full potential but they were clean; the avoidance of off-flavours was very important to their purity of expression. Where there was a lack of sanitation in Burgundy or Italy you'd see a lot of barnyard character and spoilt wine. It was hit and miss, particularly in Burgundy, because everything was attributed to the soil; there are such variations in quality, from incredibly great to incredibly poor. Now, as our technology has matured tremendously, it has allowed us to become more natural in the vineyard and the cellar."

Not all the technology is rocket science. UC Davis graduate Randall Grahm is more inclined to credit the success of the New World to a climate which helps fruit become reliably ripe, rather than to any high-tech wizardry. "Europe is more technologically advanced than we are. I mean, what technology are we talking about? Stainless steel tanks? Please."

Tim Mondavi traces the return to more classical winemaking back to the early 1970s. That was when his company started to experiment with using less sulphur than was previously thought necessary to inhibit wild yeasts and bacteria. Then, in 1974, they began to have second thoughts about the ultra-low fermentation temperatures that had been made possible by water-cooled stainless steel tanks. "At low temperatures you have more fruity floral smells, but at higher temperatures there's more colour and a rounder, richer fragrance. This was just following things we'd seen on our travels in Burgundy." Another idea that came from Burgundy, notably from the Domaine de la Romanée-Conti and Domaine Dujac, was to limit the use of the crusher-destemmer machines, at least for the company's best Pinot Noir. Instead, they used a proportion of whole grape clusters. Tim Mondavi talks appreciatively about the "wonderful spiciness" that the stems contributed to the wine.

The 1970s was when Californians started to learn Burgundian methods of making white wine. Much of the work was done at the Simi winery in Sonoma, by the winemaker Zelma Long. Between 1980 and 1984 she was assisted by David Ramey, who went on to cover two newly-created wineries with glory: first Matanzas Creek in Sonoma, then Dominus in Napa, with an intervening spell in Bordeaux at Pétrus with Christian Moueix, founder of Dominus. Californians like Ramey took the analytical, experimental approach learnt at college and applied it to detailed comparisons between Old and New World winemaking techniques. "Over 20 years, as my techniques have advanced, based on production-level controlled experiments, the traditional artisanal method has made a better wine almost every time."

Ramey says that he has made his findings available to Davis professors at technical conferences, but that they have never been interested in following up with theoretical work. He's baffled by this indifference, which he contrasts with the equivalent French institutes (citing, for example, work done in France to explain why the texture of wine changes when it's left in contact with the spent yeast cells, or the "lees"). It isn't as if Davis has been too busy with other equally useful investigations. Ramey and Paul Draper apparently set themselves the challenge of naming a single development from Davis that had helped them as top-of-the-range winemakers – and were unable to do so. For Ramey, the important developments have been fermenting white wines in barrel, maturing them on the lees, stirring the wine while it's on the lees – known as *batonnage* – and using natural wild yeasts rather than industrially-produced dried single strains. He says that academic experts tried to discourage each of these steps, claiming that they posed an unacceptable risk of spoilage.

One of the key judgements in making both red and white wine is the level of "extraction" – getting the flavouring elements in the grapes into the juice gently, without introducing the harsh flavours of the pips. Lucy Faulkner of Morris and Verdin was taken aback by the complexity of grape pressing when she helped to bring in the harvest at Dominique Lafon's estate in Meursault, in the Côte d'Or. Lucy wrote afterwards, in the Morris and Verdin wine list: "There is nothing that happens to a single grape, a single millilitre of juice, a single gram of lees that is not directed by Dominique. This year he realized the need to preserve acidity, which tends to be pressed out in the middle of press cycles and less so at the end. Press times were therefore shorter and at gentler pressures than normal."

It's this sort of decision making that makes Lucy see traditional winemaking as a highly hands-on, interventionist process. You could liken it to the concentration required in making a soufflé or scrambling an egg. But many of the new winemaking tools that appeared in the second half of the 20th century gave the grower less – not more – control over the extraction process. This is because they were invented to cut labour costs and save money rather than to make better wine.

I was given a lecture on the shortcomings of late 20th century technology in the unlikely setting of Vinovation Inc., a massive concrete shed in an industrial suburb of the little Sonoma town of Sebastopol, surrounded by state-of-the-art distillation and reverse osmosis equipment. My interlocutor was Vinovation's founder Clark Smith; a friend and collaborator of Randall Grahm and part-time Davis lecturer, who scandalized his Davis colleagues with an article that expressed the kind of criticisms that David Ramey and Paul Draper voice, but haven't set down in print.

For Clark Smith, "Electricity is the worst thing. We've taken 100 years to recover from electricity. Why would anyone pump over a tank instead of punching it down? For the same reason a dog licks its balls: because it can."

He likens winemaking to making tea. The idea is to get a well-flavoured cup without the harsh-drying tannin flavours that come from stewing the tea, or leaving it to sit for too long. Both grapes and tea leaves are natural filters, molecular sieves, which will discharge a load of coarse tannin if they're roughly handled. "We want to mix the soup. We want plenty of contact of skins and juice, but we want that mixing to be done in a gentle way."

The classic gentle form of mixing is *pigeage* – translated in the New World as "punching down" the cap or cake of skins and pips that forms on top of the wine in an open fermentation tank. You can do this with poles, but in France you're just as likely to find winemakers climbing into the fermenting vat and using their bodies to stir things up. Even as big a producer as Maison Jadot in Beaune gives pride of place to a circle of round open fermenters which are stirred with feet and legs at harvest time. Several New World growers do this too, such as David Bruce in the Santa Cruz mountains. Apparently it feels nice: a French grower who had worked in Napa compares the experience to a jacuzzi, with the heat of fermenting wine and streams of rising carbon dioxide bubbles. But it's also dangerous: carbon dioxide can cause rapid unconsciousness and there have been several deaths by drowning.

In a winery, mixing a lot of wine by *pigeage* is hardly an option, even using poles rather than legs. However, in Burgundy it is so highly regarded that a great deal of ingenuity has been shown in mechanizing the process. Roger Rageot, director of the Buxy cooperative in the Côte Chalonnaise, devised a system using mechanically-controlled steel poles. This has been widely copied, but he regards it as uncomradely to pursue competitors for breach of copyright. A refinement at Buxy is to lubricate the system with grape pip oil, so that a minor leak wouldn't cause contamination.

Most wineries use pumps to circulate wine from the bottom of the tank to the top of the cap. The problem is matching the even mixing effect of *pigeage*. If the wine just runs over and round the cap it under-extracts: a particular problem with a variety like Pinot Noir, which tends to a light colour anyway. Clark Smith is more bothered about the other extreme: "When you've got a pump doing 600 litres a minute and you're directing it through a 50mm hose at a specific spot, and you're using it to slice up the cap. The devil's in the details."

For Smith, people are repeatedly blinded to the big picture by the promise of efficiencies of cost or scale. His favourite example is the most fundamental piece of wine technology – the press. It was first described by Pliny the Elder in the 1st century AD, who said it was invented a century earlier in Greece. The oldest design you still see today is the massive square type, in which the press comes downwards. These are kept as museum pieces in many old cellars. One venerable example in the Clos de Vougeot in Burgundy was saved from destruction in 1944. The buildings were being used as a prisoner of war camp for captured Germans, who complained of the cold and proposed to use the timbers of the press for firewood. The caretaker rushed to alert the American commander, who put up a barbed wire barricade to protect this little piece of history. [1]

The early 20th century version is the "basket press" which descends, powered by electricity, onto a metal base surrounded by wooden slats, that retain the skins and seeds but allow the juice to escape. These are still highly valued in Champagne, where wine-making begins with pressing whole clusters of grapes, most of which are red Pinot Noir or Pinot Meunier, and which must be squeezed so gently that barely a trace of colour leaches from the skins into the juice. The mass of stalks and skins is compacted by the pressure from above, and staff have to use pitchforks to break it up and move it around between pressings.

This vertical press is a world away from the machines devised for bulk wine production. These work uninterruptedly with a rotary movement that tends to grind the pulp and produce coarse cloudy juice (though modern versions are less abrasive than the continuous presses of the Sixties and Seventies). The vertical presses produce excellent juice but they are slow and labour intensive. The first innovation in the design of single-batch presses was a basket press turned on its side and elongated to form a cylindrical shape. Teams of workers were no longer needed to redistribute the pressed skins; instead the whole press could be rotated and there were also internal chains to slice it through and break it up. The trouble was that this rough handling gave the juice some of the coarseness associated with continuous presses. In Champagne the new presses were binned.

A decade later came the next advance: the pneumatic press, which replaced the sideways pressure with an inflatable rubber sack that squashed the cake thinly around the inside of the tank. The juice was better but there were two practical problems. First, according to Smith, these are hellish to clean: "You need to send a kid in there." Surely not a child? "Well, a small guy." There was also a limit to the size you could build a rubber bladder before it ruptured. This was overcome in the 1980s when the rubber sac was replaced by a single membrane stretching the length of the cylinder: the "tank press". The advantage of the tank press is that it's much easier to clean and it's possible to build it large. These are the standard presses in large high-quality wineries today.

But there remains the problem of getting the grapes into a cylindrical tank. The easiest method is to pump in the slurry that is produced by a crusher-destemmer, or the bruised and sloppy mass that results from mechanical harvesting (Randall Grahm describes the films of mechanical harvesting shown to students at Davis as "viticultural snuff movies"). But to make sparkling wine from black grapes, as in Champagne, or for whole cluster pressing, as in Burgundy, you need to stuff the press with bunches on their stems, and it's time consuming to cram these through a hatch. You can't build a series of hatches without affecting the cylinder's structural integrity. However, if you turned the whole thing on its side... you would reinvent the basket press, which was exactly what happened to wine press design in the 1990s.

In fact, in their journey back to the future the new presses have overshot the early 20th century and wound up somewhere in the 19th century, in the pre-electrical era. The old square presses drained downwards through slatted wooden bases. These were replaced with a flat metal base when the presses were wired up to a motor, and the juice had to run sideways. New generation vertical presses have a permeable base, just like their wooden, unpowered ancestors. "It takes advantage of all the ideas of the tank press, except it's much easier to load," says Clark Smith. "This thing is a much better press than they had in 1850. But the whole problem was that our technological capabilities made it possible for us to lose track of what we were trying to do."

Electricity has lessened the need for wine's peculiar contributions to architecture. Where cellars deep in the ground were used to maintain cool, constant temperatures, these conditions can be created today in air-conditioned sheds. Cellars also used a system of levels to exploit gravity when transferring wine from tank to barrel. Some winemakers recreate such arrangements so they can dispense with electric pumps – Josh Jensen at Calera, for example, or Philippe Laurent at Domaine Gramenon in the Southern Rhône. Paul Draper thinks that if a pump is run slowly enough it can do the same job as gravity. However, there's one operation that he believes should still always be done by hand, never with a pump. His caution is a response to the changing nature of the grapes as they undergo vinification. When grapes are fresh and unblemished it's relatively easy to extract juice without colouring matter or tannins; this is why Champagne can be made from red grapes. It takes time to free the tannins, anthocyanins, glycocides and other phenolic compounds, and involves stirring, heat and the use of alcohol as a solvent. By the end of fermentation the solid residue – the pomace – has been subjected to all these and needs delicate handling.

"The last year that we pumped the pomace to the press was 1970," says Draper. "After a week or two of fermentation the seeds are very soft, and when you put any pressure on them at all they express harsh tannins." The technique he has used since 1970 could hardly be simpler. After fermentation the juice is drained off; then a hatch is opened at the bottom of each fermenter, the pomace is shovelled into a container and carried to the press by fork-lift. "If it's pumped out it's not what I call real wine. I'd worry about using a conveyor belt too. You spend all the money on these membrane presses that go to a maximum two atmospheres' pressure – then you pump the pomace and you've expressed into the wine the very flavours the press is supposed to keep back."

Paul Draper can afford to be fussy. He is working with low-cropped, intensely flavoured grapes from old vines. At the other end of the market over-cropping makes grapes pale and watery, and the winemaker faces the challenge of drawing some flavour from them. And at least in California and Australia such flavours won't be as mouth-puckering as they would be after a cool, damp summer in Europe. The New World's climate should give the skins, pips and stalks a certain ripeness, as long as the vines have been managed properly and are not grossly over-cropped.

With white grapes, the New World approach to beefing up flavour was once keeping the crushed grapes in contact with their skins and pips – rather as if the producers were making red wine. The skin tannins give rise to the deep yellow wines associated with Australian Chardonnays of the 1980s. The same technique was taken to Bordeaux in the late 1980s and used, in combination with selected yeast strains, to give more character to the region's dry whites, which – to the public – have always trailed a poor third to the reds and the sweet whites of Sauternes and Barsac.

The industrial winemaker uses rotary presses to get rapid extraction from red grapes. These agitate the skins and pips in the fermenting wine rather like clothes in a front-loading washing machine. Recent models are very expensive, but the Californian distributor, Conetech Inc., points out that the wine can be moved on to the press faster than from a traditional upright tank, typically in four rather than eight days – which allows more economical use of winery equipment. Some wineries will use each tank four or five times each harvest.

Rotary presses were introduced in the 1970s and gained a bad reputation in Europe and California for extracting too much too fast, rather in the way that it's easy to overcook vegetables in a pressure cooker. I saw rotary processes at the abbey of Heiligenkreutz in Austria's Thermenregion. They had been installed by the Cistercian monks who made wine there up until 1990, when they leased their facilities out to Michael Koch, a young German from the Rheinhessen. One of his first decisions was to take them out of service and limit their role to storage.

Rotary fermenters are fairly common in Burgundy, but they lack status: at the Buxy cooperative they are confined to Gamay, the lesser grape variety. Their action in tumbling and turning the pressed grapes has something in common with *pigeage*, but with the latter the pips fall to the bottom and stay there; while the rotary fermenter continues to turn them over in the wine. What's more, the internal screen tends to cut the skins, and unlike open fermenters there's no air contact during fermentation – the closed tank fills up with carbon dioxide. In the early days tanks were known to explode; one winemaker saw the stainless steel skin "rippling" when he arrived in the morning.

But the Australians stuck with this technology. They have refined the tanks' design and they are now part of the standard technique for producing that country's trademark fruity-oaky style of red wine. The grapes undergo a short, fast period of extraction which emphasizes fruit rather than chewy tannins, and the still-fermenting wine goes immediately into barrels. These fermenters are now having a revival in California. Nick Goldschmidt, Zelma Long's successor at Simi, uses open top fermenters for Pinot Noir, but he's bought rotary fermenters for his Syrah and Merlot. "You know that famous story about Harry Waugh, the wine author, when he was asked: 'When was the last time you confused Burgundy and Bordeaux?' and he replied 'Not since lunchtime.' We'd run many tastings comparing our Cabernet and Merlot and time and time again nobody could tell the difference." Nick Goldschmidt bought rotary fermenters in a successful attempt to give the Merlot a distinctive style of its own.

But the most important use of this technology will probably be to raise the standard of cheapish wines. Kevin Robinson of Rutherford Hill winery in Napa told *Wine Business Monthly* in December 1998 that the machines were invaluable in getting colour from heavily-cropped Central Valley grapes, but that "if you run mountain fruit through the rotary fermenters you can get tannic monsters." He added that they had been especially useful when phylloxera was rampant, in rescuing grapes from diseased vines that had failed to develop enough colour.

The same issue of the magazine reported the delivery of four 100-ton rotary fermenters – each of them capable of holding four truck-loads of grapes – to Kautz Ironstone Winery at Lodi, in the Central Valley. Tony Dann, the president of Conetech, which manufactured these monsters, told *Wine Business Monthly* with apparent pride that he considered them a part of the "industrialization" of California's wine business.

This is not a phrase that would have appealed either to Frank Schoonmaker or his disciple Alexis Lichine. Both passed on the European philosophy of hand-crafted wines to their American readers. "It can be made in bulk," Lichine conceded in his *Encyclopaedia of Wines and Spirits* (Cassell, 1967), "but it will not then be fine wine." Schoonmaker wrote: "Wine refuses to be a standardized factory product. It is good when natural conditions have been favourable, bad when they have been bad."[2]

Since Schoonmaker and Lichine's day it has become easier to make acceptable wine from poor grapes: as Kevin Robinson at Rutherford Hill says, the rotary press can be used to squeeze the last scrap of flavour from insipid grapes. But I'd argue that a "real wine" is one that tells a truthful story about its growing conditions, and whose concentration of colour, flavour and texture is determined in the vineyard, not the winery.

Clark Smith identifies electricity as the technology that cut the link with tradition. And he doesn't mourn: as a technologist he finds it stimulating to be forced to analyze whether traditional approaches are effective. And it obviously doesn't follow that wines shouldn't be made using electricity, any more than that they should only be shipped by barge, stagecoach or square-rigger. But where do you draw the line? Paul Draper believes that what matters more than anything else is the winemaker's intention. Nick Goldschmidt of Simi, for example, feels comfortable turning over his rotary fermenters twice a day – as often, in other words, as a small grower might perform *pigeage* – but says he wouldn't just leave them running, as some wineries do.

Refrigeration has become almost as integral to winemaking as powered presses, and it can also be used either to enhance the character of the grapes or to substitute for that character. (These tendencies can be observed in the contrasting careers of two influential Burgundians, Henri Jayer and Guy Accad.) In his *Encyclopaedia of Wines and Spirits* Alexis Lichine describes the importance of extraction in winemaking. "Colour and tannin are bound in the internal portion of the skin cells. Until these cells are killed it is very difficult to remove the pigment." He lists methods likely to cause cell death, including heat, the presence of alcohol and physical disintegration. By this stage Lichine had bought a château in Margaux, and this indeed sounds like a Bordeaux proprietor talking. In the cellars of the Médoc the wine is fermented and then kept in contact with the grape pulp so that the alcohol can dissolve colour and tannin, the family of phenolic compounds, in what is called post-fermentation maceration.

But in Burgundy there's a different tradition. Here the focus is on extracting phenols before fermentation gets underway, using the watery juice rather than alcohol as the main solvent. Far from requiring cell death, reactions in the still-living grapes appear to collaborate in this process. Hugh Johnson and James Halliday[3] report on Professor Michael Flanzy's research into "intracellular fermentation", in which the berry uses enzymes to feed on its own sugar, producing the carbon dioxide that sustains plant life and alcohol as a by-product. This only stops when the alcohol volume reaches a level that kills the living cells. Then yeasts take over, and create the enzymes that complete the fermentation.

Professor Flanzy investigated the technique used in Beaujolais, in which whole grape bunches are bundled into a vat without crushing. The intracellular fermentation gives off carbon dioxide, which forms a blanket above the grapes; these gradually liquify, as the berries on top burst from the internal fermentation and those underneath are squashed. This is the simplest way of making wine and, people speculate, an ancient one, not even requiring what Charlie Allen calls the "squishing" of grapes. This process would take place at the ambient temperature. To kickstart the main fermentation the growers used to heat some of the juice to get the wild yeasts going. In Burgundy, too, growers used heat to trigger fermentation soon after picking. But before the heating coils – or *drapeaux* – were introduced in the 19th century, it would take some time for the yeasts to start working. Anthony Hanson points out in *Burgundy* that the wine used to be made in open-sided sheds and that at harvest time, in September and October, the weather would often be turning chilly.

Refrigeration has made it possible to experiment with the effects of macerating the grapes before fermentation in Burgundy, rather than after fermentation, as in Bordeaux. The man who took it furthest was Guy Accad, a Lebanese-born oenologist who seemed set to transform the style of Burgundy in the 1970s and 1980s. At this time, wine drinkers – especially in Britain – were bafled by the way that Burgundy had gone from a robust, deep-coloured wine to something so pale it hardly seemed to qualify as a red wine at all.

There were two reasons for the change. Firstly, after Britain joined what was then the European Economic Community (EEC), community-wide *appellation contrôlée* laws banned the export sale of the old pseudo-"Burgundies", that were beefed up with Rhône. Secondly, over-productive clones and use of fertilizers were making the vines over-produce and the wines dilute.

Accad offered growers a technological solution. His advice was to buy refrigeration equipment which, as Anthony Hanson points out, had recently become available at prices small growers could afford.[4] Whether or not they were on commission, the consultant oenologists have had something of the aura of snake oil salesmen (although, unlike quack medicines, the chemicals and gizmos they offered had a measurable effect). Growers who worked to Accad's formula were able to offer big, dark wines with what Hanson describes as "blackcurrant and other piercing red fruit aromas."[4] Accad's advice was to run the cooling equipment for days on end, extracting colour and phenols over a period of ten days or more. The stalks went in to build up the tannins. Even refrigeration wasn't enough to stop fermentation starting, so another element in the formula was sulphur – and plenty of it. Red Burgundy had suddenly changed. As a buyer, Hanson wasn't especially convinced that he preferred it this way. Accad assured him that, far from being an innovation, this was a return to the old style that had been produced by the pre-phylloxera vineyards, with mass plantings propagated by *provignage*. Hanson wondered how on earth he could possibly know…

Accad made big waves in wine in the 1970s. Just as he was at the height of his fame, or notoriety, a young woman named Martine Saunier was doing the rounds of growers' cellars in the Côte d'Or. She had been born and raised in the region, in Prissé, a village some 80 kilometres to the south, and had worked in public relations before moving to California with her American husband. The marriage hadn't lasted, and she needed to support herself. First she worked as wine-buyer for a wholesaler in San Francisco, then she launched her own company. Just before Christmas 1979 she was in Vosne-Romanée tasting the 1978 vintage. One of her appointments was with a small grower called Henri Jayer, a man in his late 50s whom she'd met a few years earlier, after he began selling his wines independently. "I tasted his 1978 after tasting the DRC (Domaine de la Romanée-Conti) wines, which I thought were wonderful. But when I went to Jayer, I thought "this is really extraordinary". I went to several retailers in San Francisco and LA and they went absolutely ballistic about the wine – and that's how his fame started.

"I never advertise my wine. The way I work is by sampling. I remember flying to LA with a bottle of Jayer's Richebourg and going to one of the top retailers. Everybody was vying for the buyer's attention, but when I opened the bottle all conversation stopped and a man said to me: 'Where on earth did you get that wine?' In fact he called the head of Capitol Records and talked to his office, but his secretary said that he was in a meeting. This man said: 'Tell him this is the most urgent message he's ever going to get from me. I've got the best Burgundy I've ever had in my life.' This man from Capitol Records is now a friend of mine – and he has a great collection of Jayer."

Word spread to the Mondavi winery in the Napa Valley. "One of the things we'll always do is buy a lot of wines from the regions we think are pretty terrific," Tim Mondavi told me. "We just loved what we saw. His wines were bright, bright red in colour; we noticed the purity of fruit, a focus, a character that all derived from being very natural in the vineyards. This was during a period when Accad's style had come into vogue, with high sulphur and an emphasis on extraction. Other people were carrying out huge extractions by running the must through heat exchangers. I was really put off by both of them and the wines pretty much reflected the treatment: they were really heavy and fatigued."

Henri Jayer became a celebrity in France, but only after his reputation had become established in California. Martine Saunier says that this is almost a tradition in the Côte d'Or. "I'd say that probably all the wineries – Leflaive, Ramonet, Lafon, Jobard, Pierre Morey, Lafarge – their fame came from America. It's the American market that made these people very well off." Jim Clendenen of Au Bon Climat became one of Jayer's American disciples. "He grounded me not in production techniques, but in what you have to do to be committed to make high quality wine. He's very tough: he's tough with me, he's tough with Méo Camuzet." (This is the large-ish domaine in Vosne-Romanée, where Henri Jayer was originally a share-cropper and latterly a consultant.) "He would smell this wine and say, 'You'll never get it right.' He's very hard."

Jayer may be a stern teacher, but his warmth is also legendary. Saunier talks about his humility and his wonderful smile. His British importer, Roy Richards of Richards Walford, says: "He always had, and has retained, the ability to spin a web of magic round a tasting in his cellar. For me the thing that really marks him out is his self-evident intelligence. A generation later he would have gone to university and perhaps become a judge, like his daughter." After tasting Jayer's wines, Tim Mondavi felt he had to investigate further. "I was very impressed with his wines, so I was curious to find out more about him. This was the most natural, classic wine-growing and he turned out to be an amazing fellow. He continues to be my ideal winemaker. I've visited him a few times and I've been able to have him come to our cellars and taste. We've learned a lot from him."

When a wine becomes intensely coveted, myths arise about the producer's secrets – sometimes flattering, sometimes libellous. Jayer's theme is the need to be "as natural as possible". When Tim Mondavi visited his cellar in Vosne-Romanée he was first struck by how small it was: "It's a very tiny place, very well-organized. He's very meticulous in his care of the cellar. It's below his home; a very clean but natural environment. Good humidity. Clean, healthy, positive moulds on the cellar walls; nothing funky."

The first shock was the levels of sulphur dioxide used by his host: "I couldn't believe how low they were." There was a further surprise for Mondavi in the light of the approach he'd followed in the 1970s, when trying to make his Pinot Noirs more Burgundian. The trend in California had been towards fermenting whole clusters of grapes, as Josh Jensen does at Calera (following the practice he observed at the Domaine de la Romanée-Conti). This means that the tannins from the stalks are taken up by the wine, making it "structured" and long-lived. But Jayer was taking the berries off the stalks and, with hindsight, Tim Mondavi thinks he was right. "We were very enamoured of whole clusters, and we increased the percentage during the late Seventies and early Eighties. But then we found that the wines dried out as they aged. There was a diminution of hue – more orange and less bright. That didn't bother me, but drying tannin really did."

Everyone agrees that Jayer makes intense wines without the help of stalks to add body. Does he use cold maceration, and if so, how does he manage to dispense with the heavy sulphuring that Accad regards as necessary? Different people give different accounts. Roy Richards says he doesn't employ pre-fermentation maceration – the so-called "cold soak". Anthony Hanson says he does: holding the vat temperature to 15°C for four to five days, then letting it rise to 34°C after the colour has been extracted. According to Jim Clendenen: "Henri picks cold in the morning. His fermentation tanks are concrete vats in the garage and it takes five days to warm up." Jayer himself told the author Jacky Rigaux that "the grapes will macerate for four to six days before they start to ferment. I've noticed that when it's cold during the harvest, fermentation takes a long time to get going and the wines are fruitier. What's more, the colour's always prettier. If, thanks to temperature control, we can create the same conditions in years when it's hot at harvest time, the wines turn out equally fruity, complex and balanced."[5]

It's probably the case that people pass on different versions of Jayer's technique according to whether they were with him during a warm harvest season or a cold one. The point is that Jayer is not trying to improve on nature, he is attempting to use technology to reproduce the best possible naturally-occurring conditions. Refrigeration might be compared with chaptalization, the addition of sugar towards the end of fermentation, as recommended by Napoleon's minister of the interior, Jean-Antoine Chaptal (1756-1832). Chaptalization is yet another technique to become widely abused, in this instance to enable wine growers to escape the consequences of over-cropping; namely, producing grapes without sufficient sugar or flavouring.

But Chaptal recommended intervention on the principle that it was "to make good the conditions which would have been arrived at had conditions that year been more favourable". This apparent piece of hair-splitting is crucial. Could the wine's levels of alcohol, acidity or extraction have been arrived at naturally, or could it only be due to manipulation in the winery? Paul Draper argues that a grower's integrity is the only guarantee.

Tim Mondavi has been carrying out experiments with Pinot Noir since the mid-Seventies, both at the family's wineries and in collaboration with his friend Ken Brown of Byron vineyard in Santa Maria, which is now part of the Mondavi empire. "Whether with filtration or sulphur or acidulation, we found that the less we did the healthier the wine was. And as we tried to reproduce what mother nature was doing, we were able to develop wines that were far more expressive. The more natural we became with our winemaking – in particular using less sulphur dioxide – the more we recognized that our vineyards were tremendously divergent. And then we began to recognize the importance of dropping our yields."

Mondavi discovered that the "winemaking" – the standard, college-taught procedures – was getting in the way of the real business of letting the vineyards express themselves. He gives Jayer much of the credit for showing what "natural winemaking" should mean. When Jayer himself describes his techniques to Jacky Rigaux,[5] it's apparent that he works with great attention to detail and also, paradoxically, that winemaking is not his main concern. The fermentation takes as long as the natural yeasts and is left to finish when it wants to – from 15-18 days. He pumps over the juice for most of this period and only goes over to *pigeage* during the last three or four days. He matches the level of *pigeage* to the character of the vintage, although Jayer told Rigaux that this was barely necessary in 1983, for example, because the skins had accumulated high levels of fine tannin. The main reason for treading is to shake the pips to the bottom of the vat soon after they escape from the grape pulp: they should not free-float for more than three or four days.

But this doesn't explain why the wines are so concentrated and intensely coloured with such a light use of sulphur. Part of the reason is the absence of unripe or rotten grapes: Jayer considers a sorting table indispensable as cooling equipment. He also insists that the pickers use small containers – a maximum of 30kg – so that the grapes don't get squashed. But the determinant is the quality of the grapes themselves. The *négociant* François Faiveley told Anthony Hanson that Jayer's secret was firstly yields, secondly yields and thirdly yields – low yields. Jayer himself lists pruning, selection of the best vines for propagation and an organic approach to the vineyard as his three means of reducing yields, and it's low yields that produce the well-coloured, strongly-flavoured grapes that make richly-textured, well-balanced wine.

(1) Lichine, Alexis and Massee, William E, *Wines of France*. Alfred A Knopf, New York, 1951. (Perhaps the Americans were influenced by their French allies, who are supposed to salute the vines of the Clos de Vougeot vineyard when marching along Route Nationale 74.)

(2) Schoonmaker, Frank and Marvel, Tom, *American Wine*. Duell, Sloan and Pearce, New York, 1941.

(3) Halliday, James and Johnson, Hugh, *The Art and Science of Wine*. Mitchell Beazley, London, 1992.

(4) Hanson, Anthony, *Burgundy*. Faber and Faber, London, 1995.

(5) Rigaux, Jacky, *Ode aux Grands Vins de Bourgogne*. Editions de l'Armançon, Précy-sous-Thil, 1997.

7
MATURING THE WINE

A quarter of a century ago Burgundy's coopers, or barrel-makers, were having a tough time. Once every wine village was home to at least one cooperage – in Puligny-Montrachet alone there were four – but then the little village craftsmen went out of business and found themselves absorbed into companies employing at least ten staff. When the price of oil quadrupled following the Arab-Israeli war of 1973, the world economy went into recession. People spent less on luxuries: they drank less wine or traded down to cheaper wine. In Burgundy the consequence was a painful shakeout. As the *négociants* saw their customers vanish they cancelled their contracts with the small growers who had sold to them. The wine was traditionally delivered after two winters in the grower's cellar, by which time it would be clear and no longer likely to re-ferment after bottling. It arrived in barrels, 228-litre *pièces*, which the merchant would buy along with the wine. In a re-run of the Thirties crisis the growers tried their hand at direct sales, which meant bottling the wine themselves. One consequence was that they bought fewer barrels.

In 1977 Becky Wasserman, a young East Coast American, was living in the village of Saint-Romain, at the end of a short valley that leads up from Meursault into the Hautes-Côtes de Beaune. Saint-Romain was also the home of François Frères, one of the region's surviving cooperages; its boss, Jean François, was a friend and neighbour. Although François Frères had some distinguished customers, including Henri Jayer (who had recently begun to bottle his own wine) and the Domaine de la Romanée-Conti, the company was suffering from a lack of orders. Ms Wasserman was also feeling insecure. She had come out to Burgundy eight years earlier with her husband Dan, who left each day to work on huge white-on-white or white-on-beige post-minimalist paintings in his studio in Bouilland, a hamlet further up the valley. But the marriage was faltering and she was aware that she might soon need financial independence.

Jean François had a brainwave. For the previous 20 years one of his competitors had been sending barrels to a Californian winery, Hanzell in Sonoma. Hanzell had been created by James Zellerbach, a paper magnate and Burgundy-lover who had gone so far as to model his winery on one of the buildings of the Clos de Vougeot. In 1969 another market had opened up, when Dick Graff bought the Chalone winery and began importing his barrels from the same cooper, Yves Sirugue in Nuits-Saint Georges, to ferment his Chardonnay. California was in the midst of a wine boom, with new producers starting up almost every week. "He knew that I'd go to California for a vacation," Wasserman recalls, "so he asked if I'd sell his barrels."

She knew little about barrels. As a visual aid, Jean François equipped her with a miniature, about an eighth of the size of a regular *pièce*. "It was just to show the cosmetic look of it. I didn't know anybody in California, but I called at the Robert Mondavi Winery and met Zelma Long, who was their oenologist at the time, and she was very interested." Although Dick Graff didn't want to change his supplier, he was a mine of information. (Graff had been introduced to Becky by Josh Jensen, who had lodged with the Wassermans back in 1969 while grape-picking for their friend, Aubert de Villaine.) Becky's contacts multiplied: "People would say 'You've got to go see so and so'." Bob and Nonie Travers at Mayacamas, on Mount Veeder in Napa Valley, were among the first to sign up for a delivery, but perhaps the most important meeting was with André Tchelitscheff, the 76-year-old guru of the emerging industry.

"He had beautiful bearing and was the sort of person – I know this sounds ridiculous – who doesn't look to see what you look like, but who looks into your soul," recalls Becky. He told Becky he'd call her to account, though, if she was ever less than 100 per cent honest in her dealings with him, or with the many wineries for whom he worked as a consultant. The nearest Tchelitscheff and Wasserman ever came to falling out was over a problem at the HMR Estate Winery in Paso Robles (whose vineyard was later taken over by John Munch, of Adelaida Cellars). As Wasserman recalls: "Jean François happened to be over and we flew down, but it turned out that one of the workmen had rinsed the barrel with some extraordinary solution."

The main fear for prospective customers was that a barrel would spring a leak – when the supplier was the width of America and the Atlantic Ocean away. To allay their concerns Becky learned the art of plugging a tiny opening in a knot of wood with one or two wooden matches. There was little chance of developing Jean François' American business at a leisurely pace: the logistics of importing meant that the minimum order was a container-load of 120 barrels that were selling for 550 francs, or $100 apiece. "The problem was the barrels couldn't be delivered to individual customers for bureaucratic and technical reasons. I investigated and I thought, it can't be true! You had to have a single name on the bill of lading, so the container of barrels went to a single address which would receive it on behalf of 30 or 40 wineries. Having to find customers for 120 barrels made it rather like a jigsaw puzzle. You'd just keep calling people, and getting closer and closer to 120." This bureaucratic requirement gave rise to a kind of pyramid-selling that went beyond Wasserman's individual efforts. Customers would phone other prospective customers so that their own order could be delivered. New French oak barrels swept into California and became part and parcel of the formula for making "quality wine".

But this industry does not always warm to tradition. Richard Gibson, the technical manager of Australia's Southcorp Wines, describes natural corks as obsolete, abandoned as they were by the pharmaceutical industry in the early 20th century. So why is the wine business so attached to a maturation vessel that predates corks by at least a millennium-and-a-half? (Wine barrels can be seen on Trajan's column in Rome, carved in the 2nd century AD).

Wine cannot be sold immediately after it has fermented, for reasons that were not fully understood until as late as the 1960s. Indeed, if anything should redeem UC Davis's shortcomings, it must be the enology department's research into the secondary fermentation that occurs – usually in the spring after the vintage. The man who did much of the work is Emeritus Professor Ralph Kunkee, though in discussion it's hard to stem his stream of acknowledgements to predecessors at Davis and contemporaries at the Universities of Bordeaux and Mainz.

"When I came along" he says, "the idea was that it [secondary fermentation] only happened in red wine and that it was a kind of spoilage. But my predecessor had made a survey of a lot of wines in California, and discovered that of the premium wines neither the reds nor whites avoided a malolactic fermentation." While alcoholic fermentation is unmistakable, producing heat and great eruptions of carbon dioxide bubbles, the secondary fermentation creates only the occasional fine bubble. Louis Pasteur (1822-95) believed this was caused by a yeast but, despite his belief that "yeast makes wine, bacteria destroy it", the cause of secondary fermentation was eventually shown to be bacteria feeding on the sharp, appley malic acid in the young wine and replacing it with milder lactic acid, similar to that found in sour milk and cheese.

The Davis researchers identified the whole range of bacteria that performs malolactic fermentation in wine. "I should say there was real interest in this in the Napa, especially from Brad Webb, the winemaker at Hanzell, and André Tchelitscheff." One reason is that the research resulted in practical tools that winemakers could use to monitor progress of the malolactic fermentation, in particular what Kunkee calls using a "kind of kitchen equipment" – the cheap and easy method of paper chromatography in which different acids reveal themselves as different spots on a piece of absorbent paper[1]. The other outcome was that winemakers could now be offered cultured bacteria strains, analogous to the cultured yeast strains already in use, that could perform the "malo" simultaneously with the main alcoholic fermentation.

Perhaps I'm over-suspicious, but I am not surprised that wine technologists should want to dismiss secondary fermentation as "spoilage". In modern business, time is money – progress, to a high-volume brewer, means finding technical means of reducing lager's traditionally long maturation period. Vodka, not whisky, is the ideal modern spirit: with no ageing requirement, there's all the more money to spend on "building the brand". Similarly, the really profitable wines since the end of World War Two have been those that could be rushed onto the market: Liebfraumilch in the Sixties, or "White Zinfandel" in the Eighties.

If malolactic fermentation was just a wine fault, then the industry could feel justified in zapping it as part of the process of cleaning up wine for immediate sale. This includes knocking out micro-organisms with sterile filtration, or chemically – with sulphur – or in the US with Dimethyl Pyrocarbonate, an apparently benign cousin of the carcinogenic diethyl pyrocarbonate, which kills micro-organisms more cheaply than by filtration and then degrades into carbon dioxide. However, Ralph Kunkee and his colleagues have made wine a little more natural by offering a means of achieving malolactic fermentation without waiting – a cultured bacterium called Leuconostos oinos, commercialized as ML34[2].

With the help of instant malolactic fermentation, British supermarkets have been trying to persuade journalists and consumers that the best wines are the newest. This doesn't even mean forfeiting the taste of oak, which has been popular since the 1970s. Oak chips, for adding during fermentation, are part of the standard kit of the flying winemaker. According to the *Oxford Companion to Wine* it's now possible to buy oak chips that are impregnated with malolactic bacteria, allowing fermentation, secondary fermentation and barrel ageing to be rolled together in a single operation. Traditional growers, as you might expect, believe that a naturally-occurring malolactic fermentation – taking place typically after eight to ten months in barrel – gives much more interesting results.

Oak ageing is expensive and ties up capital. However, this procedure has become the main way of denoting a "quality wine", to the extent that even the hard-up Bulgarian industry makes a selling point of its commitment to oak. In the new Sliven winery they use the Australian technique of allowing red wines to finish fermenting in barrel. It's a far cry from 1967, when the American importer and winemaker Alexis Lichine could write: "The only reason for the French using barrels...is because formerly it was all they had."[3] The case against oak barrels was that they were unhygienic, that they didn't allow controlled low-temperature fermentation of white wine, and they did not allow the exclusion of oxygen, considered vital in making fresh-tasting "fruit-driven" wines. This view persisted as late as 1984 when Roger Rageot, director of the Buxy cooperative in southern Burgundy, opened a huge maturation cellar with space for oak *pièces*. According to Alain Pierre, the cooperative's oenologist, most of their rivals told them "forget about barrels. The future is in stainless steel."

But the tide had begun to turn long before that. In 1969, just two years after Lichine dismissed barrel fermentation, two college graduates set off on what was to become a momentous research trip round France. They were Dick Graff, who was on the point of owning Chalone Vineyards, and Rick Forman, a college friend from Davis. Rick Forman had just been hired by an expatriate English businessman, Peter Newton, who wanted him to set up a new vineyard in the Napa Valley, called Sterling. Why take on someone fresh out of college? "Beats me. I guess he did a lot of checking. I'd worked for Mondavi while I was at the university – I'd done a harvest there and at Stony Hill. There weren't too many graduates in those days, and I was actively interested in quality winemaking, not working for a bulk winemaker.

"Peter Newton grew up in London and went to school in Oxford, so with that influence from Europe he said, 'I think we want to do something traditional here. You take a whirlwind trip around France; we want Sterling to be as European as possible.'" Forman discussed it with Dick Graff, who had been to France the previous year and wanted to go back to research the use of barrels. The trip was to transform Rick Forman's life, as well as his career.

"I had been very technically orientated. But as soon as I went there I sucked it all up, like a dry sponge. I did a total U-turn and decided that my career wasn't necessarily going to be technical. I was totally overwhelmed by France. I've never been so excited in my life; I've never had anything impress me more."

The young men first spent time in Burgundy, which Dick Graff had visited before – and which was to become his lifelong passion – then went on to Bordeaux, where Rick Forman looked up Christian Moueix, another Davis contemporary. They went to Château Trotanoy, a Moueix-owned property in Pomerol, to see racking in progress. This is the process of clearing the wine by siphoning it from barrel to barrel, something traditionally carried out only when the atmospheric pressure is high, such as during a full moon. (Paul Draper bans racking at Ridge when the weather is stormy, and remembers the astonishment of a sceptical Davis graduate who broke this rule, only to discover that the lees [or sediments] had risen up and clouded the wine.) Forman noticed how much things differed from California: "They don't rack them with pumps going to big tanks; it's barrel-to-barrel racking, and very careful handling of the lees. And the sulphur additions are done in the barrel rather than added to the wine."

Forman is now a committed lover of Bordeaux, something slightly rarer in California than a passion for Burgundy or the Rhône. "I love the way they eat, the way they make wine, the architecture, the countryside. They have such a history of living with their culture." He claims to be the grower who first saw the potential in California for Merlot, the main grape of Pomerol. Now it's the third most widely planted red grape in the state.

But what Forman and Graff discovered in Burgundy was just as influential. The coopers they visited took them out to see their customers at work in their cellars. Forman had been expecting to learn about barrel maturation, but he now learned that in Burgundy they believed white wines should not only be aged but also fermented in wood. He couldn't actually see how this was being done, as he and Graff had to go back for the vintage in California. But they took notes and in October 1969 they made what may have been the first-ever Chardonnay outside Europe to be fermented in barrels.

Chardonnay and oak barrels have now been almost synonymous for a quarter of a century. But the style of wine that Dick Graff and Rick Forman learned to make is entirely different from the Australian Chardonnays I remember being impressed with in the

1980s. When I met Neville Falkenberg, chief white winemaker for Penfolds, he explained why Chardonnay used to be yellow and oaky, and why he wouldn't make it like that now.

The older style of New World oaked wine goes back to 1957 and the formula adopted at Hanzell by James Zellerbach's winemaker, Brad Webb. Despite the architecture of this estate, the winemaking wasn't especially Burgundian, but this didn't stop the oak-aged wines making a big impression. Robert Sessions, who succeeded Webb as Hanzell's winemaker, first tasted them when he worked at Mayacamas Vineyards on Mount Veeder. "You'd hear about this little place up in the hills in Sonoma that made these great wines. When I tasted them I practically fell off the verandah, they were so good."

Hanzell was a pioneer twice over: the winery was the first in California to own stainless steel tanks, which were made to an unfamiliar-looking rectangular design by the Valley Foundry in Fresno. In these tanks it was fairly easy to keep air away from the fermenting Chardonnay, which was then filtered and run into barrels. Fifteen years later came the refinement in white winemaking known as "skin contact". This involved crushing the grapes and keeping them in contact with the juice for some hours before pressing. This was bringing a red wine technique to white wine and the wine underwent corresponding colour changes. The skins sent phenols tumbling into the wine, which would darken dramatically as it aged. Paradoxically, winemakers have now learned that the more you shield the juice from the air, the darker it turns later. On the other hand the top Austrian Rieslings, like the beautiful wines made in the Wachau by Emmerich Knoll – which retain their pure, pale colour for years – are made from the juice left over from the presses, which is a disconcerting brown. The explanation is that if you oxidize the phenolic substances early on they fall out of the juice. Skin contact puts into the wine the very elements that are removed by traditional practices. The phenols don't just produce a darker colour; they can also taste coarse and bitter. It's one of those experiments that must have seemed like a good idea at the time.

Perhaps one reason for the fad is that it creates an impact that can be relied on even if the quality and flavour intensity of the grapes can't be guaranteed. This was one of the reasons that oak was embraced so widely. All sorts of methods have been devised to make wine taste oaky without the expense of oak barrels: oak chips, often supplied in something similar to tea-bags, oak essence (which is now illegal everywhere) and oak staves, that can be attached to the inside of a stainless steel fermentation tank.

One paradox of barrel fermentation is that white wine will come out less oaky than it does when passed through a stainless steel tank and followed by barrel maturation. The suggested explanation is that wine fermented in barrels is left on its lees – the spent yeasts – and that this acts as a kind of fining agent, in removing the wood tannins. [4]

The synergy between wine and wooden barrels is mysteriously neat, almost as perfect as the fit between grapes and wild yeast that is responsible for wine. Barrels are objects of great design elegance, watertight containers made without screws or nails. Even when they are too full and heavy to lift, they can be rolled and manoeuvred by virtue of the bulge in their centre. This shape has stayed constant, even though barrels have become more squat than the elongated forms used by the Normans and Romans. The bulge has nothing to do with winemaking, but it just happens to act as a perfect trap for the lees and sediment that are left behind during racking. You cannot exclude air or ferment at very low temperatures in barrels, but the parameters imposed by barrels are those that create the most classic style of white wine.

Barrels were used in winemaking for 2,000 years for storage and transportation, with little if any thought paid to their effect on a wine's taste. Mel Knox, who took over Becky Wasserman's barrel business after she became a wine-broker, has noticed French growers attributing flavours to terroir that seem to him the obvious result of different cooperage techniques. Meursault is supposed to taste "mealy", and Puligny-Montrachet "toasty". But Knox points out that the barrel maker in Meursault softens the staves with steam, whereas the craftsmen favoured by the Puligny growers bends the staves by holding them over a flame.

A new rigour was injected into traditional cooperage after Tim Mondavi and his oenologist Zelma Long caught the bug in the late 1970s. They compared the grain and flavours of American oak with French oak, and the different flavours and densities of oak trees from different French forests. In 1978 Mondavi noticed that the flavour characteristics varied according to how much the inside of the barrel had been charred. From then on he began to specify his desired level of "toast" when ordering from French coopers.

The friendship between Becky Wasserman and Zelma Long led to one of the most systematic attempts by California to unravel the secrets of Burgundy, its barrels and other aspects of winemaking. In 1979 the two women organized a course for a group of leading winemakers; it was based in the large converted barn that Becky now occupied in the hamlet of Bouilland, but the group travelled round the region on field trips.

"It was a marvellous seminar," Becky recalls. "Zelma spent months collecting questions she wanted answered: they were translated into French and each grower had a copy. We had two or three panels of growers per day; everything from seeing the vineyards to a bit of time in the cellars, and we'd sit around in the evening and discuss what had happened each day.

"Growers don't particularly talk to merchants; they rather resent merchants and journalists because they don't think they have the proper background, but they will connect with other growers, be they from Italy or California or Australia. On the very last evening we invited everyone who had received us and the

Californians brought their wines and it was very touching. We said, 'bring anyone you like' and in one case half a village arrived. My lasting memory is of Mike Richmond from Acacia hitting his head slowly against the stone wall, because not one Burgundian had the same idea as the next Burgundian. Actually, I think he was hitting his head almost every evening."

It's this intractable individualism that Wasserman identifies as the true Burgundian trait. It's not so much that Burgundy is the last redoubt of artisanal wine making. However you define this, you'll find growers going their way rather than observing every article of faith. When Californians defined "Burgundian tech-niques" as whole bunch pressing and punching down, they had somehow to accommodate Jayer, who destems and pumps over. This reassures Wasserman, who says: "The fear of many wine people is that all's going to be merged into one. This place is very important to all of us who want to see the individual survive."

But the contact with Californian winemakers has not always contributed to diversity. The two regions have moved closer together and Jim Clendenen of Au Bon Climat, in Santa Maria on the Central Coast, claims that the traffic in ideas has moved in both directions – though the American influence usually goes unacknowledged. One example he gives is *batonnage*, the practice of stirring white wine in the barrel. Ralph Kunkee believes that this was originally a means of getting a malolactic fermentation going, using the sediment as a nutrient for malolactic bacteria. It's widely regarded as a traditional Burgundian technique, one that contributes to the mouthfeel of Chardonnay and keeps the wine fresh by encouraging the yeast cells to scour up any dissolved oxygen. But Jim Clendenen is sceptical. "When they were getting into lees stirring in Burgundy they said, 'It was my grandfather's idea.' I said, 'I don't believe it's a Burgundian technique. When I first came over 25 years ago no-one did it.' But in California they had all begun stirring away like mad."

It's easier to detect the process of inventing tradition when it takes place outside France. Once the Americans had embraced French oak barrels, they started popping up everywhere. There's now a "*barrique* forum" for German growers who want the grape known locally as Spätburgunder to pretend it's still in Burgundy and is still called Pinot Noir. In a smart Italian *enoteca* the owner's voice will drop reverentially when he discusses a "Chardonnay in barrique". Neville Falkenberg has laboured to make an ultra-premium example for his employers, Penfolds, in order to match their overpriced red Grange, rather than indulge his own passion for Riesling and Semillon, the established white grape varieties of his native Barossa Valley.

"Barrel" has come to mean the 225-litre Bordeaux barrique, or the more squat 227-litre Burgundy *pièce*. But most of the world's wine regions have historically had their own distinct size: in Chablis it's half as big as a barrique; 15 per cent smaller in the United States; twice as big in Oporto and nearly three times as big in the sherry towns of Andalucía. It was not always the case – as in Bordeaux and Burgundy – that the wine was sold and shipped in the vessel used for its fermentation and maturation. In the Southern Rhône producers used big casks, *foudres* or *demi-muids*. Different German regions had different practices: in the Mosel wine was made and sold to the merchants in *füder*, 1,000-litre containers; in the Rheingau, the Rheinhessen and the Pfalz, the traditional vessel was the oval *stück*, which never left the cellar and had a hatch through which the owner climbed to scrape away deposits of tartrate crystals. The Austrian equivalents are called *fässer* and like *stücke* were permanent fixtures, used to fill bottles or small barrels for transportation. The tradition in Italy was to mature wine in the huge *botti*, with a capacity ranging from 1,000-16,000 litres.

These days farmers who decide to become full-time wine growers invest in temperature-controlled stainless steel and as many new oak barriques as they can afford. The barriques have brought changes in the style of red wines in regions as far apart as Piedmont and Chianti in Italy, Châteauneuf-du-Pape in the Southern Rhône and Bairrada in Portugal. The wine becomes "bigger" and deeper coloured, and is often ready to drink sooner than when it is kept in larger, more traditional wooden vessels. This is because barrels do much more than make wine taste of oak: they are also a natural source of oxygen and wood tannins. The tannins react with proteins in the wine to produce long polymerized molecules, creating a deep, stable colour – neither the purple of young wine or the pale, bricky colour that comes with great age – and to enhance mouthfeel.

Big wooden containers might appear to be redundant. If you want a wood influence you choose barriques; if you want to emphasize fresh, natural fruit flavours there's stainless steel. But the larger vessels have hung on in almost every region where they were once traditional, and they're even starting to appear in California. In the Kamptal a young Austrian winemaker, Martin Moosbrugger, took over an old-fashioned monastic cellar in 1996. Its vaults run underneath the early 18th-century buildings of the Schloss Gobelsburg estate, which he now leases from the Cistercian monks of Zwettl Abbey. Rather than stainless steel, the cellars are dominated by new 2,700-litre *fässer* that he had built by a local cooper. Some of the Riesling and Grüner Veltliner wines are fermented in stainless steel and moved to the casks for four to five months' settling and maturation. But two of the most serious white wines are fermented in oak.

Moosbrugger has two reasons for this practice: one is an ideological belief in using local oak from the mountain slopes of Manharstsberg: "It's part of our philosophy of making authentic wines." The other is that he wants to keep the wine on the lees, and this means that it needs contact with the air. "If you don't watch the lees very carefully, you soon get problems of off smells and flavours." For the kind of full, dry wines he wants to produce, large wooden containers give the wine exactly the right exposure to oxygen. Moosbrugger has also invented something that he calls "dynamic cellaring", a concept that has yet to be paid the usual compliment of imitation. This entails putting the wooden casks on rollers so he can push them outdoors in the depths of winter. This is a natural means of cold stabilization that in New World wineries can make heavy energy demands. Martin doesn't have conventional refrigeration. He says that this way he doesn't have to pump the wine, and that he disapproves of the coolants and anti-freeze. "How refreshing to hear that from an Austrian wine-maker" I say, making this probably the 15th year running he's heard a crack about the adulteration scandal. "Ha ha", he says.

In many other regions large oak containers are still the first choice of traditionalists, and barriques the emblem of modern international style. In Châteauneuf-du-Pape the great names – Rayas, Vieux Télégraphe, Beaucastel – are all committed to big, old-fashioned *foudres*. François Perrin of Château Beaucastel calls oak "the only material which allows wine to breathe – allowing oxidative contact in the noble sense of the word – which gives the wine refinement." The difference between his rows of giant *foudres* and the more widely-used barriques is that in big containers the process happens more slowly, leading (according to François and his brother Jean-Pierre) to a corresponding nobility and refinement in the wine. *Foudres* are even making a comeback on the southern fringes of Burgundy itself, at the Buxy cooperative, which has invested in new 2,500-litre oak tuns. Their oenologist, Alain Pierre, uses them to ferment red and white wines under the Côte Chalonnaise appellation. The result is something between the bright flavours created by stainless steel and the full small barrel treatment: Alain calls it a "wonderful balance".

It's a gamble, given the need to attract attention in a crowded marketplace and the importance of blind tastings. Big oak vessels make red wine look less expensive than it is: without the boost of wood tannins the colour tends to be lighter and there's no whoosh of coconut and vanilla. The white doesn't have the butter and vanilla aromas of small barrel fermentation, nor the exaggerated aromas you get from fermenting cold in stainless steel and excluding oxygen. The wine is what it is. I like it like this.

Larger oak containers are now starting to appear in the United States, or rather reappear, since redwood vats were widely used before the move to barriques and stainless steel. Mel Knox says that the importing business he took over from Becky Wasserman is taking increasing orders for the larger sizes: "I'm seeing a lot more sales of everything from 500-litre barrels to 3,000-gallon uprights." He links the move towards bigger barrels with the trend towards Italian grape varieties like Barbera and Sangiovese, grapes which can be overwhelmed by too much woodiness. The Rhône revival is another factor: the Tablas Creek winery (the Perrins' California offshoot) has a number of *foudres* just like Beaucastel, its parent. The theory is that Grenache tends to become over-oxidized in smaller barrels.

But the most radical move has been Tim Mondavi's decision to replace 12 stainless steel red wine fermenters with wood. When I visited the winery in February 2000 it had placed an order through Mel Knox with Taransaud, a large cooperage in the Cognac region. It was for 56 big (20,000-litre capacity) upright wooden fermenters, of the style you might still see in the cellars of the Bordeaux first growths, such as Château Mouton-Rothschild or Château Margaux. This is part of a renovation project that will cost the winery at Oakville $27 million, and will add unit costs of $12 per gallon as opposed to $6 for stainless steel, on the estimate of Patrick Mahaney, a Mondavi vice president.

The Oakville site was the first winery to be built after Prohibition. It was founded in 1966 after Robert Mondavi fell out with the family winery, Charles Krug. Oakville's trademarks were its unique architecture – loosely inspired by 18th-century Spanish mission settlements – and its technological innovation. Robert Mondavi followed the lead of James Zellerbach in going all out for stainless steel, and showed it off to the visiting public.

The winery was always conceived as a wine education centre, and part of the aim of the redevelopment is to open it up to still more visitors and give them more to see. But going over to wood has attracted criticism, some of it from an unexpected direction. At Ridge Vineyards, Paul Draper finds it difficult to see any merit in the move. "Why do it? It has absolutely nothing to do with traditional winemaking." Draper is fanatical about the detail of winemaking technology. As well as his low-speed helical pump, which one authority claims could move a tomato without bruising the skin, he bursts with pride over his customized crusher-destemmer, produced by Amos, a German manufacturer. "The idea is to get the stems off first; many machines do it the other way round. We had Dr Amos put on a half-speed motor for us." The stainless steel tanks were part of the new broom he brought to the winery in 1970, replacing redwood fermenters. He says that the problem with oak fermenters is that they are only used once a year – meaning a reliance on sulphur to preserve and clean them for the rest of the year.

The charge that I feel that Tim Mondavi has to answer is one of window-dressing. Almost all of his company's wines will still be made in stainless steel, but the exception will go on prominent display to wine tourists. His long answer places oak fermenters within the context of Mondavi's history of experiments with the European winemaking tradition. These started soon after he joined his father's company in 1974 and began with understanding malolactic fermentation, then discovering "post-fermentation maceration" as practised in Bordeaux – which found that leaving red wine in contact with the crushed skins made it richer, not bitter, as one might have predicted.

Moving to oak fermenters was a spin-off of the Pinot Noir

trials (*see* Chapter Six). The team had been looking at the short pre-fermentation maceration as practised by Henri Jayer, for example, and which was achieved mainly through leaving the grapes until a wild yeast culture had grown sufficiently to start fermentation. The value of oak was its slowness to heat up and cool down. "If you use native yeasts you'll have a lag phase, and while the yeasts are propagating there's naturally a cold soak. What we found is that the insulating quality of oak fermenters tends to retain the cold temperatures of that lag phase," says Tim Mondavi. "And at the end they hold the temperature in a very positive way, and it allows more complete extraction of flavour from the skin at the warmer temperatures. You can develop some enzymatic activities that perform a gentle extraction."

The Pinot Noir experiments led to comparative fermentations of Cabernet Sauvignon, Merlot and Sangiovese, using both open and closed-top wooden vats. One benefit was that wine which fermented in oak came into greater contact with the air, thereby preventing "reduction", the malodorous effect created by anaerobic reactions. Tim Mondavi says: "I believe that with oak fermenters there would tend to be less reduction. If you make a wine the same way but in stainless steel it will tend to become more reduced and 'steely' in flavour, though not because it picks up any flavour from the stainless steel. In oak the wine tends to have greater depth. It gives you lower yields because you lose a little bit of moisture through evaporation, and the alcohol is a little lower."

Mondavi concedes that it's a challenge to keep oak clean, but that cleanliness, good ventilation and humidity mean that they need to burn fewer sulphur candles. (Incidentally, Mel Knox points out that the dreaded wild yeast, brettanomyces, is more likely to occur in new oak barrels than in ancient vats.) "It will provide more of a challenge in terms of maintenance techniques," says Mondavi, "but I think the benefits are worth it. The trials have shown that it's appropriate. I like it."

Nor is Tim Mondavi noticeably fazed when I suggest that he is over-influenced by the fact that the wooden vats will look great. "If you look at the places where the greatest wine comes from, they're usually beautiful," he says. "There's a pride in being able to provide something that's aesthetically pleasing – isn't it nice that nature can be so attractive ?"

(1) I felt the popular and blameless Ralph Kunkee was a good person to field criticisms of Davis, and he played a straight bat (or whatever the equivalent is in baseball). On the advice to plant in the Salinas valley wine tunnel (*see* Chapter One) he said: "There are some places there where it's too wet. You can see the vines sitting in water, where there's no good drainage. But all in all it's pretty wonderful. The problem was that people shouldn't have put Cabernet there. It was very veggie. But the Pinot Noir is a success."

On AxR1 (*see* Chapter Two) he blames the growers, who were aware of the rootstock's susceptibility to phylloxera, more than his colleagues in the viticulture department. "They were well aware that there was some sensitivity, but they thought they wouldn't have to worry about the consequences for another 15 years. Something else to say about AxR1 is that some wonderful wines were made with that vigorous rootstock and there are vineyard people who say it's a pity we don't have it today." The error he's least comfortable about defending is the least publicized: the failure in supplying heat-treated stock that was not, after all, virus-free (*see* Chapter Three).

(2) Beaujolais Nouveau, which began its conquest of world markets in the 1970s, must by law undergo at least a partial malolactic fermentation. Before cultured bacteria came on the market in the 1980s Georges Duboeuf, the largest producer, had its own technique for triggering secondary fermentation. This was to inoculate with the deposits on filter pads left by wines that had had a conventional "malo".

(3) Lichine, Alexis and Fifield, William, *Alexis Lichine's Encyclopaedia of Wines and Spirits*. Cassell, London, 1967.

(4) *see* Zelma Long's article in *The University of California/Sotheby Book of California Wine*. ed. Muscatine, Doris, Amerine, Maynard A, Thompson, Bob. University of California, Berkeley, 1984.

8
DEALING WITH WINE FAULTS

Wine tasting deals with something complex and mutable; it evokes subjective responses, and this subjectivity can spill over into areas that should be strictly factual. As with poetry, contradictory statements can both be true. One instance of this uncertainty principle is the case of wine faults, or "so-called wine faults".

The New World tends to regard Europe and the Europeans as somewhat deficient in hygiene. My mother, who worked in Britain's Political Warfare Executive, once told me of the damage caused to relations with newly-liberated France after American forces came across a warehouse full of ripe Camembert. It was destroyed as unfit for consumption, in the face of agonized protest. The Californian David Ramey found in Australia that classic French wines provoked visceral disgust, earthily expressed: "F*** man, it stinks, it's completely f******* shot…"

But it's only in the New World that I've heard of the practice of deliberately creating "faults" to add interest to a bland product: namely "volatile acidity", meaning the presence of acetic acid (as in vinegar); hydrogen sulphide, the poisonous substance that smells of rotten eggs; and brettanomyces, a wild yeast that creates riding-stable smells. Richard Gibson, the technical manager of Southcorp, told me that while the presence of hydrogen sulphide was a bad fault, it could in tiny quantities be a powerful factor in creating complexity. Clark Smith of Vinovation (which offers alcohol and volatile acidity adjustment to winemakers) talked about the practice of keeping aside a tank of "brett"-contaminated wine that could be added in minute quantities. Another story I've heard about volatile acidity is too potentially libellous to reveal.

Wine critics devote much attention to faults. When Kermit Lynch learned to taste with Richard Olney at his home in Provence, his first lesson was how to spot defects. Few people can agree what makes wine good or bad; it's the ability to identify faults that is supposed to distinguish amateurs from professionals. At press tastings it is disgraceful to fail to spot evidence of cork taint; wine merchants soon learn to agree that, at the very least, "the fruit's a bit flat" and produce a second or third bottle.

But not all of us who pontificate about wine faults can spot them when challenged to taste blind. In 1999 a group of 91 buyers, writers and PR people – including several Masters of Wine – was invited to taste four cheap wines. Three had common faults (oxidation, cork taint) and one was unblemished. Only a quarter of the group identified the untainted wine. It wasn't an impossible exercise – Jane Kay, responsible for quality control at Marks and Spencer, achieved a perfect score – but it still suggested that the necessary skills and experience were confined to a small circle.[1]

Clark Smith compares America's wine and dairy industries. In his 1995 article in *Practical Winery & Vineyard*[2] Smith questioned whether the UC Davis viticulture department understood that "deliciousness" was the goal of winemaking, and discussed the analogous case of the University of Wisconsin. Here, teams of milk tasters compete to identify defects – onion grass, lactic bacteria, freezer burn. The ideal milk, he said, was totally bland, unlike in France "where low-fat milk tastes like cream. They have a completely different idea of what milk should be; 'a theory of deliciousness'."

One might conclude that "faults" aren't actually faults, but individual traits that get frowned on in our modern "zero-defects" culture. But this isn't correct either. Partly it's a question of what's appropriate. Madeira is expected to be very acetic and Rhône wine can get away with a little brettanomyces, but these qualities would be disgusting in Mosel or Muscadet. I think of faults like irregularities in flowers – the New World position, at one extreme, is like that of show judges who want pansies and violas to be as near perfect circles as possible; at the other, of course, no gardener likes plants that are deformed or mouldy with mildew.

Kermit Lynch makes an analogy with breasts and the trend to "improve" them with plastic surgery. "Modern wine is getting like breast implants. Like on television or in Hollywood movies, how often do you see an actress who hasn't had implants?" he says. "They don't look like real breasts and they don't behave like real breasts. But from a distance most men will look at a woman who has had a breast job, it's an automatic reaction. And wines are like that. If they're alcoholic and oaky then the first reaction is 'Wow! I can smell that!' It's just when you get closer you see that there's no reality there."

This debate is the flip-side of the polemic of "non-interventionist winemaking". Not many winemakers will boast that they use technology to manufacture qualities that weren't present in the grapes: instead they deploy sulphur, single-strain yeasts, filters, centrifuges, tartaric acid, ion exchangers, reverse osmosis machines and spinning cone columns as weapons in a war on wine faults. Are they all works of the devil – anathema to natural wine, just as "faults" are to the technician?

Sulphur is a tough case to argue against. It is an ancient form of intervention which, like barrels, dates back to the Romans. Sulphur is the traditional way to disinfect a wooden vessel. You burn a "candle" of the yellow element which is bound to a central wick: the foul smoke it creates is sulphur dioxide, which combines with any available oxygen and also kills or inhibits the growth of bacteria and wild yeasts. Sulphur is also used in the vineyard, and even biodynamic growers rely on it to deal with fungal diseases.

Mechanical harvesting makes sulphur indispensable: without relatively large quantities the liquescent mass shaken off the vines would oxidize and spoil. Then there is the accountant's desire to get maximum return from their firm's investment in fermenters – if you make wine in batches rather than all at once, the grapes are crushed and the juice is stored with lots of sulphur, to stop the fermentation starting. Once the equipment is free the sulphur is removed (with, for example, the spinning cone column).

Sulphur is produced in all fermentation processes and is present in every cell of every living creature. But then radioactivity is "natural"; dioxin is "natural". Asthmatics may be grateful for attempts to reduce or eliminate sulphur in wine, as it can trigger asthma attacks.[3] High sulphur wines also cause headaches. Low sulphur and sulphur-free wines have a kind of sweet, innocent purity about them. They can also be undrinkable.

Martin Ray, the Californian pioneer of single varietal wines, believed in working without any sulphur. The result could be very good or very bad. The problem was that he refused to admit the latter possibility. Before he joined Ridge, a young Paul Draper fell foul of Ray. "In the Sixties I remember buying some wine for a very high price, $16 or $18, and taking it back to the shop. They called Martin Ray; they said he refused to compensate them for any bottles but they agreed with me that it was vinegar. I didn't talk to Ray but they held the phone out so I could hear what he was saying: 'Obviously your customer is a total neophyte and has never drunk fine wine in his life. How dare you intimate such things about my wine.'"

Draper hasn't been tempted to abandon sulphur dioxide, but one of his Santa Cruz neighbours was. In the late 1950s David Bruce, then a young dermatologist, had been "enthralled" with the intensity of flavour and abundance of aromas in Ray's wines. "I was going round picking up these bottles and one of the wine shops got hold of him and said, 'this young kid is trying to buy all

your wine', so he invited me to his pre-vintage party in 1958."
The event followed a routine familiar to Ray's friends and regular
guests, who often included Charlie Chaplin and John Steinbeck.
Bruce describes how it began at three in the afternoon, when the
host was still going round the vineyards in his tractor gathering in
the harvest, "pulling grapes with the prospect of making sparkling
wine. He finally got out of his tractor and introduced himself and
we sat outside at a kind of picnic table and his wife brought out
bottle after bottle of wine. There were 16 or 17 people there. It
went on from three in the afternoon till three o'clock in the
morning, and of course Martin Ray did more than his share of the
drinking, and the more he'd drink the more he'd hold court and
pass comments on all the personalities in California winedom."

In 1961 David Bruce bought a vineyard 16 kilometres as the
crow flies from Martin Ray's. "To begin with," he says, "I followed
some of his methods in winemaking: early on, for example, the
use of sulphur dioxide in wines. You have to be terribly clean in
the process, but for some years I used no sulphur dioxide. Now we
use it very modestly, rarely over 60-80 parts per million (ppm)."
Meanwhile, Bruce somehow fell from favour with his mentor. "He
found that I had a friend who had a friend who had a friend who
he didn't like, so he wouldn't invite me back any more."

Ray probably had the wrong kind of personality to inspire a
following of disciples, although he won his crusade for controls
over bogus varietal labelling. His other campaign was boosted by

the United States' restriction of the term "organic" to grapes rather than wine. The proposed definition of "organic" wine would allow only 90ppm of sulphur dioxide as opposed to the 350ppm otherwise permitted. So, Fetzer's Bonterra range can claim only to be "made from organically grown grapes", while Frey Vineyards and Organic Wine Works in Santa Cruz eschew sulphur dioxide. Tony Coturri in Sonoma says he could obtain certification but chooses not to, preferring to emphasize wine quality above ideological correctness. The Coturris are Italian by origin and Tony links the dislike of sulphites to family traditions. It is certainly true that Italian home winemakers, *see* Chapter Six, are suspicious of additives of any kind and Italian expatriates I know in London put great emphasis on finding "natural" wines.

The French routinely use sulphur, although a number of good growers are opposed to it, including Domaine Gramenon in the Southern Rhône, Pierre Overnoy in Jura, Pierre and Catherine Breton at Bourgueil in the Loire, and Jean Foillard and Marcel Lapierre at Morgon in Beaujolais. A crucial influence was Jules Chauvet (1902-1989), an oenologist and wine merchant based in the village of La Chapelle de Guinchay.

Chauvet was an indefatigable researcher and a gifted taster. Professor Emile Peynaud, author of the classic *Le Gout du Vin*, described him as *"nôtre initiateur à l'analyze olfactive"*[4]. Chauvet had two quirks, a love of cigarettes (surprisingly widespread in the wine trade) and a belief that tasting was better done out of doors, even in the rain. Kermit Lynch, who met Chauvet in 1987, describes him as "a gracious, guileless man with a poetic streak which he seemed to want to repress." Chauvet loved to experiment and tried some extremely interventionist ideas, including heat-extraction and adding glycerine. In 1951 he compared a Pouilly-Fuissé made without sulphur with the same wine conventionally made, and found it much finer and more aromatic. From then on he always made some of his wines without sulphur.

From 1982 until his death Chauvet was assisted by Jacques Néauport, who had taught English and had recently returned from a teaching stint in the north of England. There he came across CAMRA, the campaign for real ale, which inspired him to champion the cause of authenticity in French wine. Chauvet and Néauport concluded that the main role of sulphur is to inhibit bacteria which otherwise trigger malolactic fermentation before alcoholic fermentation gets underway. Néauport now works as a consultant, and promotes a combination of carbon dioxide (to exclude oxygen) and refrigeration (to promote pre-extraction fermentation and limit the bacterial count). He says that there are two essentials in making wine without sulphur: extreme cleanliness – as found in a lager brewery or dairy – and constant laboratory checks on microbial activity.

Another aspect of this method is the use of natural rather than cultured yeasts, a question of honour for many New World producers who want to rival the top European wines. Néauport is not especially gung-ho about their chances. He says that where he lives in the Ardèche the local yeasts are useless, and he is still smarting from criticism rained on him by grape growers who followed his methods – described in a newspaper article – in a difficult year with low yeast populations.

It is essential to have good local wild yeasts ("*une patrimoine levurienne*"), but the yeast population that grows outside the established regions sometimes contains rogue organisms that create off-flavours. In New Zealand, however, Néauport reports tasting a delicious Sauvignon Blanc made without sulphur and using wild yeasts, so they obviously exist.

Yeasts and sulphur are related issues. The guaranteed way to make a "clean" wine is to use high levels of sulphur to zap all microbial activity in the grapes, and then inoculate with a commercial yeast strain with a high sulphur tolerance. These offer a fast, reliable and predictable fermentation and the makers also claim the ability to create specific and desirable aromas. One counter-argument is that single yeast strains reduce complexity. Wild yeasts are genetically diverse and spontaneous fermentation always brings different species and many sub-species into action.

You can try to get this complexity with cultured yeasts. Jeff Cohn, for example, makes white wines for the ex-veterinarian Kent Rosenblum, in a vast hangar-like winery in the middle of a naval base at Alameda, in the San Francisco Bay area. He was especially pleased with the effect of a cocktail of commercial yeasts he used in his top-of-the-range Chardonnay, though I felt the effect was a bit showy. The next day David Ramey told me why he believes wild yeasts make better wine. It's not just that there are lots of different strains; it's that they work slowly, one taking over from another. A mixture of selected yeasts will, by contrast, be a collection of organisms that are essentially similar.

Wild or "ambient" yeasts are dear to those who describe wine in terms of complex natural systems. Claude Bourguignon says that microbial life in the soil transmits its distinct character to the vines. Another unique living community then transforms the grapes in a way that is unpalatable to rival micro-organisms, though not to mammals. The Danish winemaker/researcher Peter Vinding-Diers lays great store by the notion that yeasts are an extension of terroir and that the greatest vineyards are those with the best local varieties.

But Josh Jensen at Calera makes almost an opposite argument in support of the same case. He says that countless numbers of these creatures live in the outer atmosphere, rising with air currents and falling in endless showers onto the land: this means, surely, that you can manage perfectly well without industrial single-strains. There's no doubt that natural yeasts work, and that few really great wines are made with their single-strain counterparts, but it's harder to explain why – not least because there is no money to be made from research into a free resource.

Yeast and sulphur are just two of a long list of permitted wine additives. You also hear gossip about flavourings. One case that surfaced in the mid-1990s involved an English proprietor, David Ealand, who submitted samples to the English quality wine scheme. Tasters found that his "Luxter's Old Dessert" wine had a penetrating aroma of peaches – something evident in two successive vintages. The Wine Standards Board was called in and took the unusual step of sending off samples for analysis in Germany. When the analyst at Würzburg University's department of food chemistry, Professor Peter Schreier, reported finding synthetic flavourings, the board prevented Mr Ealand from selling his wine. They also prosecuted him under European Union wine law.

The case was written up by Christopher Booker, *The Daily Telegraph*'s anti-EU voice, in a tone that was familiar from the campaign to "save" consumers from being put off substandard British chocolate by Brussels-inspired labelling. For Booker the crucial point was that, because of its high level of alcohol, "Luxter's Old Dessert" was not a wine at all, and was therefore not subject to EU law. An appeal court judge agreed, and the conviction of the winemaker, Peter Arguile, was "trenchantly" quashed. Booker explained that Arguile had "inadvertently tipped a minute quantity of peach flavouring essence back into a tank containing dessert wine." Whoops. Since two successive vintages were affected, we must take this as a case of lightning striking twice in the same place.

Professor Schreier finds little evidence of adulteration in the course of his duties. Occasionally he sees cases involving the ester 9-Ethyl Butanoate which creates forward, fruity flavours, and he points out that you cannot monitor the use of spinning cone column technology, which subtracts flavour elements from wine. By law, these should be added back only to the wine they were taken from in the first place – such as when making low-alcohol wines – but as yet there is no technique capable of checking this.

In any case, there's plenty of scope for modifying the taste of wine using legal additives. Certain yeasts create a fresh "estery" character, especially if the wine is fermented at low temperature. Pectolytic enzymes help to clear grape juice, but also accentuate fruitiness, and this is especially marked when they are added after fermentation. Vitamin C, also known as ascorbic acid, has the same effect and is also quite legal. Oenological tannins, from various tree barks, are a cheap way to substitute or supplement the effects of barrel ageing in creating a supple mouthfeel in red wines. Oak chips, unlike oak essence, are a legal flavouring. Such techniques are known to their admirers as "skilful winemaking".

These additives mostly correct insipidity (although ascorbic acid is an anti-oxidant and can be used with sulphur dioxide to protect machine-harvested grapes). The two key additives counter the effect of too much or too little sun. Sugar, legal in much of Europe but largely banned in the New World, raises alcohol levels. Tartaric acid is both an additive and a by-product of wine.

It's limited in Europe, but came into use after phosphate fertilizers adversely affected grapes' natural acidity. Tartaric acid is widely used in the Americas, South Africa, Australia and New Zealand, to protect wine from infections and stop it tasting "flabby".

When Europeans and Australians stoop to hand-to-hand conflict, among the first weapons are the sacks of various white powders lying around their respective wineries. Robert Parker, the American guru, wades in on the European side, berating the excessive acidulation of many Australian and Californian wines – which he compares to biting into a lemon or lime. New World winemakers wonder whether their critics will be as hostile to "chaptalization", or sugar addition.

It would appear not, but chaptalization is a subject for some soul-searching. It is banned altogether in southern Europe and in higher quality German wines. But sugar is part of the formula for making Burgundy and helps camouflage the loss of natural sugars caused by over-cropping. That doesn't mean people refrain from speaking out against the practice. One high-profile opponent is Hubert de Montille in Volnay, and Jules Chauvet was also against it. When he met Kermit Lynch in 1987 Chauvet lamented the trend towards soupy, alcoholic Beaujolais and sang the praises of the low-degree wines that proliferated before the war.

(I find highly acidified wines nastier than over-chaptalized ones. Sugar added during fermentation turns to alcohol, often increasing glycerol in the process. Tartaric acid just sits on top of the flavour of overripe grapes like clumsily-applied make-up.)

The most contentious issue of all is not what's put in but what's taken out. The process of subtraction starts earliest with white grapes. Especially if they are machine harvested it will be necessary to clean up the juice before fermenting it, otherwise the freshness of the fruit flavours will be lost. The industrial approach is to fine with bentonite clay, and stand the juice in refrigerated tanks (the low temperature is needed to prevent fermentation starting) or clear it with a centrifuge. If you've hand-harvested and have whole bunches of disease-free grapes, it's possible to put the juice straight into the fermentation vessels, and sometimes without having to settle it out in tanks. The reason is that slowly pressed whole bunches produce very clear juice, and the mass of intact stems act as a natural filter. A centrifuge can also be useful in clearing red wines after fermentation but before the malolactic fermentation. Again, it's an option preferred for the cheap, high-volume wines, but one criticism is that the process physically breaks up the bigger molecules in red wine.

Like cultured yeasts, filtration is a German technology, embraced in the postwar period by all of the world's teaching institutes. Here the front-line between the New World and Old World zig-zags all over the place. In the 1984 edition of his *Connaissance et Travail du Vin*, Professor Emile Peynaud argues that wine should always be fined or filtered, or both. "Clarity achieved spontaneously is never sufficient," he warns (advice that writers do well to heed). The staunchest defence of the practice is made by an Englishman and an Australian; Hugh Johnson and James Halliday in *The Art and Science of Wine*, while the most vigorous attacks come from Robert Parker and Kermit Lynch. The Americans are involved not just as commentators but as customers and business partners with French growers. Filtration is often immediately followed by bottling, and importers and agents influence both the decision whether to bottle – rather than sell in bulk – and how to bottle.

Before the coming of domaine bottling, filtration was not an issue for growers. They sold the wine to the *négociants* and left it in their hands from that point forward. For centuries wine had been filtered through hemp sacks, which effectively took out the sediment and removed yeasts, the relatively big micro-organisms. But the most important tools for making wine clear and stable were time, during which tannins and proteins reacted together and precipitated out, and the wine's own acidity, which prevented bacteria from multiplying.

Time is money, and it's not surprising that wine merchants should have looked for an alternative which would also eliminate the possibility of contamination. One approach, taken by Maison Louis Latour in Beaune, was pasteurization or heat treatment, which kills bugs but markedly influences the taste of wine. But the real breakthrough was made by a pair of newcomers to the business, Theobald and Georg Seitz, who set up as wine brokers in

1887 in the small town of Bad Kreuznach in the Nahe, in the heart of the wine country of southwest Germany. The brothers were hearing frequent complaints about the cloudiness in their bottled wines, even though these wines had been clear before they went through the filter. The culprit would have been micro-organisms in the hemp sacking. Theobald had the alarming-sounding idea of mixing an asbestos slurry with the wine and then sieving it all through a wire mesh lined with silk fabric. This was effective, and almost overnight created a new business and a new industry. Asbestos was the key, and continued to be used in most filters until well into the 1970s.

The biggest single development took place in 1914 when the company developed a filter sheet that was fine enough to remove all bacteria, rather than the 99 per cent previously achieved. This was presented to the German army in 1916 and issued to troops in a portable version, to protect them from water-borne diseases.

Sterile filtration has transformed medicine and many food processes, including brewing, fruit juice extraction and the dairy industry. It is also essential in certain wine styles. Crisp dry wines from hot regions must have malolactic fermentation blocked to retain the highest possible levels of acidity. But without having gone through a secondary fermentation they are vulnerable to bacterial attack in the bottle; the wine has to be sterile filtered as a precaution. The sweetened style of German wine produced since the 1950s also needs to be free of bacteria.

Exponents of filtration claim that it removes the suspended particles and contaminants without harming the flavour of the wine. (A Seitz poster from the 1930s shows the technology evicting a host of micro-organisms with what seem to have been intended as Jewish faces.) Johnson and Halliday call unfiltered artisanally-made wines "bacterial time-bombs"[5]. This seems to suggest that wine should contain no bacteria. But if the wine is stable, it can and should have a measurable bacterial count: this is the condition of all natural foods, even "pure" mineral water. The war on bacteria is in some cases being waged at the expense of public health, depriving people of desirable immunities.

Another problem is that in order to remove bacteria a filter has to be very fine, with pores at least ten times smaller than those needed simply to make the wine look clear. At this level you start taking out the larger molecules, which is more than just a theoretical significance: the wine actually looks different and tastes different too. Defenders of routine filtration say that the effect is short-lived. Kermit Lynch disagrees, based on tasting the library of comparative bottlings created since 1981 by his Châteauneuf growers, the Brunier family of Vieux Télégraphe. He told me: "I've seen cases where the filtered wine is dead and the unfiltered wine is vibrant."

It wasn't a Burgundy or Rhône grower who alerted Lynch to this issue, it was through tasting the Zinfandels made in the 1970s by Joe Swan (*see* Chapter Two), one of the first producers to put "unfined and unfiltered" on the label. Swan's son-in-law Rod Berglund claims that Swan discovered the difference by tasting in France with growers in their cellars. Lynch has found that small growers can be the worst offenders in filtering the goodness out of their wines – "the little old winemaker who thinks he doesn't know anything" is the most likely to be dazzled by the high-tech solutions offered by the diploma-wielding oenologist.

But technology is still required to guarantee the quality of unfiltered wines. Thomas Jefferson toured French wine regions during his spell as American ambassador in 1792. He wrote to his friend Henry Shaff, a Philadelphia merchant, that "Chambertin, Vougeot, Beaune are red wines of the first quality and are the only red wines of Burgundy which will bear transportation, and even these require to be moved in the best season and not exposed to great heat or great cold. I think it next to impossible to have any of the Burgundy wines brought here in a sound state." Even today, Lynch treats wines like perishable goods, using refrigeration for their entire journey to the United States.

In its most advanced form filtration can do much more than remove particles or micro-organisms. "Crossflow filtration"[6] uses a filter with holes that can be as small as a five-thousandth of the 0.1 micron width of conventional filters. When a filter is this fine it is no longer possible to push wine through it: the particles immediately clog up the holes. So, the liquid is driven rapidly past the filter, a movement forcing some liquid through and at the same time sweeping the holes clear. It's a technique modelled on the human body – it is the flow of blood along capillary vessels that keeps the kidneys' membranes clear – and one of its main applications has been in kidney machines. It is also at the heart of reverse osmosis, a technology that can correct wine faults like vinegariness ("volatile acidity"), sulphides and excess alcohol. The principle is that the filter is now so fine that you remove everything apart from water in unfermented juice, or water, alcohols and other liquids in wine. Reverse osmosis is used in France mainly to concentrate unfermented grape juice, in order to make ultra-dark and alcoholic wines – in turn removing the need for chaptalization.

Clark Smith of Vinovation has taken the technology to the US and found new applications for it. The point is that while you cannot remove elements from wine by distillation without making it taste cooked, it is entirely possible to do so once you've removed all the proteins, tannins and colouring matter. He says: "The central debate about crossflow applications and other high-tech wine production innovations is not anymore about whether they work, it is about whether we will go to hell if we use them... Reverse osmosis submits wine to terrific pressures and 'sheer forces', but it also opens doors to natural yeast fermentations, lower sulfites and longer [grape] hang times, all old ideas which have been considered too risky of late." Winemakers are guilt-ridden and confused about using Clark's services and it was a condition of being allowed round his facility that I instantly "forgot" any names I saw written on tanks or order forms. A few days later I met a "natural" winemaker who, a year or two earlier, had used Vinovation's reverse osmosis technology to fix a vintage with volatile acidity problems. Again I was sworn to the strictest secrecy on the issue.

There is hardly a mood of greater openness at Vinovation's competitor, Conetech, over its spinning cone column. This device looks something like a wartime V2 rocket, minus the pointed nose. It is the most successful single development to have emerged from Australia's Commonwealth Scientific and Research Organization (CSIRO). Its inventor, Don Casimir, first described the principles in a paper he published in the mid-1970s. Casimir claims that its precursor was the system used by Norsk Hydro to isolate heavy water at the Vemork hydro-electric power station – an installation that was successfully attacked early in 1943 by Norwegian partisans under command of the British Special Operations Executive. The raid was intended to thwart any German attempt to develop a nuclear bomb, and became the subject of the 1965 action film *The Heroes of Telemark*. A little of the romance was destroyed, however, when a retired engineer from the plant told me that the distillation system (comparable to the spinning cone) was not introduced until 1960; the wartime system had used electrolysis.

The spinning cone addresses the same problem as

Vinovation's reverse osmosis technology: how to separate out the constituents in wine without damaging it in the process. While reverse osmosis was first used to desalinate seawater, the spinning cone was designed for fruit juice processing – the original aim was to preserve the fragile aromas of passion fruit juice. One solution would have been to heat the juice and distil the aromatic substances, but this would have ruined the flavour of what was left behind. Instead Casimir used kinetic energy, whizzing the juice in a thin film round a series of inverted cones at approximately 40°C, under low atmospheric pressure. The lightest elements are stripped by a neutral gas, while the heaviest move to the bottom.

In wine, the cone's first use was to remove sulphur dioxide from grape juice, so that it could be stored and fermented when convenient. Sulphur dioxide is almost gaseous, so it is the first substance to come off. A later application was in making low-alcohol wines: the flavouring elements were removed, then the alcohol, and then the wine was reassembled. But in California, by far the biggest application is in reducing alcohol levels.

Although the spinning cone may not descend from a Nazi secret weapons programme, the device retains a covert air. As Paul Franson wrote in *Wine Business Monthly* in May 1988, "most winemakers get laryngitis when asked about it." One of Conetech's clients is a highly respected medium-sized producer whose reliance on the spinning cone is an open secret in the industry. But when I spoke to the winemaker in question he claimed to have been looking at the possibility of making de-alcoholized wine, before admitting using the equipment to reduce alcohol levels: "it's something we don't like to talk about."

Clark Smith takes a refreshingly different approach. Firstly he talks openly about the pros and cons of technical interventions, and admits that taking out volatile acidity (VA) is not always a good idea: "There were five European studies of our VA process; one was a nice Pinot Gris and the rest were crap. Sometimes when you take the VA away all the other off-flavours are even worse." On the other hand he remains an enthusiastic pioneer in California of oxygen additions to newly-fermented wine. This technique, called *microbullage* in French, was developed in the 1980s by Patrick Ducornau in Madiran, in southwest France, in order to soften tannins and improve the mouthfeel of the hard red wines common to the region.

Smith becomes almost lyrical at times about the benefits of alcohol reduction. He describes one particular instance of an exercise called "sweet spot tasting", which involves taking an excessively alcoholic wine and employing reverse osmosis and distillation to reduce the alcohol level to eight per cent. This low alcohol wine is then blended back with the original batch and a variety of different possible alcoholic strengths are evaluated.

"We had a Chardonnay from the Stag's Leap district that I think was 15.5 per cent alcohol. They gave us a previous vintage which they hadn't de-alcoholized, it had been 14.2 per cent, and they said 'That's what we want, an identical wine.'" Smith's team created 24 samples, ranging from 12.5 per cent to 14.8 per cent, jumping in steps of a fifth of a per cent alcohol.

"This was a really interesting tasting. When wine is too alcoholic it tends to be hot and quite bitter, but if you find a harmonious balance point the wine becomes sort of sweet. At 14.2 per cent the wine was really terrible, but we found practically a dead ringer for the previous wine at 14.6. This is what we call a Californian Montrachet – in your face, harmonious and round.

"Then we didn't find anything at all until 13.5 per cent. The funny thing is that when you get lower than a sweet spot the wines become weak and salty, but then you might find another good wine. And as you approach it, it starts getting hot and bitter; kind of like dialling in a radio station – just when you're approaching it the static is worse.

"At 13.5 we found a Meursault style, much more elegant. So we kept on going and down around 12.9 we found a Grand Cru Chablis: acidic backbone and all the floral character that at 14.6 you can't smell at all." Clark claims that you can demonstrate this property of alcohol in reverse if you start with a light, fragrant wine: "All you have to do is put a little vodka in it and all the cool region character evaporates."

Clark recognizes that this process would horrify many wine lovers. Growers are meant to select the best vines for their terroir, agonize over the best training system, labour with secateurs, spend sleepless nights monitoring fermenting vats... They are not supposed to draw up a seat before a technician who asks what kind of wine they plan to make that day, and then punches the appropriate numbers in on a keyboard. Many producers question whether the kind of winemaking-by-numbers that Clark describes can actually mimic the great white Burgundies, as he claimed. "Clark's a very clever guy," one told me, "but that must be the dumbest thing he's said."

Clark Smith's defence is that he's the one working in the true spirit of peasant winemaking, which he claims isn't "hands-off" at all, but simply about achieving results. He embarks on a hilarious riff about Californian versus New Orleans chefs and how they would approach making stuffed crayfish. In the hands of a celebrity Californian chef this would all be about showing off simple ingredients and making an elegant presentation of the raw materials. In New Orleans you would get a brown gloop that didn't bear any resemblance to what had gone into it – but would be the most delicious thing you had ever tasted. He believes his clients are dedicated to "getting as close to the wine as possible" and that this makes them like old-fashioned Burgundians.

I have my doubts about this. Bob Haas, for example, recalls that in Burgundy in the 1950s the wines were much less fussed-over than they are today, since the two-way exchange with California got off the ground. And alcohol reduction has created a new style of wine, based on leaving grapes on the vine to become super-ripe and then using technology to bring the wines back into balance. But I'm not sure I actually like these wines, whatever the much-invoked artisans or peasants make of them.

But I do like Clark Smith. At least he's searching his soul about what he does for a living. And how else can you react to someone who asks if you're going to do an exposé of him, then shrugs his shoulders and relaxes because, as he says: "Everybody knows that I'm the bad guy."

(1) The exercise preceded the debate on "Terroir versus technology" referred to in Chapter One. It was sponsored by a Portuguese cork manufacturer, which led some press victims to question its validity, though I can't see why, precisely. For the record I spotted the "clean" wine and the oxidized sample, but not the cork taint.

(2) Does UC Davis Have a Theory of Deliciousness? Smith, Clark, *Practical Winery & Vineyard*, July-August 1995.

(3) Adverse Reactions to Wine. Gershwin ME et al, *Journal of Allergy and Clinical Immunology*. Vol 73, No 3, pp411-420.

(4) ed. Néauport, Jacques, *Jules Chauvet, ou le talent du vin*. Jean-Paul Rocher, Paris, 1997.

(5) Halliday, James and Johnson, Hugh, *The Art and Science of Wine*. Mitchell Beazley, London, 1992.

(6) The Crossflow Comix. Smith, Clark, *Practical Winery & Vineyard*, March-April 1998.

9
MAKING
MONEY

"We are not open for tastings or tours. Our wines are sold by mailing list and our current vintage is sold out. If you're calling to be placed on the waiting list this is to let you know that there is an extremely long waiting list and our production is tiny. Rarely does an opening on the list occur." (Voicemail message of a fashionable Napa Valley producer.)

Nikolaihof, on the south bank of the Danube, is an estate where you become especially aware of wine's spiritual dimension. It is a former monastery, incorporating the massive walls of an early Roman structure, from where the Benedictines founded the great abbey of Göttweig in 1074. Christine Saahs stood me in the ancient courtyard of her family home and invited me to stretch out my arms. She believes that it's possible to feel the energy rising from the point where the Roman priest used to stand at the altar of the Imperial cult.

We talk about the way wine's history is so closely linked with monks, especially the Cistercians. This 11th century order was an offshoot from the Benedictines and was so strict that its abbey at Kloster Eberbach on the Rhine was deliberately constructed on the shady side of a hill, to deny the brothers the pleasures of a sunny day. One of the new Cistercian rules was that the order should live by its own labour, rather than by tithes. To make this possible the Cistercians oversaw a revolution in agricultural technology. Their most enduring achievement was viticultural, creating great wine estates in Burgundy, in the Rhinelands and alongside the Danube in Austria. But sourly I argued against making too much of the link with the sacred. I said it struck me that the wine was simply an effective way of turning capital – the land – into tradable assets. Wine was also a perfect commodity, with the highest value of all agricultural products. What's more, when wine is stored it gains rather than loses value. Christine demurred: "What you say may be true. But wine is also something that set people's hearts free and liberated them from old, rigid ways of thinking. Wine is an essential, original part of Christianity." Later she extolled the virtues of biodynamic vine growing. But didn't simple economics mean that this risky, labour-intensive approach could only be a rich person's hobby? "If we choose to spend our money this way, is it worse than using it on keeping race horses or running expensive cars?" she asked, smiling.

But I'm uncomfortable with the way that wine doubles up as an investment medium or status symbol. It has happened because Frank Schoonmaker, Bob Haas and the rest did their job all too well in communicating an enthusiasm for wines that are produced only in small quantities – the likes of Krug in Champagne, Pétrus in Bordeaux, the Domaine de la Romanée-Conti in Burgundy. They then became the preserve of a few by virtue of their price. Just as oil money dislocated and transformed the Middle East, the grander wine producing regions have experienced the mixed blessings of being hit by a wall of money. Champagne, which before the Second World War was poor and communist, is now comfortable and right-of-centre thanks to deals that guarantee growers the highest grape prices paid anywhere in the world. In Burgundy, long before the Americans turned up brandishing their chequebooks, the growers of the Côte d'Or were the poor cousins of their southern neighbours who reared white Charolais cattle.

My visit to Becky Wasserman in Burgundy had been put off for a day so she could attend the funeral of one of her friends – "a stubborn old coot but a marvellous grower" – from Pommard, who had died in his eighties. His breakthrough had come in the late 1930s when the family managed to scrape the funds together to buy a horse to work their vineyards. Even the great Domaine de la Romanée-Conti was not immune from the general poverty that followed in the wake of phylloxera; their wine business was subsidized by general farming.

It was the same story at Domaine Leflaive in Puligny. Vincent Leflaive, who died in 1993, told Simon Loftus, the author of *Puligny-Montrachet: Journal of a Village in Burgundy* (Penguin, 1992) how all the *vignerons* had grazed cows and pigs. The village of Puligny had been without a mains water supply until as recently as 1955. In this world of hand-to-mouth living there was little social gap between struggling vignerons and impecunious artists. Becky Wasserman remembers a "lovely period" after she came to live in Burgundy in 1968, with her post-minimalist artist husband Dan. The young Aubert de Villaine had an apartment in

Beaune, and would drop in once or twice a week to be fussed over by Becky's Hungarian mother. Then the Wassermans would go out with de Villaine to taste in the cellars of the region's greatest names: de Vogüé, Rousseau, Hubert de Montille, Jacques Seysses and Alain Roumier. In the 1960s these wines were still an affordable luxury.

The young American Richard Olney may have been an impoverished expatriate painter at the start of that decade, but he could still sometimes buy Montrachet and La Tâche and enjoy the friendship of France's top gastronomes. "Except when going out, I dressed in rags and received in rags. My studio-dining room was a shabby little affair from which the lingering scents of oil paint and turpentine were never absent. It was a mystery to me how people from worlds so foreign to mine could be so charmed."[1] But this mutual attraction was nothing new. Baron Philippe de Rothschild has his place in history as both a pioneer of château bottling in the Médoc and a friend of leading artists, out of which came his decision, after the Second World War, that each Mouton-Rothschild vintage would be adorned with a label designed by a contemporary painter.

This common ground has now been lost. Artists today are likely to be sponsored by Becks beer and Absolut vodka. They would look elitist – and they'd damage their careers – if they were seen hobnobbing with château-owners. Wine at this level now requires the sort of income generally only enjoyed by the more sober professions[2] and, like opera, is the duller for it. Expensive wine is undemocratic, more so than expensive meals or works of art. Visual masterpieces may fetch high prices but they are on free display everywhere, while great chefs can reach a mass audience by writing cookery books. The money charged for some wines actually seems to diminish them by inviting pretentiousness and hyperbole. Is the experience of any bottle more profound than a bargain-priced CD of Bob Dylan's *Blonde on Blonde*, or a free visit to a public art gallery, or a trip to the cinema?

Silly prices suggest that wine is a form of art because it behaves in a similar way in the marketplace. Its price is inflated because – unlike books, records or films – the production of an individual wine cannot be expanded to meet demand. Some wine people reject comparisons with fine art, others embrace them. Clark Smith of Vinovation likes to compare wine with music, an entirely abstract form, and enjoys lampooning his ex-colleagues at UC Davis for their "philistinism". One tease is a parody of the "flavor wheel" produced by Professor Ann Noble to aid wine analysis, by grouping smells and tastes. He illustrated his article "Does UC Davis have a theory of deliciousness?"[3] with a wheel grouping strings, woodwind, percussion and so forth as a supposed aid to creating an orchestral masterpiece.

But it is striking that Clark Smith's most apt comparisons come from the era of Bach, Mozart and Haydn, composers we consider great artists, but who would themselves have failed to understood the way that we use the word "art" today. Clark takes "art" to mean a preoccupation with formal qualities: texture, aromas and balance in wine corresponding to a composer's use of texture, melody, rhythm and harmony. His definition of a great winemaker is someone who gets as "close to the wine" as possible, if necessary using expensive technology (Clark's for example) to tweak the flavours and achieve an individual version of perfection.

Clark is often right about things, but this approach strikes me as banally commercial. And while the money paid for "great wine" may encourage winemakers to think of themselves as artists, the effect of high prices is to discourage risk taking. As Clark's friend Randall Grahm observes: "Americans don't want to have to worry about the vagaries of a vintage. They don't want to spend $30-$50 and be disappointed." The winemaker John Olney (Richard Olney's nephew) argues that "when your number one priority is making money you're going to make a bland product."

Jim Clendenen believes that the market penalizes him for his enthusiasm for elegant, balanced wines. His response is a cuvée called "Why Not?", sold in a heavy, pretentious bottle and made according to the formula for a big, expensive, international-style Chardonnay – overripe grapes, lees stirring and "200 per cent new oak" (i.e racked into another set of new barrels for the malolactic fermentation). "It's big and clumsy and stupid and everybody loves it. Effectively I'm saying 'Put your money down and I'll make the wine you want. If you want a big, stupid, obvious wine then you pay a serious price for it and I'll be perfectly happy.'"

We live in a world where there is a vested interest in saying that something is "art", because that's where the money is. It's the over-familiar language of "sample the timeless art of hospitality in our Business Class", a syndrome Mel Knox irreverently calls "The Art of Lighting my Farts". Perhaps it's in response to this that the art world today restricts the term "artist" to people who try to change the way we see things – and it's a category which turns out retrospectively to unite quite a lot of composers, from Palestrina and Monteverdi to Beethoven and Wagner.

The preoccupations of all these composers go beyond music. (Monteverdi's operas were part of a project to revive the art of Classical Tragedy; Beethoven's symphonies contain coded revolutionary messages, while Wagner was a mystical nationalist.) Terroir is the winemaker's equivalent: it supplies an agenda that supplements the sensations created by the passage of a liquid over the winemaker's tongue and responds to other external realities: a vineyard, a climate, a region, a tradition, a growing season. Such an approach also introduces a moral dimension – a sense that the means are as important as the result, and that the wine should be a true and transparent record of what went into it.

Jim Clendenen reacts not with aesthetic disgust but with moral outrage to the idea of making a "big" unbalanced wine and then using technology to put it back into balance. "When you purposely pick your grapes out of balance it's a more heinous violation than using fungicide, herbicide or irrigation. Purposely picking grapes in bad condition and having to rectify them – if it isn't simply an accident of nature – is like going to work planning to rob the owner of your company." Whether or not wine is a work of art, Clendenen sounds more like an artist talking than a luxury goods manufacturer.

The moralizing tone is one legacy Richard Olney bequeathed to his fellow Americans. Olney was the link between French campaigners for real food and wine, the founders of *Cuisine et Vins de France* and the *Revue du Vin de France*, and the generation of Californians who embraced wine in the 1970s. Olney taught Kermit Lynch the skills of wine tasting; Lynch in turn introduced Randall Grahm to Burgundy. Lynch took me out to lunch at Chez Panisse, the successful, influential Berkeley restaurant founded in 1971 by another of Olney's friends and admirers, Alice Waters.

"The biggest criticism, the worst thing Richard could say about anyone was they were a whore," Lynch told me. "He never did anything because he had to. He hated tasting notes and he detested scores and points for the reason that we all know – they are totally meaningless." We were drinking a mature bottle of Vieux Télégraphe, the Châteauneuf-du-Pâpe made by the Brunier family, old friends of Lynch. He reflected that the Bruniers could make a lot more money if they also went in for low-volume, high-priced special releases, though the effect would be to deprive the flagship wine of the best *parcelles* of grapes. "They've always refused to play that game. If they did a little cuvée of 200 cases they could charge five times their normal price for it. But they don't. There you get into what Richard hated, "whores" – people doing things because they can get money for it; not because it's better, not because the results will be great, but because it pays."

Chez Panisse isn't to everyone's liking. David Darlington writes that its "hip but privileged movieland atmosphere" makes him feel "about as comfortable as a snake being poked with a stick."[4] Well David, why don't you just saddle up and git, and leave us Champagne socialists to enjoy ourselves (the house Champagne is biodynamic, as it happens). The décor is Pacific redwood/ Japanese and with a public food-preparation area staffed by jolly young people. While I waited to interview Alice Waters the flower vases were being imaginatively filled, with evergreen, small-flowered scented climber *Clematis armandii* used as a cut flower. Meanwhile the restaurant's wine buyer and a wine importer were talking about asking French suppliers to go organic, and how they often turned out to be organic anyway, without saying so on the label.

This was no coincidence. Alice Waters was taking a fresh look at the Chez Panisse wine list. "I'm looking to have people with integrity about what they're doing, who are going to take care of the land for future generations – not people who are simply manipulating the soil to take advantage of this moment in time when people are interested in wine." Alice wasn't shy in raising this, not even with the Domaine de la Romanée-Conti. I hadn't gathered from Aubert de Villaine that he was making the estate fully biodynamic, but Alice Waters was confident that he had taken the plunge: "Kermit Lynch is a good friend of Aubert and we were just having lunch together and talking about this. He's very interested in this."

I'm worried by the idea of progress without struggle – the notion that privileged people consuming nicer food will somehow make the world a better place. But Alice Waters' point is that by caring about what we eat we learn to care about the world around us, and about each other. She made this connection in Paris, where she lived as a student aged 19, having left her native New Jersey. "I had an apartment at the bottom of the market street and I walked through the market every day and it changed my life, and I wanted to eat like that and I wanted to live like that. I knew that that sense of community that I felt in Paris had something to do with food, because people gathered in restaurants."

Chez Panisse was an interpretation of local restaurants she had got to know in France. It caught the mood of its era and was an overnight success. "We tapped into the idealism of the Sixties, the time of the Free Speech Movement here in Berkeley. It was when we felt we could change the world. I was uncompromising. I'm so glad we made some impact but it wasn't what I was looking for. I was just determined to have a little French restaurant. Now after 25 years we have this community of people that care about each other. It's the customers that come in, it's the fish guy, it's the baker, it's the vegetable people. We can never take them for granted. That's one of the problems in France; they've taken a lot of their food for granted, that it's always going to be there. People need to be supported and encouraged – it's like any relationship. I'm determined never to take any of these guys for granted. They're doing something remarkable for us."

I felt kindly disposed but a little superior in this environment: how Californian to mistake antipasti and hand-made goats' cheese for real politics. But it soon became apparent that it wasn't Alice Waters who attributed innate virtues to food, independent of its social context – it was me. I mentioned that I cooked for my children and that they weren't especially interested, and pestered me for junk food. She asked if I got them involved in choosing and cooking the food, and laying the table. "They need to be brought into the big picture. You can't just get them in at the end." I was too ashamed to admit that often I don't even get them to sit at table.

"We need to teach these values to schoolchildren from the very beginning, from pre-school," she said. "It isn't happening at home any more. They need to know how to take care of the land, they need to know how to feed themselves and to connect with other people. It's hard when the culture is telling them to get it on the run. But when they have an authentic experience and they go into the garden and pick it themselves and they bring it into the kitchen and cook it, then they want to eat it. They like serving it to their friends and they like cleaning up from the table," (cue gasps of disbelief from me). "They like the candles lit on the table, they like making it a sacred moment when people talk about things that are important to them."

Waters speaks from experience. A few years ago she noticed that a school she passed on her way to work had a depressing and neglected playground. On impulse she went in to talk to the school principal to suggest that the children might be interested in turning the yard into a vegetable garden. This was the genesis of the "Edible Schoolyard" project at Martin Luther King Jr Middle School. Since then the Robert Mondavi winery has got involved to the tune of a $50,000 annual contribution, which is funding a cafeteria where the children will serve food they have grown and cooked themselves, and where they can receive the region's farmers. Alice Waters sees this as a useful counter-blow to the trend for fast-food chains to set up in school canteens, and it's her informal equivalent of work that in France is done through the Ministry of Culture. "They've got a SWAT team that goes into the schools. One week they take them to a farm and then they do 'blind tastings'."

Her point that food is central to how we live, in shaping the landscape and environment, in nourishing our bodies and in providing a framework for social life. But she is neither a food nor a wine bore. "I love pure, simple wine that you buy in a big container – if it's made well, if it's real wine. I just hate manipulation." This is a taste shared by lots of the grandest French growers. Emmanuel Reynaud, who makes Châteauneuf's most sought-after wine, Château Rayas, also produces a jug wine from the high-cropping young vines at Château des Tours, where he lives. His aim is to ensure that his neighbours, who enjoy quantity rather than quality, have something to drink that's free from chemicals and additives. Many Bordeaux proprietors divide their attention between a star name in a top appellation and an estate in a more humble sub-region, where they turn out good everyday wine. So, for example, Château Marjosse in the Entre-Deux-Mers benefits from the same skills that Pierre Lurton uses to make the St Emilion Premier Grand Cru Cheval Blanc; and when Jacques Guinaudeau took over Château Lafleur in Pomerol he came equipped with years of experience at Château Grand Village, a Bordeaux Supérieur property where he still makes the wine. Aubert de Villaine told me he often felt his heart was not in the Côte d'Or at all, but the unglamorous Côte Chalonnaise to the south. There, at a property in Bouzeron he bought in 1973, he pours his energy into making the best possible Aligoté, a white variety that Jancis Robinson describes as "lower middle quality" and "not at all fashionable".[5]

It isn't only French proprietors who dislike the idea that their custom is limited to the super-rich. Paul Draper of Ridge has no interest in making "bottles that aren't being bought to be drunk, but as a rarity, a collector's item. It all goes back to why you're doing it. Is your vision to produce something that people find delicious and want to enjoy with their friends and family, or is it to become well-known, to find fame? If you step in to the wine business today you may come in with the money you've earned in another business, and see wine as the ultimate form of one-upmanship. One great advantage we had was that when we got started nobody in the wine business in the States was famous, so it was pretty easy for us to get on the track of making something that was good and enjoyable."

But the demand now well exceeds the supply. Draper and his colleagues face requests from their many wholesalers to put up their prices in response.[6] They just say no, and warn that unless the mark-up stays reasonable Ridge will find another agent. Paul Draper wants to be able to go on selling to the same people he always has: professionals, academics and their students. "And a few years ago we found a group of poets when I was visiting New York – a number of our best known poets, and they were all Ridge fans. They were all sitting around drinking Ridge Zinfandel."

Ridge sold up some years ago to a Japanese pharmaceutical magnate, a fine wine lover who is content to keep an arms-length relationship. This benefactor does not ask the estate to do more than show a profit, and doesn't require its prestige to be bolstered by pretentious prices. The outcome isn't always so happy when a famous name falls into corporate hands. The most-cited villain is Heublein (later part of the British-based multinational IDV) who swallowed up Almadén, Paul Masson and the celebrated Beaulieu and Inglenook vineyards in Napa. In *The Wines of California* (Faber and Faber, 1999) Stephen Brook cites two crass ideas from Heublein executives for making Beaulieu more profitable: they suggested replanting the vineyard with Gamay and making the estate's sparkling wine with Thompson's Seedless, on the grounds that this cost $50 a ton as opposed to $900 for Chardonnay.

Beaulieu's winemaker managed to thwart these intentions. But Heublein had milked Almadén and Paul Masson for profit, trading on customer brand loyalty rather than on the content of the bottles. "Those brands had a pretty good reputation for fruity drinking wines," says Paul Dolan, the managing director of Fetzer. "Then the quality just became worse and worse until there wasn't any quality left." It's especially ironic that the legacy of two of the great 19th century French pioneers of wine in California should be the outright fakes made under the Almadén label and sold as "wines with natural flavors" (*see* Chapter Four) and the insipid industrial stuff sold in Paul Masson carafes.

As an English wine writer, this is a difficult story to tell. The big corporations are so much a part of our landscape that it is hard to achieve balance or perspective. Journalists who work in this field are children of the wine boom that hit California and Australia in the Sixties and Seventies, reaching Britain a little later. James Halliday's *A History of the Australian Wine Industry 1949-1994* (Winetitles, 1994) tells the story of an extraordinary period of corporate activity at that time. The new players included Philip Morris, Reckitt and Colman, Heinz, Allied Vintners and Rothmans. These multinationals came and later went, but left enduring structural changes.

This was a period of investment in new technologies, creating the vast installations (reminiscent of oil refineries) that cluster throughout the Barossa Valley. The vineyards were mechanized; a new region, Coonawarra, was planted with a system of "minimal pruning" that dispensed with a labour force bearing secateurs. At every level the wines got worse. Halliday writes: "Many of the major companies (Penfolds being an honourable exception) bowed to market pressure and "stretched" the volume of wine going into their leading brands, with a sharp decline in quality the inevitable result." Even premium wines suffered in the eyes of critics, like the English writer Andrew Jefford, who dislike the taste that results from heavy additions of tartaric acid. The other change in Australia was in the ratio of ownership to production. France's vineyards cover eight times the area of those in Australia, but the former has around 140 times as many wineries.

The new big wine firms invested in marketing and promotion on a scale that dwarfed the efforts of their fragmented European rivals. In Britain the wine trade has traditionally been peopled with hobbyists and enthusiasts. In the 1980s and 1990s they began to enjoy glad-handing on an unprecedented scale. One landmark was the Masters of Wine (MW) tour of Australia that Hazel Murphy, the industry's lively British representative, first organized in 1985. Journalists in the UK were invited to judge at competitive tastings, and acted as tour guides on the series of Wine Flights that Hazel ran throughout the Nineties for trade buyers. She made a point of not telling MWs, journalists or buyers what to think of the wines; however, such hospitality may, I think, have engendered a sympathetic outlook. An acquaintance of one of Britain's wine writers describes the effect of this high living on her friend. "One day he was working as a waiter. The next day he had an airline ticket in his pocket and he was an international wine expert. It made a really big impression on him."

For whatever reason, it became fashionable among British wine writers to scold European producers and praise the New World, particularly Australia. It became received wisdom that new producers had replaced tired, faulty wines with a fresh, clean, fruity style that was winning over a new generation of drinkers. This would be of marginal interest if it wasn't for the fact that many of the new, exciting and heavily-promoted wine brands are rubbish. Recently, the British wine trade magazine *Harpers* invited me to speak in a debate. They wanted someone to attack wine brands and, although I don't regard brands *per se* as the problem, I agreed to participate. In the event I felt rather like those soldiers on training exercises who role-play terrorists or protestors; but the real revelation was the blind tasting of Britain's best-selling branded wines. I had expected these to be cleverly made techno-wines, but in fact most assembled were fruitless, characterless and even nasty, with some odd cardboardy chemical flavours. The buyers and journalists privately agreed that the wines were awful, but no-one got up and said this, either from the platform or the floor. A mixture of parables rubbed together in my flu-laden consciousness, from the Emperor's New Clothes to the Case of the Dog who Didn't Bark in the Night. Had we been tasting Bordeaux or Muscadet of such poor quality the gathering would have been in lynching mood.

Speaking at the brands conference was an uncomfortable experience. If you are going to argue an unpopular line then it should come from the heart, and I felt as if I was in a school debate. But, in retrospect, I felt I had put forward a valid case. My proposition was that a "brand" is anything that allows the seller to price something above the going rate – and wine is rich in such profit potential. It is often sold as a simple commodity – a bottle of "house red" in a restaurant, a glass of "dry white" in a pub. But frequently other qualities are on offer too, be they a grape variety, a wine region or a grower. The brands "Henri Jayer" or "Château Pétrus" can generate levels of added value that will appear mouthwatering to outsiders, including restaurateurs and wine merchants. The smart company men with whom I shared the platform were familiar with the suggestion that firms might suck brands dry; and later Paul Dolan of Fetzer confirmed that this exploitation happens all the time.

In Europe, the small farm has epitomized virtue ever since Virgil and Horace began writing at the time of the emperor Augustus. The image on the label used by the French small growers' association, the *Confédération Nationale des Caves Particulières*, conveys a pride in sturdy independence, depicting a peasant in a traditional smock, labouring single-handed under the weight of a barrel. Paul Dolan's great-grandfather tried to export this ideal to the New World, when he founded the Italian-Swiss Colony in Sonoma County in 1881. He planned to employ agricultural workers from Piedmont and Italian Switzerland on a grape farm and give them the opportunity of sharing the ownership of the land in return for their labour. The wines were successful, winning no fewer than ten medals in the first quarter-century of the project, and the colony created a settlement – now one of California's historical sites – with the appropriately Piedmontese name of Asti. "They created quite a business and my grandfather and uncle managed it in their turn," says Dolan. But the collective ideal was never realized. "The workers really wanted to be paid regular wages."

However, the family tradition of business idealism lives on and was rekindled for Paul Dolan when he discovered the ideas of Paul Hawken. Hawken's extraordinary career began at the age of 19, as a press coordinator for Martin Luther King's desegregation march on Montgomery, Alabama. The following year, 1966, he opened America's first business to specialize exclusively in organic food, creating contracts over the following seven years with farmers in 37 states. The book that made an extraordinary impression on Paul Dolan was Hawken's *The Ecology of Commerce* (Harperbusiness, 1993).

"I'd been on my own adventure, which was living a life of integrity and one that made a difference. When I read Paul's book I knew that how I was going to make a difference was through business. It really transformed my thinking about what business can be. He drew attention to the responsibility that business has for the environment, because it's business that has the major impact on the environment through the decisions it makes day-to-day." When I spoke to him, Paul Dolan had organized a wine industry conference to take place in three months' time and he had booked Paul Hawken to speak. It would be the first time that the disciple had met his hero although, he said, "he knows about me and the work I've done."

This seems only fair in view of the political "right-on-ness" of the Fetzer vineyards. Under Paul Dolan's guidance, 790 hectares of vineyards are now organic. There are recycling centres; Fetzer composts all its grape residues; it uses recycled paper for stationery and recycled glass bottles. Even the labels are made with treeless paper printed with soya ink. The company has set up anti-alcohol abuse programmes for young people and signed up to a supplier of "green" electricity, generated entirely from wind, biomass, hydro and geothermal plants. "In addition," says Dolan, "we've made a commitment to reduce our energy use by 25 per cent." There has been a project with the University of California to recycle waste water for irrigation rather than using clean water. Recently, the State of California awarded the company a grant to test the use of commuter vans (running on natural gas), to save staff using their petrol-fuelled cars to get to work.

Until 1992 Paul Dolan was the winemaker. He was promoted to chief executive when the Fetzer family sold the business to the Brown Forman corporation (who make Jack Daniel's). How did this Southern dynasty receive Paul Dolan's pet causes? (While no-one is surely losing sleep over soya ink, green electricity adds substantially to production costs.) "They love what we're doing," he insisted. "The business has grown so much and we're taking the environmental lead."

In Europe today the "charismatic businessman" often turns out to be a crook or megalomaniac, but Daddy Warbucks is still alive and well on the other side of the Atlantic. The supportive Forman family belong to a long tradition of idealists, that runs from Dr John Harvey Kellogg to Steve Jobs of Apple Computers. What's more, the very qualities that make wine ripe for corporate plundering also make it a good testbed for green capitalism.

The grounds for determining how much people should pay for a bottle are subjective. Dolan's task is to defend the price of his brands – the conventional Bel Arbor and the organic Bonterra range – so that he can maintain their quality and not be driven into a cost-cutting spiral of decline. To be America's greenest mass-market winemaker makes good business sense: it gives the company a point of difference and maintains the brand's value.

Does Fetzer's environmentalism have the wider value that Dolan believes? Does it make any difference in the big world? When a jet's emissions are tearing up the chemical balance of the upper atmosphere, does it matter if some of its passengers are enjoying a 25 cl bottle of organic wine?

I think it does. There is no alternative to air travel for rapid transport, but wine is a product wrapped in ambiguity. What can a real wine offer that cannot be had from one of Canandaigua or Gallo's "speciality wines", that is, sweetened and acidulated solutions of ethanol and water? Robert C Fuller, professor of religious studies at Bradley University in Peoria, Illinois, suggests wine lovers have created a form of religious belief, with their own values and rituals[7]. Or, as the barrel importer Mel Knox puts it: "Wine provides some kind of meaning. In a post-religious age we see this whole thing of people looking for values – looking for identity, and something they do it with is the products they buy." Other analogies can be made with fashion, fine art or pop. Hard liquor for the generation that grew up under Prohibition was a symbol of the liberty of the individual. In turn, their children drank wine to differentiate themselves from their parents, and to express a a greater sense of cosmopolitanism – in particular a willingness to embrace the Catholic Mediterranean culture that has historically provoked visceral antipathy in white Protestant America.

Today, wine reflects environmental concerns and big players realize this. Southcorp already makes an organic range, while Gallo and Mondavi are, like Fetzer, enthusiastic about organic viticulture. The industry's leaders are happy to be lectured by Paul Hawken on their responsibilities: this must be worthwhile and Hawken has to be right over the central importance of orthodox, mainstream businesses. After all, who still believes that the world will be saved by the state, or by an "alternative society" that develops outside the conventional centres of power?

But perhaps wine is most appealing when it evokes possibilities that are not forthcoming from other products. Both America and Australia have begun to imitate the appellation system, through which French producers and consumers invoked the power of the state against the untrammelled rights of commerce. The hero of wine lovers is the vigneron, whose work begins with the soil and ends with the direct sale of the vineyard's produce: someone in whom manual and intellectual labour are united. As we have seen, this model of wine production is not simply a European idea that has found admirers in the New World, but a joint creation. Without Schoonmaker, Lynch and Saunier the world would not have heard of d'Angerville, Tempier and Jayer.

Meanwhile the farmers' market movement, of which Alice

Waters is a leading supporter, is making American farmers more like French wine growers. It is a tendency the big companies are monitoring. Mike Paul of Southcorp told the Harpers brands debate of his worry that wine would become more like the mainstream food industry, just as food production was becoming more diverse and more concerned about authenticity – more like wine, in fact.

In a free market, money tells us a lot about people's values and about the state of supply and demand for any commodity. Part of the message conveyed by the unearthly prices asked for wines from small producers is a positive one – that people who dedicate themselves to the highest quality farming will make a living, even if they lack the resources of the big capitalist enterprises. This process began in Burgundy, but thanks to the enthusiasm of wine lovers, small farmers all over Europe are managing to defy the economics of agribusiness and make an independent living.

Or, as Henri Jayer told Jacky Rigaux[8]: "Nature is my guide and, for me, wine has never been a matter of making money. Today I would say that it was still possible to make a good living with five hectares of vines. This is a scale on which it's possible to keep on top of all the variables involved in making great wine and to pamper the vineyards so that they can give birth to superb and distinctive wines. The search for quality will always be linked to respect for the vine. This is not a discovery of the 20th century. If today we lay so much stress on quality, low yields, organic approaches, minimal spraying and so on, this is because vine growers in Burgundy have been too seduced by profit and are too little aware of the risks of exhausting the soils.

"During the past 20 years, even during the past 10 years, I've wondered if it was me that was out of step. Today, happily, I meet young vignerons who come to taste my wines, who listen to me, who invite me to their properties. I haven't been preaching in the desert."

(1) Olney, Richard, *Reflexions*. Brick Tower Press, New York, 1999.

(2) Paul Draper remembers selling cases of Ridge to people who were fairly obviously marijuana barons in the 1970s. They always paid cash.

(3) Smith, Clark, Does UC Davis have a theory of deliciousness? *Practical Winery & Vineyard*. July-August, 1995.

(4) Darlington, David, *Angels' Visits: An Inquiry into the Mystery of Zinfandel*. Henry Holt and Company, New York, 1991.

(5) Robinson, Jancis, *Vines, Grapes and Wines*. Mitchell Beazley, London, 1986

(6) American law after Prohibition required that liquor wholesaling and retailing should be separate businesses, and that they should be self-contained operations in each state, with no interstate sales.

(7) Fuller, Robert C, Religion and Wine. Quoted by Barr, Andrew in *Drink: A Social History of America*. Carroll and Graf, New York, 1999.

(8) Rigaux, Jacky, *Ode aux Grands Vins de Bourgogne*. Editions de l'Armançon, Précy-Sous-Thil, 1997.

APPENDIX ONE

DO IT YOURSELF

In the introduction I owned up to the fact that I hadn't made any kind of alcoholic drink since I was ten (though each year I think about getting a cider press to mop up the windfalls of a friend with an apple orchard). But those who do get involved say that it gives them a new depth of understanding about wine – as well as lots of cheap drink.

Home winemaking is at the roots of much of the wine traditions both of Europe and the New World – just as the origins of the modern beer industry lie in the brewing that used to be a feature of taverns and large households. French and Italian farmers often kept a small vineyard just to supply their family with wine, while home winemaking preserved California's vineyards during Prohibition – the fruit was transported across the continent to the Italian communities of the East Coast. Ernest and Julio Gallo founded their enterprise on this business, as Barney Fetzer would in the 1960s. And as we've seen, Joe Swan, a pioneer of both Zinfandel and the Burgundian varieties, began as a home winemaker.

BUYING GRAPES

The starting point is good grapes. In the UK these will come from growers in southern Italy or Sicily and will be on sale from September onwards in areas with a large Mediterranean population – St Albans, Tottenham and Harringay. Two outlets worth trying in London are **Mamma Roma**, 377 Holloway Road, London N7, tel: 020 7609 1740, and **LC Imports**, located opposite Pentonville Prison at 419-421 Caledonian Road, London N7, tel: 020 7607 1236. It's also worth asking at **New Covent Garden Market**, London SW8, tel: 020 7720 2211.

If you are travelling in Europe in the autumn it's feasible to return home with a car-load of wine grapes. The wine writer Merlin Holland has a regular deal with a grower in Burgundy, but if you're imitating Holland it would be best to do your deals and reconnaissance on separate trips.

UNITED STATES

In America you can buy directly from a farmer, but Jeff Cox, the author of a best-selling guide to home winemaking, thinks that the pick of the crop goes to those who buy collectively, for example through some of the many home winemaking clubs. Try the **Central Coast Home Vintners Association**, **Wine and Stein** of Paso Robles, the **Orange County Wine Society**, the **Sacramento Home Winemakers** and the **LA Cellarmasters**. Two useful contacts are the **American Wine Society**, based in Rochester, NY, tel: 716 381 9092, and **Winemaker Magazine**, in Vermont, tel: 802 362 3891.

WINEMAKING SUPPLIES

In September and October the delicatessens in Clerkenwell, the old heart of London's Italian community, have winemaking equipment, including plastic barrels, crushers and corks. Another UK source is **Vigo Vineyard Supplies**, Hemyock, Devon, tel: 01823 680230. In the US contact **Napa Fermentation Supplies**, Napa, CA, tel: 707 255 6372, www.napafermentation.com or **The Compleat Winemaker**, St Helena, CA, tel: 707 963 9861

ON A GRANDER SCALE

An alternative is to hire professionals to make wine for you. In England and France there are various "vine leasing schemes". As practised at **Shawsgate Vineyard** in Suffolk (01728 724060) this means taking out a contract to rent any number of rows of vines, each of which will yield about 150 bottles a year. The winemaker Rob Hemphill makes the wine either dry, medium dry or medium, and you get personalized labels. You can tend the vines as you like, or pay the vineyard to do it for you. As well as the attractions of Shawsgate wines – which are pretty good – customers will be pleased to hear that they pay neither VAT nor alcohol duty.

In America some enthusiasts lease part of a site from a farmer. To find a suitable vineyard, try one of the many local growers' associations. For a list of these contact the **California Association of Winegrape Growers** in Sacramento, tel: 916 924 5370. With a minimum area of about an acre it is feasible to give the farmer detailed instructions, for example on the use of sprays or the planting of cover crops.

You can then transport your grapes to a "custom crush" plant, which will make them into wine, again at your direction, in lots as small as a single open top fermenter. Two such facilities are Central Coast Wine Services, Santa Maria, tel: 805 928 9210, and The Napa Wine Company, Oakville, tel: 707 944 8669, www.napawineco.com.

PLANT YOUR OWN VINEYARD

The British face no restrictions on bringing in vines from France (although it's more complicated to bring in plant material from non-EU countries). Otherwise, English vineyards are the best source of wine grapes. Try **Three Choirs Vineyard** in Gloucestershire, tel: 01531 890223, **The English Wine Centre** at Alfriston, near Lewes, East Sussex tel: 01323 870164, **Tenterden Vineyard**, East Sussex, tel: 01580 763033, **Shawsgate** in Suffolk, tel: 01728 724060 or the UK's only organic wine maker, **Sedlescombe Vineyard** in East Sussex, tel: 01580 830715, and at www.tor.co.uk/sedlescombe One advantage is that you can try the wine to see how the unfamiliar grape varieties that will grow in England can actually taste like.

The legal restrictions on importing vines into America are described in Chapter Three. Rather than becoming a "suitcase importer" try contacting growers: as in Britain, it can be worth asking established vineyards if they have plants for sale. **Tablas Creek** (chapters One and Three) is an example of an estate that also has a nursery business. Californian grapevine nurseries include: **Sonoma grapevines**, tel: 707 542 5510, at various sites north of Santa Rosa, and at www.sonomagrape.com If you want to take home winemaking further then invest in *From Vines to Wines* by Jeff Cox (Storey Books, Vermont 1999) which lists American nurseries specializing in mail order.

MAKE WINE IN FRANCE

There's a long tradition of Anglo Saxons buying into France's vineyards, from Alexis Lichine coupling his surname to Château Prieuré in Bordeaux, to the Mondavi company's controversial attempts to turn virgin forest in the Languedoc into vineyards. If you are buying a farmhouse in a winemaking region you may well find that one of the fields used to be planted with vines.

Alternatively you can buy a wine estate, through a French estate agent. The best properties are not likely to come on the market; vendors will be people who couldn't make a go of it. Your dream will be to find a great piece of land that for some reason has been in less-than-capable hands, though you'll have the commercial disadvantage of a poor reputation. There are advantages in looking in a tourist area, like the Dordogne or Provence, in the hope that you can make substantial sales from the cellar door. Otherwise, warns Jonathan Malthus, the proprietor of Château Teyssier, the St Emilion Grand Cru, you'll spend at least half your time trying to sell the wine.

The super-rich will buy an established Château with a winemaking team in place, through a Paris merchant bank. With only several hundred thousand pounds to spend, you'll have to do most of the work yourself, though these days almost any estate will have a modern cellar – ie stainless steel fermenters. You'll need an oenologist – ideally someone open-minded and who doesn't impose a set formula, such as François Serres in Narbonne. There won't be time to learn on the job, so learn how to make wine by doing at least two vintages as an unpaid worker on someone else's property. But the key, says Malthus, is youth: "Don't do it as a retirement project, it's too much hard work."

APPENDIX TWO

WINES AND WHERE TO BUY THEM

Many of the people who feature in this book are pioneers and their wines enjoy the prerogative of an inaccessible price level; these are listed on the following pages either in sterling or dollars, probably for the benefit of the rich, or plain reckless. Nonetheless, real wine doesn't have to be expensive. In France, for example, growers' wines are often overpriced in the Côte d'Or, but not in southern Burgundy, Beaujolais, the Southern Rhône or the Languedoc. Some leads are given in my earlier book *The Wild Bunch*. Here, too, I've tried to include some affordable examples.

TRACING A RETAILER

Finding wines in the United States is complicated by laws that often prohibit retailers and wholesalers from operating in more than a single state. To find a local stockist, try phoning the winery or visiting their website; this may reveal the state wholesaler, who in turn will know where a local retailer is situated. What a business. It's also worth trying www.winesearcher.com

Many wines are now sold on the internet and in the US useful websites such as www.wine.com www.wineshopper.com or www.winetasting.com can sell directly to some states, but not others. Unless otherwise indicated, the producers sell from the cellar door.

Certain retailers in the US and Britain sell several of the wines discussed. (To avoid repetition most contact details are given in full in the first instance.)

US MAIN STOCKISTS

Hi Time Wine Cellars, 250 Ogle Street, Costa Mesa, CA, tel: 949 650 8463. www.hitimewine.com

K&L Wine Merchants, El Camino Real, Redwood City, CA 94061, tel: 650 364 8544. www.klwines.com

Pops Wines and Spirits, 256 Long Beach Road, Island Park, New York 11558, tel: 516 431 0025. www.popswine.com

Sam's Wine and Spirits, 1720 North Marcey Street, Chicago, IL 60614, tel: 312 664 4394. www.samswine.com

Sherry Lehman, 679 Madison Avenue, New York, NY 10021, tel: 212 838 7500. www.sherrylehman.com

Wally's Wines and Spirits, 2107 Westwood Blvd, Los Angeles, CA 90025, www.wallywine.com

UK MAIN STOCKISTS

Berry Brothers and Rudd, 3 St James St, London SW1, tel: 020 7396 9600. www.bbr.co.uk

Bibendum Wine, 113 Regent's Park Road, London NW1, tel: 020 7722 5577. www.bibendum-wine.co.uk

Lay and Wheeler, Gosbecks Park, Gosbecks Road, Colchester CO2 9JT, tel: 01206 764446. www.layandwheeler.co.uk

Morris and Verdin, 10 The Leathermarket, Weston Street, London SE1, tel: 020 7357 8866. www.morris-verdin.co.uk

Noel Young Wines, 56 High Street, Trumpington, Cambs, tel: 01223 844744. www.nywines.co.uk

Raeburn Fine Wines, The Vaults, 4 Giles Street, Leith, Edinburgh, EH6 6DJ, tel: 0131 332 5166/0131 343 115. www.raeburnfinewines.com

CHAPTER ONE (CHOOSING A SITE)

Adelaida Cellars, 5805 Adelaida Road, Paso Robles, CA 93446, tel: 805 239 8980. Cabernet Sauvignon 1997 $25; Pinot Noir Hoffman Mountain Ranch 1998 $32; Old Vine Zinfandel 1997 $24. There's currently no UK importer, and most sales are ex-cellar door.

Alban Vineyards, 8575 Orcutt Road, Arroyo Grande, CA 93420, tel: 805 546 0305. US stockists include The Wine House, Los Angeles, tel: 310 479 3731 and Crossroad, New York. The UK importer is The Wine Treasury, 69-71 Bondway, London SW8 1SQ. Central Coast Viognier 1997 £18.80; Estate Viogner 1997 £23.76; Estate Grenache 1997 £26; Estate Roussanne £26.50; Lorraine Vineyard Syrah 1997 £29.35. Also, try www.wine.com

Calera Wine Company, 11300 Cienega Road, Hollister, CA 95023, tel: 831 637 9170. US wholesalers include Chambers and Chambers in San Francisco. UK importer is Bibendum Wine, (see "UK main stockists"). Bibendum have two Pinots from the 1996 vintage, at £27.08 for the Reed vineyard and £35.83 for Jensen, which is a bargain compared to US prices, although at first glance it might not appear to be.

Gérard and Jean-Louis Chave, 37 Avenue St Joseph, 07300 Mauves, France. John Alban's chief influence in the Rhône. Their Hermitage Rouge 1996 is £41 at Yapp Bros, Mere, Wiltshire, tel: 01747 860423. www.yapp.co.uk The Hermitage Rouge 1997 is approximately $95 at Sherry Lehman, (see 'US main stockists'), and LA Wine Company, 4935 McConnell Avenue, Unit 8, Los Angeles, CA 90066-6756, tel: 310 306 9463. www.lawineco.com

Château Rayas, 84230 Châteauneuf-du-Pape, tel: 04 90 83 73 09. Rayas' Châteauneuf-du-Pape 1996 £89 at Berry Bros and Rudd (see "UK main stockists"), Châteauneuf-du-Pape 1997 $69.99 at The Wine Exchange, 2368 North Orangemall, Orange, CA 92865. www.winex.com

Two leading producers of Condrieu, the wine that converted John Alban to the Rhône, are: **Yves Cuilleron**, Verlieu, 42410, Chavanay, tel: 04 74 87 02 37. Condrieu Les Eguets Vendange Tardive 1997 £27.99 at Oddbins Fine Wines in the UK, www.oddbins.co.uk Condrieu Les Chaillets 1998 £22.33 at Bibendum. Les Chaillets 1995 $40.94 at Hi Time Cellars (see "US main stockists"). And **Pierre Dumazet**, Route Nationale 86, 07340 Limony, tel: 04 75 34 03 01. Try Bibendum for, example, the Côte Fournet 1997, which is listed at £22.50.

If you doubt the existence of terroir, one test is to taste wines made by the same producer that differ only in the vineyard site. You could go up and down the range made by **Domaine Daniel Rion,** Prémeaux, 21700, Nuits-Saint-Georges, tel: 03 80 62 31 10. US stockists include Hi Time and Sherry Lehman. The UK importer is Morris and Verdin, (see "UK main stockists"). The bargain in the Rion line-up is a simple Bourgogne AOC called Les Bons Batons, which sells for under £10.

It's cheaper to try the same exercise in Beaujolais, where, for example, the **Duc** family makes long-lived wines in both the St Amour and the Chénas appellations. **Domaine des Ducs**, La Piat, 71570 Saint-Amour-Belleville, tel: 03 85 37 10 08. Both wines sell for £8.75 at Bibendum.

German Rieslings are undervalued, but show some of the most precise vineyard differences. The best way to explore these are through two superb and idiosyncratic lists, one American and one Scottish. The American is the importer **Terry Thiese**, 8601 Georgia Avenue, Suite 910, Silver Springs, MD 20910, tel: 301 562 9099. His 160-page catalogue is more interesting than many wine books; but it is also rather frustrating for ordinary consumers who can't directly order, say, Kurt Darting's Dürkheimer Nonnengarten, Ungsteiner Bettelhaus and Dürkheimer Speilberg for a spot of comparative drinking. They may have no option but to go through their home state's wholesalers and retailers. In Britain customers can go direct to **Gelston Castle Fine Wines** of Galloway and London, tel 01556 503012.

CHAPTER TWO (PLANTING THE VINEYARD)

Cotat Frères, Chavignol, 18300 Sancerre, tel: 02 48 54 04 22. Les Culs de Beaujeu 1998 and Les Monts Damnes 1998 are another example of different vineyards making different wines. Both £12.97 from Noel Young Wines (see "UK main stockists"). Hi Time Cellars sometimes have certain Cotat wines.

Chehalem Winery, Route 1, Box 99C, Newberg, Oregon 97132, tel: 503 538 4700. www.chehalemwines.com New York wholesaler is Scott Martin Wines,

1981 Marcus Avenue, New Hyde Park, NY 11042. Pinot Gris 1999 $15; Pinot Noir 1998 $25. In their home state there's Avalon of Oregon, 201 SW 2nd Street, Corvallis, OR 97333, tel: 541 752 7418, who list the cuvée that Harry Peterson has named after his Burgundian friend: Chehalem Pinot Noir Rion Reserve 1997 sells at $36.

Peter Michael, 12400 Ida Clayton Road, Calistoga, CA, tel: 707 942 4459. www.petermichaelwinery.com UK importer is The Vineyard at Stockcross, tel: 01635 589405. www.thevineyardcellars.com Most sales are ex-cellar door. The Peter Michael blend named after the ubiquitous poppies is Les Pavots Cabernet Sauvignon/Franc/Merlot 1997, which sells at $85; the Belle Cotes Chardonnay 1998 sells at $55.

Au Bon Climat, Santa Maria Mesa Rd, Santa Maria, CA 93454, tel: 805 937 9801. Jim Clendenen's wines are well-stocked in California, at The Wine Cask, 813 Anacapa Street, Santa Barbara, CA, tel: 805 966 9463, and at www.winecask.com The Duke of Bourbon, 20908 Roscoe Blvd, Canoga Park, CA 91304, tel: 818 341 1234, www.dukeofbourbon.com The Wine House, 535 Bryant Street, San Francisco, CA 94107 tel: 415 495 8486, and www.winehouse-sf.com La Bouge de Cote Estate Chardonnay 1998 $25, La Bouge dau Dessus Estate Pinot Noir $25. Morris and Verdin are the UK importers.

Bannockburn Vineyard (the winemaker Gary Farr) Midland Highway, Bannockburn, Victoria 3331, Australia, tel: 03 52 81 1363. UK importers are Négociants UK, Harpenden, Herts, tel: 01582 462859. Retailers include Tanners, 26 Wyle Cop, Shrewsbury, SY1 1XD, tel: 01703 234500, also at www.tanners-wines.co.uk and Ballantynes, 3 Westgate, Cowbridge, CF71 7AQ, tel: 01446 774840, www.ballantynes.co.uk

Joseph Swan Vineyards, 2916 Laguna Road, Forestville, CA 95436, tel: 707 573 3747. Raeburn Fine Wines stock Stellwagen Zinfandel 1997 at £16.99 (see "UK main stockists"); K&L Wine Merchants stock Ziegler Zinfandel 1997 at $22.99, (see "US main stockists").

Simi, 16275 Healdsburg Avenue, Healdsburg, CA 95448, tel: 707 433 6981, www.simiwinery.com Alexander Valley Merlot 1997 $20; Russian River Valley Estate Chardonnay 1997 $35. Stockists include Pops Wines and Spirits (New York) and K & L Wines, (Redwood City) UK importer/distributor is Grants of St James, tel: 0191 224 0955

CHAPTER THREE (SOURCING THE VINES)

Château de Beaucastel, 84350 Courthézon, France, tel: 04 90 70 41 00. Châteauneauf-du-Pape 1997 £19 at Justerini and Brooks, London SW1, tel: 020 7493 8721. Wines are imported into the US by Bob Haas Vineyard Brands, 2000 Resource Drive, Birmingham, AL 35022, tel: 205 980 8802. Retailers include Sherry Lehman and Sam's Wines and Spirits (see "US main stockists" for both).

Domaine Weinbach, Riesling Cuvée Theo 1997 £13.50; Riesling Grand Cru Schlossberg £25, Cuvée Sainte Cathérine £25, at Justerini and Brooks, London SW1, tel: 020 7493 8721. US importer is Bob Haas Vineyard Brands (see above) and retailers include Hi Time Wine Cellars.

Tablas Creek, 9339 Adelaida Road, Paso Robles, CA 93446, tel: 805 237 1231. Mistral Wines, 3 Junction Mews, Sale Place, London W2 1PN, tel: 020 7262 5437. Tablas Creek Vineyard Rouge 1997 and Tablas Creek Vineyard Blanc 1998 are $35. Distributed by Bob Haas Vineyard Brands, see above.

Jade Mountain, PO Box 596, Angwin, CA 94508, tel: 707 226 7373. Distributed by Chalone Wine Group, tel: 707 254 4200 for local distributor. Mourvèdre 1998 $16.50, Napa Syrah 1997 $24, Viognier 1998 $34.32. UK importer is Morris and Verdin.

Dominus, PO Box 3327, Yountville, CA 94599, tel: 707 944 8954. The US distributor is Chateaux and Estates Wines, tel: 212 572 1362, which stocks the Dominus 1997 at $100. US retailers include K&L (Redwood City) and Wally's (Los Angeles). The UK importer is Corney and Barrow, 12 Helmet Row, London EC1V 3QJ, tel: 020 7251 4051.

Adelsheim Vineyard, 16800 NE Calkins Lane, Newberg, Oregon 97132, tel: 503 538 3652. Oregon Pinot Noir 1998 $25, Seven Springs Pinot Noir $35, Elizabeth Reserve Pinot Noir $30. Phone the winery for local suppliers. No UK importer, but contact Avery's of Bristol, tel: 01275 811100.

CHAPTER FOUR (CHOOSING GRAPE VARIETIES)

Domaine Michel Lafarge, Volnay, 21190, Meursault, tel: 0380 21 61 61. Côtes de Beaune Villages 1997 £13.50, Volnay Premier Cru Clos du Château des Ducs 1997 £37.50, at Raeburn Fine Wines. US stockists include K&L (Redwood City).

Mount Eden Vineyards, 22020 Mount Eden Road, Saratoga, CA 95070, tel: 408 867 5832. Old Vines Pinot Noir 1997 (from a vineyard, now grubbed up, planted by Martin Ray in 1942) $50; Estate Chardonnay 1997 $45; Estate Cabernet Sauvignon 1997 $28. Certain wines are available through www.wine.com, or from K&L. There is no UK importer.

Domaine du Marquis d'Angerville, Clos des Ducs 21190, Volnay, tel: 03 80 21 61 75. Volnay 1997 £300 per case, including VAT, at John Armit Wines, London W11, tel: 020 7727 6848. US stockists include Pops (New York) and K&L (Redwood City).

Bonny Doon, 10 Pine Flat Road, Bonny Doon, Santa Cruz, CA 95060, tel: 831 425 4518, www.bonnydoonvineyard.com has a list of wholesalers in every state. Big House Red 1998 and Pacific Rim Dry Riesling 1998 $10; Le Cigare Volant 1997 (The Bonny Doon take on Châteauneuf-du-Pape) $28. UK importers are Morris and Verdin.

CHAPTER FIVE (GROWING THE GRAPES)

Coturri Winery, 6725 Enterprise Road, Glen Ellen, CA 95442, tel; 707 525 9126, www.coturriwinery.com Albarello Sonoma Red 1997 $17, the Chauvet Zinfandel 1997 $21, through Pops Wines and Spirits, New York, (see "US main stockists").

Pierette et Jean-Claude Rateau, Chemin des Mariages, 21200 Beaune, tel: 03 80 22 52 54. Beaune Premier Cru 1997 £14.40 at Vintage Roots (organic wine specialists) Reading, UK, tel: 0118 976 1999, www.vintageroots.co.uk Or try John Armit Wines, London W11, tel: 020 7727 7133 and Gelston Castle, Galloway, 01556 503012. US stockists include Classic Wine Imports, 99 Rivermoor Street, West Roxbury, MA, tel: 617 731 6644, and The Stacole Company, 1082 South Rogers Circle, Boca Raton, FL, tel: 561 998 0029.

Nikolaihof (owned by the Saahs family) Nikolaigasse 77, 3512 Mautern, Austria, tel: 027 32 82 901.

Clos de la Coulée de Serrant (Nicholas Joly), Château de la Roche aux Moines, 49170 Savenièrres, France, tel: 02 41 72 22 32. Coulée de Serrant Savennières 1997 £25.69 at Raeburn Fine Wines and Bibendum. A selection of Nicholas Joly's 1995 wines are listed on www.wine.com

Domaine Leflaive, 21190 Puligny-Montrachet, tel: 03 80 213 013. Puligny-Montrachet 1997 £34.35; Puligny-Montrachet Premier Cru Les Perrières £46.95; Bâtard-Montrachet Grand Cru 1997 £103.80, at Lay and Wheeler (see "UK main stockists"). Domaine Leflaive's wines are available in the US on www.wine.com

Pierre Morey (the winemaker at Domaine Leflaive), 9 Rue Comte Lafon, 21190 Meursault, tel: 03 80 21 21 03. Bourgogne Chardonnay 1996 £11.90 at Justerini and Brooks, London SW1, tel: 020 7493 8721. Monthélie 1997 £16.40 and Meursault Les Tessons 1997 £33.90 at Lay and Wheeler. Le Montrachet Grand Cru 1997 £220 at Justerini and Brooks.

Fetzer Vineyards, 12625 East Side Road, Hopland, CA 95449, tel: 707 744 1521. Fetzer wines are widely distributed in the UK and US.

Frey Vineyards, 14000 Tomki Road, Redwood Valley, CA 95470, tel: 707 485 5177, www.freywine.com Also available at branches of Safeway and Realy's, plus Whole Foods and other health food stores. Chardonnay 1998 $10.50, Zinfandel 1998 and Syrah 1997 are $10.

Ceago, 2002 McNab Ranch Road, Ukiah, CA 95482, tel: 707 468 0377.

Frog's Leap Wine Cellars, 8815 Conn Creek Road, Rutherford, CA 94573, tel: 707 963 4704. Wines are available in the UK at Lay and Wheeler and Morris & Verdin and online at www.wine.com In the US try Dean and Deluca chains in New York, St Helena, Charlotte in North Carolina, and Washington DC, Sam's in Chicago and various Whole Foods supermarkets.

CHAPTER SIX (MAKING THE WINE)

David Ramey, 1784 Walm Springs Road, Glen Ellen, CA 95442-9434. UK importers are Morris and Verdin and Noel Young. Hyde Chardonnay 1997 £28.80; Hudson Chardonnay 1997 £29.70.

Domaine des Comtes Lafon, Clos de la Barre, 21190 Meursault, tel: 00 3 80 21 22 17. Lafon's Meursault wines are rare and expensive, selling at between £30-£60. UK importers include Lay and Wheeler, Morris and Verdin and Tanners, 26 Wyle Cop, Shrewsbury, SY1 1XD, tel: 01703 234500, and at www.tanners-wines.co.uk Also, Adnam's Wine Merchants, Southwold, Suffolk IP18 6JW, tel: 01502 727220.

The US retailer is The Wine Cask, 813 Anacapa Street, Santa Barbara, CA, tel: 805 966 9463, www.winecask.com Lafon has just bought a property in the Mâconnais, La Grande Chapeau in the village of Tilly-la-Martine, which will be a more affordable source of white Burgundy.

David Bruce, 21439 Bear Creek Road, Los Gatos, CA 95030, tel: 408 354 4214. San Francisco Wine Exchange, tel: 415 546 0484. Central Coast Pinot Noir 1998 $18; Russian River Reserve Pinot Noir 1998 $32, and Santa Cruz Mountain Estate Pinot Noir 1998 $50.

Henri Jayer has, since retirement, been working with his nephew Emmanuel Rouget, in Flagey-Echèzeaux, 21700 Vosne-Romanée. His wines are imported by Martine's Wines, 285 Bel Marin Keys Blvd, Novato, CA 94949, tel: 415 883 0400. In the UK try Raeburn Fine Wines.

Domaine Méo-Camuzet, 11 Rue des Grands Crus, 21700 Vosne-Romanée, tel: 03 80 61 11 05, www.meo-camuzet.com

Robert Mondavi, 7801 St Helena Highway, Oakville, CA 94562, tel: 707 963 9611. Mondavi wines are widely distributed. In the UK the Reserve wines are sold by, among others, Berry Brothers and Rudd and Tanners of Shrewsbury, tel: 01703 234500, www.tanners-wines.co.uk Within the Mondavi fold is **Byron Vineyards**, 5230 Tepusquet Road, Santa Maria, CA 93445, tel: 805 937 7288, but their wines are only on sale in UK restaurants.

Ridge, 17100 Monte Bello Road, Cupertino, CA 95015, tel: 408 867 3233. Much of Ridge's business is now done ex-cellars. Montebello (largely Cabernet Sauvignon) 1996 $150, Santa Cruz Mountain Chardonnay 1998 $30, as are Lytten Springs and Geyserville (largely Zinfandel) 1998. Adnam's Wine Merchants, Southwold, Suffolk IP18 6JW, tel: 01502 727220, and Morris and Verdin.

CHAPTER SEVEN (MATURING THE WINE)

Emmerich Knoll, Unterloiben 10, 3601 Loiben, Austria, tel: 02 732 79 3 55. Riesling Ried Loidenberg Federspiel £15.50, and Riesling Ried Schutt Smaragd £23.50, both at Raeburn Fine Wines. Also, try www.drinks.com

Mayacamas, 1155 Lokoya Road, Napa, CA 94558, tel: 707 224 4030, www.mayacamas.com Chardonnay 1997 $32, the Sauvignon Blanc 1998 $18. Call the winery for details of stockists.

Chalone Winery, Stonewall Canyon Road and Highway 146, West Soledad, CA 93960, tel: 831 678 1717. The corporate office is 621 Air Park Road, Napa, CA 94558, tel: 707 254 4200 for details of local stockists in the US. The Chardonnay 1998 is $31, the Pinot Noir 1998 $35. The UK importer is Bibendum.

Saintsbury, 1500 Los Carneros Avenue, Napa, CA 94559, tel: 707 252 0592. Also on sale at www.winetasting.com and its own website www.saintsbury.com which gives information on local state distributors. Wines are available at Sam's in Chicago and Wally's in LA. Pinot Noir Garnet 1999 $17, Pinot Noir Brown Ranch 1998 $75. UK stockist is Justerini &Brooks, tel: 020 7493 8721.

Hanzell, 1844496 Lomita Avenue, Sonoma, CA 95476, tel: 707 996 3860, www.hanzell.com Knightsbridge Wines, Chicago, Sherry Lehman, New York. Try also www.wine.com Chardonnay 1997 $42, Pinot Noir 1996 $40.

Buxy Cooperative, 71390 Buxy, France, tel: 03 85 92 03 03. Wines are widely distributed in the UK, but there is no major US importer.

Acacia, 2750 Las Amigas Road, Napa, CA 94559, tel: 707 226 9991. Call Chalone for US stockists (707 254 4200). Chardonnay 1998 $21, Pinot Noir 1998 $24. UK importer is Bibendum.

Casa de Saima in the Bairrada region of Portugal makes traditional and underpriced wines, which are released after long maturation in big oak vessels. Almost everything sells for under £10/£15 apart from the 1995 Garrafeira, which is £25, from Gauntley's of Nottingham, tel: 0115 911 0555. UK importer is Raymond Reynolds, tel: 01663 742230. The US importer is Martine Saunier at Martine's Wines, 285 Bel Marin Keys Blvd, Novato, CA 94949, tel: 415 883 0400.

Schloss Gobelsburg, Schlosstrasse 16, 3550 Gobelsburg, Austria, tel: 02 734 24 22, www.gobelsburg.at Wines from Ben Ellis Wines, Wheelers Lane, Brockham, Surrey RH3 7HJ, tel: 01737 842 160. Riesling Zobinger Heligerstein 1999 £12.75; Grüner Veltliner Ried Lamm 1998 £14.75. The US importer is Terry Thiese, 8601 Georgia Avenue, Suite 910 Silver Springs, MD 20910, tel: 301 562 9099.

Içi là-bas Les Révéléés Oregon Pinot Noir 1998, Mendocino Pinot Noir 1998, and Philipinne Mendocino Chardonnay 1998 are all around $35. *See* Au Bon Climat (Chapter Two) for stockists.

CHAPTER EIGHT (DEALING WITH WINE FAULTS)

Domaine Gramenon, 26770 Montbrison-sur-Lez, Rhône, tel: 04 75 53 57 08. Côtes du Rhône Le Gramenon 1998 £7.40, Côtes du Rhône Les Laurentides 1998 £9.95; Côtes du Rhône 1998 La Sagesse £12.25, at H&H Bancroft, London SW8, tel: 020 7627 8700. US stockists include John's Grocery,

401 East Market Street, Iowa City, IA 52245, tel: 319 337 2183. Try online at www.johnsgrocery.com or at Sam's Wine and Spirits, Chicago.

Jean & Agnes Foillard, Morgon, France. Wines through Kermit Lynch Wine Merchant, 1605 San Pablo Avenue, Berkeley, CA 94702, tel: 510 524 1524.

Marcel Lapierre, Domaine des Chénas, 69910, Villi-Morgon, France, tel: 04 74 23 89, www.marcel-lapierre.com Morgon 1999 $20 and Domaine de Prieur $18, through Kermit Lynch (*see* above).

Domaine du Vieux Télégraphe, 3 Route de Châteauneuf-du-Pape, 84360 Bédarrides, tel: 04 90 33 00 31. The proprietors are Kermit Lynch's friends, the Brunier family. The 1998 White is $34, the Red $38, the Vieux Mas des Papes White/Red is $25 and Le Pigeoulet Red, White and Rosé are under $15. UK stockists include Berry Brothers and Rudd.

Domaine Tempier, 83330 Le Plan du Castellet, tel: 04 94 98 70 21. This is the property that launched some prominent Americans, including Kermit Lynch and Richard Olney, on their exploration of France and French wine. Located in Bandol, the property makes dense wines from Mourvèdre that are designed for long keeping, and a typically Provençal rosé. Wines available in the US through Kermit Lynch Wine Merchant, 1605 San Pablo Avenue, Berkeley, CA 94702, tel: 510 524 1524. UK stockists include Gauntley's of Nottingham, tel: 0115 911 0555.

Rosenblum Cellar, 2900 Main Street, Alameda, CA 94501, tel: 510 865 7007. Wines sold by Sam's, Chicago and Big John's in New York. Paso Robles Zinfandel Richard Sauret Vineyard 1998 $18, the Sonoma Valley Zinfandel Samsel Vineyard 1998 $30.

Clark Smith makes a Cabernet Franc which sells in New York through Jeff McKay, tel: 917 750 9463. His Winesmith Cabernet Franc 1996 is $25-30.

CHAPTER NINE (MAKING MONEY)

Château Marjosse, Tizac de Curton 33420, tel: 05 57 74 94 66. This is the home of Pierre Lurton, who makes the premier St Emilion, Château Cheval

Blanc. The Bordeaux 1998 is £6.25 from The Wine Society, Gunnels Wood Lane, Stevenage, Herts, tel: 01438 741177.

Château Lafleur is home to the Château Grand Village, made by Jacques Guinaudeau. His range includes the Château Grand Village Rouge 1996, Bordeaux Supérieur, available at £90 per case including VAT from John Armit Wines, London, tel: 020 7727 6846.

Château des Tours, Quartier des Sablons, France, tel: 04 90 65 41 75. This is the home of Emmanuel Reynaud, who makes Château Rayas (*see* Chapter One notes). Vacqueyras 1997 £11.50 at Yapp Brothers, Mere, UK, tel: 01474 860423. His less expensive Vin de Pays de Vaucluse and Côtes du Rhône are available at Bibendum.

The owners of the **Domaine de la Romanée Conti** property in the Côte Chalonnaise are Aubert and Pamela de Villaine, Bouzeron, 71150, Chagny. The Aligoté de Bouzeron 1998 is £9.73, the Mercurey Les Montots 1998 £12.97, both from Corney and Barrow, 12 Helmet Row, EC1V 3QJ, tel: 020 7251 4051. The US stockist is Kermit Lynch Wine Merchant, 1605 San Pablo Avenue, Berkeley, CA 94702, tel: 510 524 1524.

FRANK SCHOONMAKER
(1905-76)
Two Personal Tributes

A personal memoir by Peter Sichel

I met Frank in Algiers in the fall of 1943, maybe a little later. He had been in Spain under diplomatic cover working for OSS and his responsibility was to run the underground railway to get allied pilots, who had parachuted into France after their plane had been hit, back to the allied services. This was a high priority throughout the war. It took almost a year to train a qualified pilot, and there was always a shortage of them during the war.

The Spanish authorities had gotten wind of Frank's real job and he was declared *persona non grata* and booted out. OSS sent him to Algeria to work as a civilian in the Algiers station. I don't remember what his function there was, but I believe he worked in counter-espionage. I knew him in Algiers, but not well. We both went into southern France shortly after the invasion in St Tropez/St Raphael on 15 August 1944, and shortly thereafter Frank was in a serious car accident and hospitalized in or around Grenoble.

I was involved in getting him to the hospital in time and he always later claimed that I saved his life, which was not true. It was true, however, that I saw to it that he got the right medical attention and that he had plenty of Cognac to help him recuperate. I had little to do with him for the rest of the war, though he was attached to the same unit of OSS as I was. He worked with some Spaniards, but I have no idea what he did. I was too busy recruiting German POWs to train and send back into Germany as spies; and anyhow, we were pretty well compartmentalized.

I did not see Frank again until we were both in the wine business in New York in the early Sixties. (I had stayed in OSS/CIA until 1959 then returned to the family business.) I saw a fair amount of him in New York in the Sixties and Seventies and was at his memorial service in New York. He had a lot of health problems – cancer, his heart etc. – but he finally married a marvellous woman, an Austrian refugee, who looked after him well. He had been a heavy drinker and was extremely argumentative, but we always had a wonderful relationship, perhaps because of our common love of German wine. I had been after him to revise his book on German wine, but he never did. I finally did it at the urging of his widow after he died.

Frank was a personality: lots of charm, if he wanted to use it. He was a good conversationalist, a lady's man, but he didn't have much luck with his liaisons, until his final marriage. He was erudite, opinionated and not a good businessman, but he ultimately sold his business and made enough money that way. He wrote like a dream and really should have remained a travel writer, the thing he knew best.

Tribute to Frank Schoonmaker at the time of his death
by Jacques, Marquis d'Angerville

The news of his death is hard to take in: how could so imaginative a spirit be extinguished with a single blow? For 40 years the name of Frank Schoonmaker has been tied up with every new development that has shaken the world of wine. How hard it is to do justice to such a subject in just a few lines, or to evoke the quality of his intelligence, strange and complex as it was scintillating.

He had a writer father who taught literature in a university; a mother who had attended the Sorbonne at the end of the 19th century and who had been a very active member of a society promoting female emancipation, and an aunt who studied under the sculptor Bourdelle. In such a setting, how could Frank Schoonmaker do other than develop that faculty he possessed to such a high degree: intellectual curiosity, an undeniable artistic sense. As someone fascinated by European civilization, he gave up his studies to discover the old continent for himself and to undertake a bicycle journey from Casablanca to Algiers. Naturally he was drawn to find out about wine - his first teacher was a small-scale grower from the Côtes de Provence, with whom he stayed as a lodger, and who would fine him a day's wine ration for each slip he made in judging bottles submitted for his assessment.

Once back in the United States he had the idea of sharing his passion for Europe with his countrymen, by writing *Through Europe on Two Dollars a Day*, followed by *Come with me to France*. To tell the truth, there is scarcely a mention of wine in these two first works, but it is our good fortune that before be became the expert taster that we have all known, Schoonmaker should have been a journalist in the best sense: an excellent writer of dense, clear and exact prose, who could convey an argument in a minimum number of words, someone whose learning made him able to put basic information in a form that was individual and intriguing, the master of a style that was at once free of affectation and sloppiness.

"A wine book, like a good wine, needs no introduction – it is self-contained," he wrote in the preface to his *Complete Wine Book*, the result of a project he was commissioned to carry out by a New York daily newspaper on the event of the repeal of Prohibition. In researching it, Frank Schoonmaker made the acquaintance of the founder of the *Revue du Vin de France*, at the restaurant, Le Roy Gourmet, that he never failed to visit when in Paris. Raymond Baudoin enabled him to discover the wine regions, not just as an intelligent amateur but as a professional insider, and initiated him into the mysteries of the *Appellation d'Origine Contrôlée* legislation that was then coming into effect. After his return to New York in 1934 he railed against the poor wines on offer post-Prohibition, against the fakers whom he didn't shrink from naming in articles for *The New Yorker*.

He was too practically-minded to be satisfied exclusively with literary work, and so founded, with several friends, a wine importing business known as Bates and Schoonmaker. This was at the same moment that F Wildman, Albert Connet and Ridgeway Knight took the same career move, having also concluded that the wines on sale in America did not represent what they had been able to taste in Europe. Side by side with Raymond Baudoin, who was by now a friend, Schoonmaker travelled France's vineyards looking for growers who wanted to bottle and market their wines. These trips, which began in 1935, were interrupted only by the war, which he passed working for the American information services. After landing at St Tropez he liberated Baron Leroy at Châteauneuf-du-Pape, became the first American to reach Lac Léman, and then enjoyed the hospitality in Vienna of his old friend Fernand Point. After demobilization he went back to his business, always looking to recruit new growers, who, once taken on, were not dropped. At a time when almost hardly anyone could resist uniformity and convenience, he had the courage to embrace individuality and innovation, and leave the beaten track.

He had numerous American followers: Alexis Lichine, Robert Haas, Morton Shiekman and so many others learned from him and tried to follow in his footsteps. His status with the government – which frequently sought his advice – and with wine professionals derived from the fact that he was totally in command of a subject that he had taken on, learnt and understood. He belonged to the category of witness that Pascal said he was disposed to believe, because they weren't afraid to take a stand.

Schoonmaker never wanted to remove the creator from his work – behind each bottle he saw the face, the character, the temperament of the winemaker, and he had the ability to convey them. The feelings that all who knew him are experiencing at the news of his death come, perhaps, from the human aspect that he never neglected in his relations with his suppliers, who were unused to being treated with such respect.

In his field, Frank Schoonmaker had a voice that will continue to resound. Now that it has fallen silent, this one grower, on behalf of so many others, expresses a need to say thank you. Koestler has written that when a lock finds the right key, the world is turned upside down. We will have to find out, as French wine growers, if we can find in the United States another key that fits so marvellously well.

BIBLIOGRAPHY

Barr, Andrew, *Drink: A Social History of America*. Carroll and Graff, New York, 1999.

Benson, Robert, *Great Winemakers of California*. Capra Press, Santa Barbara, California, 1977.

Blue, Anthony Dias, *American Wines*. Doubleday, Garden City, New York, 1985.

Bourguignon, Claude, *Le Sol, La Terre et Les Champs*. Sang de la Terre, Paris, 1989.

Brook, Stephen, *The Wines of California*. Faber and Faber, London, 1999.

Clarke, Oz, *New Classic Wines*. Websters/Mitchell Beazley, London, 1991.

Darlington, David, *Angels' Visits: An Inquiry into the Mystery of Zinfandel*. Henry Holt and Company, New York, 1991.

De Villers, Marq, *The Heartbreak Grape: A California Winemaker's Search for the Perfect Pinot Noir*. Harper Collins West, New York, 1994.

Halliday, James, *A History of the Australian Wine Industry, 1949-94*. Winetitles, Adelaide, 1994.

Halliday, James, *Wine Atlas of California*. Viking, New York, 1993.

Halliday, James and Johnson, Hugh, *The Art and Science of Wine*. Mitchell Beazley, London, 1992.

Hanson, Anthony, *Burgundy*. Faber and Faber, London, 1995.

Hawken, Paul, Lovins, Amory B, and Lovins, L Hunter. *Natural Capitalism: The Next Industrial Revolution*. Earthscan Publications, London, 1999.

Heinic, Lionel, *Si Bandol AOC m'avait contée*. Scriba, Avignon, 1992

Johnson, Hugh, *The World Atlas of Wine*. Mitchell Beazley, London, 1994.

Joly, Nicolas, *Le Vin du Ciel à la Terre*. Sang de la Terre, Paris, 1997.

Kennedy, Philip, *The Wine Song in Classical Arabic Poetry*. Clarendon Press, Oxford, 1997.

Klein, Naomi, *No Logo*. Flamingo, London, 2000.

Kolisko, Lily, *The Moon and The Growth of Plants*. Kolisko Archive Publications, Bournemouth, 1978.

Lichine, Alexis with Fifield, William, *Alexis Lichine's Encyclopaedia of Wines and Spirits*. Cassell, London, 1967.

Lichine, Alexis with Massee, William E, *Wines of France*. Alfred A Knopf, New York, 1951.

Loftus, Simon, *Puligny-Montrachet: Journal of a Village in Burgundy*. Penguin, London, 1992.

Matthews, Patrick, *The Wild Bunch: Great Wines from Small Producers*. Faber and Faber, London, 1997.

ed. Muscatine, Doris, Amerine, Maynard A, Thompson, Bob, *The University of California/Sotheby Book of California Wine*. University of California, Berkeley, 1984.

ed. Néauport, Jacques, *Jules Chauvet, ou le Talent du Vin*. Jean-Paul Rocher, Paris, 1997.

Norman, Remington, *Rhône Renaissance*. Mitchell Beazley, London, 1995.

Olney, Richard, *Reflexions*. Brick Tower Press, New York, 1999.

Olney, Richard, *Romanée-Conti: The World's Most Fabled Wine*. Rizzoli International Publications, New York, 1995.

Peynaud, Emile, *Connaissance et Travail du Vin*. Translated by Spencer, Alan, as Knowing and Making Wine. Wiley, New Yotk, 1984.

Ray, Eleanor, with Marinacci, Barbara, *Vineyards in the Sky: The Life of Legendary Vintner Martin Ray*. Heritage West Books, Stockton, CA, 1993.

Rigaux, Jacky, *Ode aux Grands Vins de Bourgogne*. Editions de l'Armançon, Précy-Sous-Thil, 1997.

Robinson, Jancis, *Oxford Companion to Wine*. OUP, Oxford, 1999.

Robinson, Jancis, *Vines, Grapes and Wines*. Mitchell Beazley, London, 1986.

Schilthuis, Willy, *Biodynamic Agriculture: Rudolph Steiner's ideas in practice*. Floris Books, Edinburgh, 1994.

Schoonmaker, Frank and Marvel, Tom, *American Wine*. Duell, Sloan and Pearce, New York, 1941.

Schoonmaker, Frank and Marvel, Tom, *The Complete Wine Book*. Simon and Schuster, New York, 1934.

Smart, Richard, *Sunlight into Wine: A Manual of Viticultural Practice*. Winetitles, Adelaide, 1992.

Sullivan, Charles L, *Like Modern Edens: Winegrowing in Santa Clara Valley and Santa Cruz*

Mountains, 1978-1981. California History Center, 1982.

Thun, Maria, *Work on the Land and the Constellations*. The Landthorn Press, East Grinstead, 1990.

University of California, *Grape Pest Management*. University of California Press, Oakland, 1992.

Waldin, Monty, *Organic Wine Guide*. Friends of the Earth and Thorsons, London, 1999.

Wilson, James E, *Terroir: The Role of Geology, Climate and Culture in the Making of French Wines*. Mitchell Beazley, London, 1998.

ed. Winkler, Albert J et al, *General Viticulture*. University of California Press, Berkeley, 1974.

Wright, Hilary, *The Great Organic Wine Guide*. Piatkus, London, 2000.

Useful web sites

www.smartwine.com Access to articles from the present and back issues of *Wine Business Insider* and *Wine Business Monthly*, plus a useful links page.

www.terroirs-b.com The Bourguignon's terroir website offers links to Claude Bourguignon's *Laboratoire d'Analyse Microbiologique des Sols* and excellent Burgundy and Beaujolais producers, such as Méo-Camuzet, Jean Thévenet and Marcel Lapierre of Villi-Morgon. Thanks to an English language version, you can savour such language as 'It was urgent to give word to the most famous of vignerons of Burgundy that will fight until its last blows against modern temptations of a viticulture technique.'

wineserver.ucdavis.edu – UC Davis's excellent wine website

www.winepros.com.au Australian page fronted by Len Evans and James Halliday, with news service and comprehensive access to Jancis Robinson's *Oxford Companion to Wine*.

www.waite.adelaide.edu.au/AWRI Website of the heavyweight Australian Wine Research Institute. Find out, for example, how to avoid the bite of agrochemical residues.

www.wineloverspage.com An American wine journalists' site for wine consumers, with tasting notes, information on tasting, interpreting labels and lots of articles.

www.practicalvineyard.com Website of *Practical Winery & Vineyard* magazine. Current and recent articles: for example, the Mondavi Winery's detailed comparisons of the results of different spacing regimes (*see* Chapter Two.) Not a light read, but illuminating.

For **wine merchants' websites**, see Appendix Two.

INDEX

Acacia 194
Accad, Guy 168, 170-2, 175
acetic acid 206-7
acidity 89, 99, 157, 206-7, 220
acidulation 176
additives 12, 98-100, 103, 153,
    206-13, 215-18
Adelaida Cellars 35, 262
Adelsheim, David 83-5
agrochemicals 10, 24, 27-8,
    122-32, 146, 170
Alban, John 18, 23, 28-33, 41,
    43-4, 86
Alban Vineyards 263
alcohol levels 20, 224, 226-8
aldehydes 20
Aligoté 244
Allen, Charlie 152, 169
Almadén 87, 98-9, 112, 246
American Viticultural Areas
    (AVAs) 101
Amerine, Professor Maynard 22, 42
Anagrus epos 128, 145
Angerville, Dom. du Marquis d'
    88, 104, 254, 267
Angerville, Jacques, Marquis d'
    90, 105, 107-8, 110, 119, 275-7
anthocyanins 163
anti-freeze 198
appellation contrôlée 87, 100-105,
    170
Aramon-rupestris cross (AxR1) 54-8
Arguile, Peter 216
asbestos 221
ascorbic acid 217
Aubert, Mark 50, 55-6, 58-9, 82, 94
Au Bon Climat 60, 173, 194, 265

Australia 9-10, 19, 22-3, 28, 49-52,
    103, 164-5, 218, 246-7, 248
Austria 133, 165, 191, 196, 197-8

Bacteria 184-6, 209, 213, 220-2
Bairrada 196
Bannockburn Vineyard 61, 265
Banyuls 89
Barbaresco 118
Barbera 199
Barolo 118
Barossa Valley 247
barrels 180-4, 192-7, 199
    charred 192-3
    fermentation in 156, 186-8,
        191, 199
    maturation in 189, 191, 195-7
    oak 183, 186-7, 191
    racking 188-9, 192
barriques 195, 196-7, 198
Barsac 102
Bates and Schoonmaker 107, 108
batonnage 156, 194-5
Baudoin, Raymond 87-8, 105-7,
    111, 112
Beaucastel, Ch. de 34, 86, 90-1,
    198, 200, 266
Beaujolais 26-7, 168, 218
Beaulieu 89, 246
Beaune 103, 104, 132, 223
Bel Arbor 253
Benson, Robert 22
bentonite clay 219
Berglund, Rod 69-70, 72, 223
Bernard, Raymond 84-5
Bernkastel 103
Bettane, Michel 15, 81-2, 91, 109

biodynamic viticulture 12, 26,
    132-9, 142-50, 209, 233
Bioletti, Frederic 56
biological controls 128, 145
Bize-Leroy, Lalou 77
blending 104, 114, 117-19
Boek, Ken 75-6
Bollinger 53
Bonny Doon 94, 119, 267
Bonterra 212, 253
Booker, Christopher 216
Bordeaux 102, 103-4, 168, 188, 244
Botrytis cinerea 129
botti 196
Bouchard 103
Bouchet, François 132
Bourgueil 212
Bourguignon, Claude 23-8, 37,
    132, 149-50, 215
Bouzeron 244
Breton, Pierre and Catherine 212
brettanomyces 203, 206, 208
Brook, Stephen 246
Brouilly 27
Brown, Ken 176
Brown, Martha 138
Bruce, David 158, 210-11, 269
Brunier family 239
bunch rot 129
Burgundy 18, 19, 52, 71, 101,
    103-4, 106-7, 144, 159, 160,
    162, 168, 169-78, 180, 188,
    193, 199, 223, 256
Busby, James 76
Buxy Cooperative 159, 165, 186,
    199, 271
Byron Vineyards 176, 270

Calera Wine Company 38-44,
163, 174, 215
California 9-11, 18-23, 28-46, 51,
55-8, 86-7, 95, 111-12, 114-20,
124-5, 132-49, 181-3
work force 51-2, 123, 128-9
Callaway 127
Canandaigua 99, 253
Capus, M. 101-3, 112
carbon dioxide 169, 184, 213
carcinogens 129, 186
Carneros 21, 69, 93
Casa de Saima 271
Casimir, Don 225-6
cat-tails 141
Ceago 141, 143-5, 268
cellars 162
Central Coast 21
Central Valley 166-7
centrifuges 209, 219
Chablis 195
Chadwick, Alan 137-9, 141-2,
148
Chalone Winery 22, 42, 181,
187, 270
Chambertin 106-7, 223
Champagne 12, 160-1, 163, 233
Chanson 103
chaptalization 176, 217-18, 224
Chardonnay 39, 58, 69, 70, 114-
15, 164, 189-90, 215
Châteauneuf-du-Pape 34, 117,
196, 198, 239
Chauvet, Jules 212-13, 218
Chave, Gérard and Jean-Louis 263
Chehalem Mountain Vineyard
59, 60
chelation 26-7
Cheval Blanc 244
Chez Panisse 239-44
Chianti 196

Cistercian Order 18, 104, 165,
197, 232-3
Clarke, Oz 14
Clendenen, Jim 51, 60, 173, 175,
194-5, 237-9
climate 31, 40, 41-6
Clos de la Coulée du Serrant 130,
268
Clos des Mariages 132
Clos du Val 55, 56, 152
Clos de Vougeot 160, 181
Cluny Abbey 104
Cohn, Jeff 214
cold soak 175
Coldstream Estate 36
Colombo, Jean-Luc 32
Condrieu 29
Conetech 164, 167, 225, 226
coolants 198
Coonawarra 23, 103, 247
cooperage 180-1, 189, 192-3
corks 183
cork taint 207
Cotat, François 49-50
Cotat Frères 48-9, 264-5
Côte de Beaune 130
Côte Chalonnaise 159, 199, 244
Côte d'Or 19, 39, 58, 104, 136,
157, 171, 234
Coturri, Tony 124, 212
Coturri Winery 140, 267
Counoise 91
Covelo 139, 141-2, 148
cover crops 124, 126, 144-5
crusher-destemmer 155, 161
Cuilleron, Yves 263
Curnonsky 130
Currado, Alfredo 118

Danielak, Doug 86, 288
Dann, Tony 167

Darlington, David 12, 116, 240
deficiency diseases 131-2
Delmas, Jean 81
Demeter 139
demi-muids 196
Dijon 104
Dimethyl Pyrocarbonate 185
distillation 227
Dokuchaiev 25
Dolan, Paul 244, 250-53
Dominus 89, 90, 155, 266
downy mildew 53
drainage 129
drapeaux 169
Draper, Paul 9, 12-15, 50, 82, 116,
117, 156, 163-4, 168, 176, 188,
200-201, 210, 244-5
Drouhin 59, 103
Ducs, Dom. des 264
Dujac, Dom. 36, 155
Dumazet, Pierre 263
Durand-Ruel, Paul 110
dynamic cellaring 198

Ealand, David 216
ecology 25
Edmunds, Steve 86
electricity, use of 158, 162-3, 167,
168-70, 252
Entre-Deux-Mers 67, 244
esters 20
European Economic Community
(EEC) 170
extraction 156, 163, 166, 168-9,
171

Faiveley, François 178
Falkenberg, Neville 190, 195
Faller, Theo and Colette 90
Farr, Gary 49-50, 60-1
Farr, Simon 13

fässer 196
Faulkner, Lucy 152, 156-7
faults 206-30
fermentation 174
  alcoholic 184, 186
  barrel 156, 186-8, 191, 199
  intracellular 169
  large wooden containers 197-203
  malolactic 184-6, 194, 201,
    213, 221
  oak chips 186, 191
  post-fermentation maceration
    168, 174-5, 201
  pre-fermentation maceration 175
  rotary processes 164-8
  secondary 184-6
  tanks 155, 190, 196-7, 199, 200-1
  temperature 155, 168-70,
    174-5, 199
fertilizers *see agrochemicals*
Fetzer Vineyards 75, 124, 139,
  140-1, 143, 212, 250-1, 254,
  257, 268
field grafting 102
filtration 14, 69, 176, 185, 209,
  219-23
fining 219-20
Flanzy, Professor Michael 169
flavescence dorée 127
flavours, added 98-100, 103,
  215-17
Foillard, Jean & Agnes 212, 272
Forman, Rick 187-9
foudres 196, 198-9
François Frères 180
François, Jean 180-3
Franson, Paul 226
Fresno 114
Frey Vineyards 139-41, 212, 268
Frog's Leap Wine Cellars 147,
  268-9

füder 196
Fuller, Robert C 253
fungal diseases 129, 145-6, 209
fungicides *see agrochemicals*

Gallo 21, 124-5, 253-4, 257
Gamay 112
gas chromatography-mass-
  spectrometry (GC-MS) 20
Geelong 49, 60-1
Germany 103, 195, 196, 220-2
Gibson, Richard 183, 206
glassy-winged sharpshooter 75,
  127-9
Gluck, Malcolm 122
glycerol 218
glycocides 163
Goheen, Dr Austin 81, 84, 85
Goldschmidt, Nick 165-6, 167-8
Golino, Deborah 79-80, 92-3
Gonatocerus ashmeadi 128
Gouges, Henri 88, 104
Gould, Henri 89
Graff, Dick 22, 181-2, 187-9
Grahm, Randall 34, 86, 92, 93-4,
  114-20, 154, 157, 161, 237, 239
Gramenon, Dom. 163, 212, 271-2
Grand Village, Ch. 244
Grange 65
grape varieties 53-8, 74-96, 112-20
gravity, use of 162
Gregory, Clay 67-8
Grenache 117, 200
Grüner Veltliner 197
Guillot, Jean-Gérard and
  Jacqueline 134
Guinaudeau, Jacques 244

Haas, Bob 18, 23, 34-5, 78, 85-95,
  107-8, 115, 229, 233
Hall, Chafee 42

Halliday, James 14, 36-7, 169,
  220, 222, 247
Hanson, Anthony 28, 101, 169-
  71, 175, 176
Hanzell 181, 185, 190, 271
Haraszthy, Agoston 75-6, 78, 79
Harlan, Mount 35-44
harvesting 52, 177
hand 219
mechanical 161, 209, 217-19,
  247
Haut-Brion, Ch. 81
Hawken, Paul 250-1
Heiligenkreutz 165
Henschke, Prue and Stephen 64-5
herbicides *see agrochemicals*
Hermitage 104
Heublein 246
Hill of Grace 64
HMR Estate 87, 182
Hochar, Serge 15
Hoenisch, Dick 92-3, 126
Hoffman, Dr Stanley 42
home winemaking 153-4, 257-60
Hooper, Stuart 50
Howard, Sir Albert 136, 138
Le Huet-Lieu 146
Hunter Valley 35, 58
hydrogen sulphide 206
hydroponics 19, 25
hygiene 154, 206, 213

Içi là-bas 271
Inglenook 78, 246
Integrated Pest Management
  128-9
internet, buying wine on 261-73
ion exchangers 99, 209
irrigation 19, 23, 62, 125, 129,
  145
Italy 195, 196

Jacob, Harry 56
Jade Mountain 266
Jadot, Maison Louis 104, 133, 158
Jayer, Henri 10, 48, 168, 171-8, 180-1, 194, 202, 249, 254-6, 269
Jefferson, Thomas 223
Jefford, Andrew 247
Jekyll, Bill 19
Jensen, Josh 18, 19, 23, 28, 35-44, 115, 163, 174, 182, 215
Jobard 173
Johnson, Hugh 14, 42, 44-5, 169, 220, 222
Johnstone, Russell 122
Joly, Nicholas 130-2, 136-7, 144

Kamptal 197-8
Kautz Ironstone Winery 167
Kay, Jane 207
Kloster Eberbach 232
Knoll, Emmerich 191, 270
Knox, Mel 11, 192, 199-200, 203, 238, 253
Koch, Michael 165
Kolisko, Lili 134
Kramer, Matt 18
Krug 233
Krug, Charles 200
Kunkee, Professor Ralph 184, 185-6, 194

Labelling 8, 98, 100, 114, 211
lacewing 145
La Chapelle de Guinchay 212
La Crema 69
La Cresta 79, 113
Lafarge, Dom. Michel 105, 173, 267
Lafite, Ch. 104
Lafleur, Ch. 244, 273
Lafon, Dom. des Comtes 173, 269
Lafon, Dominique 133, 157

Langhorne Creek 103
Lapierre, Marcel 212
La Tâche 104, 235
Latour, Maison Louis 78-9, 220
Laurent, Philippe 163
leafhopper 127-8
leaf removal 129
lees 156, 188-9, 191-2, 194-5
Leflaive, Anne-Claude 12, 131, 132-3, 136, 146, 149
Leflaive, Dom. 12, 81, 130-3, 173, 234, 268
Leflaive, Joseph 130-1
Leflaive, Olivier 81
Lefranc, Charles 87, 98
Le Pin 13
Les Gaudichots 104
Les Pavots 57-9
L'Espiguette 84
Lett, David 83
Leuconostos oinos 186
Lewis, Don 63
Libourne 89
Lichine, Alexis 88, 109, 167-8, 187
Lider, Lloyd 56
Liebfraumilch 185
limestone 37-9
Livermore 78, 111
Loftus, Simon 234
Loire 144
Long, Zelma 65, 68, 83, 155, 181-2, 192-3
Lowe, David 63
Lurton, Pierre 244
lutte raisonée 136
Luxter's Old Dessert 216
Lynch, Kermit 69, 114, 207-8, 213-14, 218, 219, 222-3, 239, 241, 254
Lytton Springs 68

McCloskey, Leo 21
maceration
    post-fermentation 168, 170-5, 201
    pre-fermentation 175
Madeira 208
Mahaney, Patrick 200
Mahoney, Francis 93
Margaux, Ch. 168, 200
Marjosse, Ch. 244, 272-3
Martini, Louis 111
Masson, Paul 78-9, 113, 244
Matanzas Creek 155
Matrot, Dom. 88
maturation 180-204
Mayacamas 182, 190, 270
mechanization 59-60, 67, 247
Médoc 168
Mendocino 79, 127, 139
Méo-Camuzet, Dom. 173, 269
meristem culture 93
Merlot 189
Meursault 58, 156, 192
Meza, Javier 144-6
Michael, Peter 50, 54-6, 57-8, 82, 94, 265
microbullage 227
mildew 53, 126, 129, 145
Millton, James 135
Mitchelton 63
mixed planting 124, 126, 143, 144-5
ML34(2) 186
Moët & Chandon 12, 59
Moltke, Freya von 137
Mondavi, Robert 10, 67-8, 136, 172, 176, 181-2, 200, 243, 254, 270
Mondavi, Tim 152, 154-5, 172-4, 176, 192-3, 200-3
monoculture 124-5, 128, 141

Montille, Hubert de 218, 235
Montrachet 235
moon, phases of 134, 148, 188
Moosbrugger, Martin 197-8
Morey, Pierre 173, 268
Morgon 27, 212
Morris, Jan 139
Mosel 118, 196
Moser, Lenz 67
Moueix, Christian 89, 90, 155, 188
Mount Eden Vineyards 267
Mourvèdre 117
Mouton-Rothschild, Ch. 200, 235
multinational companies 247
Munch, John 33-5, 50, 51-2, 182
Murphy, Hazel 248
Musar, Ch. 15
Muscatine, Doris 152-3

Napanook 89
Napa Valley 21, 40, 55, 67, 127,
   147, 155
Néauport, Jacques 26, 213-14
Nebbiolo 118
négociants 103-5, 180, 220
Neill, Richard 122
Newton, Peter 187-8
New Zealand 135, 218
Nikolaihof 133, 232, 268
9-Ethyl Butanoate 216
nitrogen-fixing 144, 150
Noble, Professor Ann 236
Nuits-St-Georges 103, 181

Oak
   ageing 186-7
   barrels 9, 183, 186-7, 191
   chips 186, 191, 217
   essence 191, 217
   fermentation 197-203
   large oak containers 198-203

staves 191
Oakville 200-1
oidium 53
Olmo, Dr Harold 79, 84
Olney, James 82-3
Olney, John 237
Olney, Richard 52, 77, 82, 104,
   207, 235, 239
Onish, Ken 108
Oporto 195-6
Opus One 67
Oregon 18, 38, 59, 83-6
organic viticulture 23, 26, 122-5,
   132-3, 135-6, 138-48, 176-7,
   211-12, 240-1, 251-6
Organic Wine Works 212
organochlorines 130
Overnoy, Pierre 212
oxidation 190-1, 195, 196, 199
oxygen, added 227

Paper chromatography 185
Parcé, Dr André 89
Parker, Robert 14, 30, 218, 220
Paso Robles 42, 87
pasteurization 220
Pasteur, Louis 184
Paul, Mike 19-20, 254-5
Pectolytic enzymes 217
pedology 25
Penfolds 65, 190, 195, 247
Perrin family 34-5, 85-6, 90, 92,
   117, 198-9, 200
persimilis spider mite 145
pesticides see agrochemicals
Petaluma 69
Peterson, Harry 59, 60
Peterson, Joel 69, 119
Pétrus, Ch. 13, 88-9, 155, 233, 249
Peynaud, Professor Emile 212, 219
Pfalz 196

Phelps, Joseph 136
phenolic compounds 163, 169,
   171, 190-1
pheromones, use in organic
   viticulture 136
phylloxera 53, 55-7, 101, 166, 234
pièces 180-1, 187, 195
Piedmont 118, 196
Pierce's disease 127, 129
Pierre, Alain 187, 199
pigeage 158-9, 165, 168, 176
Pinguet, Noël 146
Pinot Noir 36-7, 39, 43, 83-4, 94,
   114-15, 201
Piper, Tom 124, 143
pips 156, 158, 163, 164, 176
piquette 101
planting 48-72
   density 52-3, 57-68, 72
ploughing 130-1, 144
Pouilly-Fuissé 213
polyphenol 20
pomace 163
Pomerol 188-9, 244
Ponsot 88
Portet, Bernard 55, 56, 59-60,
   152-3
potassium 131, 150
powdery mildew 129, 145
Prémeaux 18, 59
presses 159-65
Prohibition 106, 111, 116, 200,
   253, 257
proteins 220
provignage 52-3, 171
pruning 71-2, 129, 148, 178, 247
Puligny 58, 234
Puligny-Montrachet 130, 180, 192
punching down 158-9, 194

Quarantine rules 74-5, 79-80, 93

Racking 188-9, 192
Rageot, Roger 159, 187
rainfall 31, 40
Ramey, David 18, 30, 90, 99, 155-6, 206, 215, 269
Ramonet 173
Rateau, Pierette et Jean-Claude 132, 136, 268
Ravenswood 69, 119
Rayas, Ch. 198, 244, 263
Ray, Eleanor 113-14
Ray, Martin 11, 42, 79, 89, 113-14, 119, 210-12
red spider mite 136, 145
redwood vats 199, 201
refrigeration 168-71, 176, 198, 213
regionality 22-3
regional names, protection 101
Remelluri, Bodegas 148
retailers, wine 261-2
reverse osmosis 209, 224-6, 227
Revue du Vin de France (RVF) 87, 105, 106, 109, 239
Reynaud, Emmanuel 244
Rheingau 196
Rheinhessen 196
Rhine 117
Rhône 29, 117, 144, 196, 199-200, 208
Rhône Rangers 34, 86, 117
Richards, Roy 173, 175
Richebourg 172
Richmond, Mike 194
Ridge 15, 40, 50, 68, 82, 117, 188, 200, 244-5, 270
Riesling 117, 118, 191, 197
Rigaux, Jacky 175, 177, 255
Rioja 148
Rion, Dom. Daniel 264
Rion, Patrice 18, 20, 30, 59, 60
Robinson, Jancis 76

Robinson, Kevin 166-7
Rodale family 136
Rodale Press 136
Roederer, Louis 79
Romanée-Conti, Dom. de la 10, 36, 77-8, 104, 149, 155, 171, 174, 181, 233-4, 241, 273
rosé 112
Rosemount 14
Rosenblum Cellar 272
Rosenblum, Kent 214
roses 126
Rothbury Estate 63
Rothschild, Baron Philippe de 235
Rouchet 118
Roumier, Alain 235
Round Valley School 139
Rousseau 235
Russian River 71, 125
Rutherford Hill 166-7
Ryman, Hugh 64

Saahs, Christine 133, 232
Saahs, Nikolaus 133
St Emilion 244
St Helena 111
St John, Cornelia 86
Saint-Romain 180
Saintsbury 270
Salinas 44-6
Sancerre 48-9
Sangiovese 199
San Joaquin 114, 127
San Jose 112
Santa Barbara 60, 124
Santa Cruz 89, 113, 127, 137
Saunier, Martine 171, 173, 254
Sauzet, Etienne 88
Schae, Dr Jutte 133
Schloss Gobelsburg 271

Schoonmaker, Frank 87, 105-12, 114, 117, 119, 131, 167, 233, 254, 274-7
Schreier, Professor Peter 216-17
Schuster, Michael 13
sediment 192
Seguin, Professor Gérard 31
Seitz, Theobald and Georg 220-1
sélection massale 77-8
Sessions, Robert 190
Seysses, Jacques 235
Shaff, Henry 223
Sibertsev 25
Sichel, Peter 108-10, 274-5
Simi 155, 166, 168, 266
Sirugue, Yves 181
skin contact 190-1
skins 158, 164, 168
Sliven 186-7
Smart, Dr Richard 61-8, 72, 76, 99-100
Smith, Clark 157-8, 159, 161-2, 167, 206-8, 224-5, 227-30, 236-7, 272
sodium 99
soil 18-39, 66-7, 91, 95
erosion 125
Soil Association 136, 138
Soledad 118
Sonoma 21, 40, 54, 79, 124-5, 127, 140, 155, 157, 250
sorting tables 177
soupe 104, 119
Southcorp 11, 19, 21, 23, 183, 206, 254-5
Spätburgunder 195
spinning cone columns 209, 217, 225-6
Spurrier, Steven 15
stainless steel tanks 155, 190, 196-7, 199, 200-1

stalks 155, 161, 170, 174
Steger, Lynn 56-7
Steiner, Rudolph 133, 134, 136,
    137-8, 142, 147-8
Sterling 187-8
stück 196
sugar, added *see chaptalization*
sulphur 123, 145, 153, 155, 171,
    174-6, 185, 189, 201, 203,
    209-14, 216, 224
sulphur dioxide 209-13, 217, 226
Sutter Home Winery 11
Swan, Joseph 69-72, 79, 222-3,
    265
Syrah 58, 117

Tablas Creek 35, 78, 86, 92-3, 95,
    199-200, 266
Tamm, Curtis 22, 42
tannins 158, 164, 168, 171, 174,
    176, 191, 196-7, 217, 220
Taransaud 200
tartaric acid 89, 132, 209, 219,
    218, 247
tasting wine 206, 207
Tchelitscheff, André 69, 87, 89,
    182, 185
Temecula 127
Tempier, Dom. 254, 272
terpenes 20
terra rossa 23
terroir 14-15, 18-46, 58, 117-18,
    192
Thackrey, Sean 86
Thermenregion 165
Thomas, Ferdinand 48-9
Thompson's Seedless 99, 244
Thun, Maria 133-5, 148
tillage 126
toasty flavour 192-3
To-Kalon 67, 78

Tours, Ch. des 244, 273
training systems 65-7, 71
Travers, Bob and Nonie 182
treading 152-3, 176
Trinchero, Bob 12
Trotanoy, Ch. 188
Turley, Helen 50

University of California, Davis 41,
    45-6, 55-7, 79-80, 81-3, 125-8,
    156, 184, 207, 236

Van Steenwyck family 50
Vietti 118
Vieux-Télégraphe, Dom. du 198,
    222, 239, 272
Villaine, Aubert de 10, 15, 132,
    136, 149, 234, 241, 244
Vinding-Diers, Peter 215
vines 18
Vinovation 157, 206-7, 224-30,
    236-7
Viognier 29, 37
viral diseases 79-81, 93-4
vitamin C 217
Vogüé, Robert-Jean de 59, 235
volatile acidity 206-7, 224, 227
Volnay 105
Vosne-Romanée 10, 48, 136, 171,
    174
Vougeot 223
Vouvray 146

Wachau 191
Washington 118
Wasserman, Becky 180-3, 193-4,
    234-5
Waters, Alice 239-44, 254-5
Waugh, Harry 166
Webb, Brad 184-5, 190
weeds 144

Weinbach, Dom. 90, 266
Wente Brothers 45, 111
Wente, Eric 45
Why Not? 237-8
Williams, John 147-8
Wilson, Richard 139
winemakers 50, 152-3
Winkler, Professor Albert 22, 42
Wiseman, Colonel Frederick 131

Xyella fastidiosa 127

Yeasts 58, 156, 169, 184, 195, 203,
    209, 213-15, 217
yield 176-7, 255
York, Alan 141-6, 148, 149

Zeldin, Theodore 100
Zellerbach, James 79, 181, 190,
    200
Zinfandel 11, 68, 70, 116-17,
    185, 222
Zwettl Abbey 197

ACKNOWLEDGEMENTS

In this book I've tried to look at big subjects through a narrow focus. There's a small cast of characters and noticeable absentees, so I'd like to acknowledge those who gave generous help but who are not correspondingly prominent. The most obvious example is Robert M Parker Jr, who chatted entertainingly at length on the phone. But I find Parker too pertinent to a book about wine, America and France, and as a walk-on part he unbalances the overall design. Perhaps I don't feel up to assessing his influence, or that, in the words of Chou En Lai's much-quoted verdict on the French Revolution, "It's too early to say."

I spent some enjoyable hours with two excellent winemakers and Rhône Rangers, Doug Danielak of Jade Mountain and Randall Grahm. Other missing persons will I hope, accept my apologies, among them Paul Draper of Ridge. Draper does appear here, but I could fill a chapter with great stuff that didn't get in. Perhaps in future he can explain to me again the connection between "real wine" and the way tomatoes finish ripening on your window-sill.

Anthony Hanson and Stephen Brook made my job much easier by writing Burgundy and The Wines of California respectively, great books to take on the road. Anthony Hanson also dug out irreplaceable texts for me from his large library. By contrast, Sally Duerdoth's hospitality in Burgundy almost stopped me doing any work at all. I'd also like to thank John McLaren and Ann Pemberton of the Wine Institute of California for securing funding from their colleagues in Washington; while University of California, Davis provided two of my most pleasant and helpful contacts, Dick Hoenisch and Debbie Golino, and its eminence grise, Emeritus Professor Ralph Kunkee, turned on the charm.

Final thanks go to Becca Spry, Adrian Tempany, Hilary Lumsden, Lavinia Osbourne, Phil Ormerod and Colin Goody at Mitchell Beazley, to Tessa Hunkin for asking Clifford Harper to do the illustrations and to Helen Spence, my editor.